INTEREST GROUP POLITICS IN AMERICA
A New Intensity

H. R. MAHOOD

Memphis State University

Prentice Hall, *Englewood Cliffs, New Jersey 07632*

Library of Congress Cataloging-in-Publication Data

Mahood, H. R.
   Interest group politics in America : a new intensity / H.R.
Mahood.
      p.   cm.
   Bibliography: p.
   Includes index.
   ISBN 0-13-475575-8
   1. Lobbying--United States. 2. Pressure groups--United States.
I. Title.
JK1118.M298 1990
324'.4'0973--dc20   89-33050
                                                      CIP

Cover design: 20/20 Services, Inc.
Manufacturing buyer: Bob Anderson

 © 1990 by Prentice-Hall, Inc.
A Division of Simon & Schuster
Englewood Cliffs, New Jersey 07632

Printed in the United States of America

10 9 8 7 6 5 4 3 2 1

ISBN   0-13-475575-8

Prentice-Hall International (UK) Limited, *London*
Prentice-Hall of Australia Pty. Limited, *Sydney*
Prentice-Hall Canada Inc., *Toronto*
Prentice-Hall Hispanoamericana, S.A., *Mexico*
Prentice-Hall of India Private Limited, *New Delhi*
Prentice-Hall of Japan, Inc., *Tokyo*
Simon & Schuster Asia Pte. Ltd., *Singapore*
Editora Prentice-Hall do Brasil, Ltda., *Rio de Janeiro*

CONTENTS

PREFACE

It is a largely unappreciated fact of life that our politics are group-based. National policy making is increasingly monopolized by growing numbers and types of organized interests. Virtually all segments of our society have established associations or other types of organizations to articulate and represent their interests before selected governmental decision makers. This situation will undoubtedly continue well into the 1990s.

Paradoxically, political scientists have generally been lethargic about examining the interest group explosion and its meaning for our political system. The pioneering though polemical work of Arthur Bentley early in this century established no school or sustained interest in group-based politics. It was not until David Truman's restatement of the Bentleyian thesis of political groups that political scientists began to inquire into the contribution of organized interests to national politics. Given, of course, the variety of methodological approaches that were taken by such investigators as Robert Dahl, Harmon Zeigler, Robert Salisbury, Theodore Lowi, and Terry Moe, differing conclusions were inevitable. Some of these investigators noted positive contributions of groups to both our political system and its institutions, while others were quite critical and negative. Despite their controversial nature, these studies have contributed to a more accurate and complete assessment of the nature and political activities of organized interests.

The 1970s and 1980s witnessed a surge of group formation and political activity, and Washington's officialdom found itself under increased pressure from a growing army of group spokesmen. This phenomenon, however, is not all that well chronicled or discussed in existing political science literature. Indeed, emphasis is frequently on such micro matters as types of group benefits, qualities of group leadership, organizational stability, etc.

What is needed is relatively more up-to-date accounting and analysis of the pressure group system in general. In this context, we need to become aware of new forces contributing to group formation, highlight some of the more visible and influential groups in today's national politics, explore new strategies and tactics currently in vogue among today's lobbying organizations and make note of the growing role of interest groups in national elections. These and related tasks can provide the basis for a relatively more accurate assessment of organized interests in the political life of our nation. The main purpose of this publication, then, is to refocus on this new generation of interest groups and lobbies presently not all that well analyzed or understood. Given the fact, too, that today's interest group universe is vast and complex, we also see our mission as one of separating out and identifying a number of general themes concerning organized interests and their activities. By doing so, we can better predict what the consequences are for our political system in general and national policy making specifically.

In order to perform the above-listed tasks, this book is organized into three parts. Part I (Chapters 1 through 4) is introductory and deals with a number of subjects such as the recent explosion of organized interests, some prevailing theories of interest groups, lobbyists and lobbying, various key interests in selected policy areas, various lobbying techniques and strategies, plus an in-depth analysis of political action committees (PACs). These data will provide the reader with both an awareness and an appreciation of the changing group universe as well as the growing influence of these organizations in contemporary national politics.

Part II (Chapters 5 through 7) discusses and illustrates the increasing interest group interaction with the legislative, executive, and judicial branches. This section also draws attention to the changing nature of government itself, as well as to the changing focuses of policy making. Governmental decision making today is much more complex and atomized than it was in the late 1940s and the 1950s. Part III (Chapters 8 and 9) deals with the recent public interest group movement and provides a detailed look at some of the representative organizations resulting therefrom. The public interest movement is responsible for a greatly expanded national agenda. Finally, Chapter 9 summarizes a number of themes from earlier chapters and notes various consequences of group-based politics on our national politics. The recent transformation in our politics is largely the result of complex and highly interrelated organized interests. It is the aim of this book to help the student better understand this important change.

The author wishes to acknowledge the contribution of Ralph Rossum for his comments on earlier drafts. Jim King and David Cox also made valuable editorial contributions. Patricia Vasser and Jernice Green contributed vital typing and computer skills. The encouragement and expertise of Karen Horton, Dolores Mars, and Judy Winthrop of Prentice-Hall are greatly appreciated. Errors and omissions are the responsibility of the author.

I am also grateful to the reviewers: Michael A. Baer, University of Kentucky; Christopher J. Bosso, Northeastern University; and Dennis L. Thompson, Brigham Young University.

CHAPTER ONE
THE GROUP BASIS
OF POLITICS:
A New Era

A PARTICIPATION
REVOLUTION

The politics of modern America cannot be fully described or understood without appreciating the role of political interest groups. Indeed, since the nation's founding, interest groups have pervaded the American political scene. Recent years, though, have witnessed an escalation of both the kinds and the numbers of politically active groups. As one report notes,

> this [group] expansion takes the form of: (1) involvement of an increasing proportion of the population in political activity; (2) the development of new groups and of new consciousness on the part of old groups, and ethnic minorities; (3) the diversification of the political means and tactics which groups use to secure their ends; (4) an increasing expectation on the part of groups that government has the responsibility to meet their needs; and (5) an escalation in what they conceive those needs to be.[1]

Public officials have attested to the presence and heightened activities of organized interests. Former cabinet member Joseph Califano, for example, observes that

> Washington has become a city of political molecules, with fragmentation of power, and often authority and responsibility, among increasingly narrow, what's-in-it-for-me interest groups and their responsive counterparts in the executive and legislative branches. This is a basic—perhaps the basic—fact of political life.[2]

And Senator Edward Kennedy has proclaimed,

> The . . . problem is that the Senate and House are awash in a sea of special interest lobbying and special interest campaign contributions. . . . We're elected to represent all the people of our states and districts, and not those rich enough or powerful enough to have lobbyists holding megaphones constantly to our ears.[3]

An ever broadening range of organized interests—tobacco farmers, Vietnam veterans, feminists, right-to-lifers, gays, religious conservatives, nonsmokers, environmentalists, and endless others—are well organized and active within the nation's political system. Since the mid-1960s, then, there has been

> an explosion of interest group activity in Washington, either with national program perspectives or for the purpose of preserving existing programs;
>
> an increasing diversity of organizations, including those seeking benefits distinctly different from traditional ones;
>
> and both an expansion and diversification of lobbying and other political activities by organized interests.

A major theme of this book is that along with the expansion of politically active groups there has been a significant transformation in their strategies of influence. Groups and governments are increasingly intermeshed, and their linkages more and more widespread.

In the pages that follow, interest group politics will be examined in greater detail. In the process, efforts will be made to draw a number of generalizations about the contributions of groups to national politics and the implications of their activities for our democratic institutions. In this way we can more accurately assess the role of groups in national policy making. Also, we can better comprehend the consequences of this heightened organizational activity for American politics in the years immediately ahead.

Several tasks must be completed, however, before we can more accurately evaluate the role of organized interests in national politics. These tasks will take up the remainder of this publication. Included among them are an examination of the factors in group formation, analyses of evolving strategies and tactics characteristic of today's pressure politics, an examination of interest group–political party interaction in present-day electoral politics, and the changing bases of government–interest group relationships in recent years.

DEFINING SOME TERMS

Before moving on to the main concerns of this chapter, we need to define some of our terms so that we can better understand the kinds of political organizations and politics that will be discussed in the remainder of the book. First, *interest groups* or *pressure groups* are defined primarily as membership organizations with political goals. These organizations demonstrate a good deal of variety in their purposes, objectives, and levels of political influence. *Organized interests* consist of a number of cooperating organizations—consumers, environmentalists, farmers, veterans, and so forth—having a common goal. *Pressure politics,* frequently viewed negatively, are characterized by an array of conflicting organizations interacting with public officials. It involves both give and take of political influence.

Finally, what are "private" versus "public" interests? Chapter 8 will demonstrate that a number of organizations emerged in the late 1960s and the 1970s representing broadly held interests—consumers, environmentalists, law firms, and others. A *public interest group* is one that seeks a benefit enjoyable by society as a whole (a public good) and not just by the immediate membership—for example, lower taxes, open government, or more citizen participation in policy making. Benefits can be either substantive or procedural. A private organization, by contrast, seeks gratification principally for its own members (a private good).

In the rest of this chapter we will examine theories of group formation and the contributions groups make to national politics, analyze group benefits as factors in the formation and maintenance of, and look at interest group–political party relationships as they exist today. By doing so we will contribute to an analytical framework for better understanding the nature and consequences of our group-based politics.

EARLY COMMENTATORS ON GROUPS: MADISON AND TOCQUEVILLE

James Madison was the first political writer to perceive and analyze the interests of the "factions" emerging in the new nation. He defined these factions as follows:

> a number of citizens, whether amounting to a majority or minority of the whole, who are united and actuated by some common impulse or passion, or of interest, adverse to the rights of other citizens, to the permanent and aggregate interests of the community.[4]

Factions, in his view, were a disease common to all systems of popular government—a disease that wrought injustice, instability, and confusion and caused governments to perish.

Madison perceived two methods of "curing the mischiefs of faction"—removing their causes and controlling their effects. He viewed neither as a viable option for popular government. Eliminating the causes of faction would be impossible, for the seeds "are sown in the nature of man." On the other hand, suppressing the effects of faction could destroy liberty—a remedy worse than the disease.

For Madison the answer lay within the framework of the new governmental system—a federal republic. Federalism could be a powerful antidote to "minority" factions and a key ingredient in the cure for "majority" factions. Though apprehensive about both, Madison was primarily concerned with controlling majority factions. Certain constitutional devices would enable government to suppress majority factions and protect its citizens' property and ultimately their political liberty. But how? Madison's argument was threefold.

First, he reasoned that the sheer number and variety of factions in a broadly constituted nation would make it "less probable" that a majority of the whole would seek to invade the rights of others. Additionally, the more factions, the more likely they would cancel each other out.

Second, federalism—a system whereby power is divided between the nation and the states—would result in "aggregate interests" being referred to national authorities and local interests being referred to state legislatures for solution. This delegation of power would prevent a "factious leader" in one state from spreading to others and eventually dominating the entire nation.

Finally, Madison contended that the most effective remedy for the ills of factions lay in a system of national checks and balances. Such safeguards would fragment power sufficiently to ensure that no single branch or level of government could be co-opted by those whose purposes were antithetical to the rights of all.

Madison conceived of minority factions as small, scattered, loosely organized groups that represented particular interests as opposed to broad social or economic concerns. Because of their relatively specialized goals, he argued, minority factions would be incapable of dominating decision making in the national government:

> If a faction consists of less than a majority, relief is supplied by the republican principle, which enables the majority to defeat its sinister views by regular vote. It may clog the administration, it may convulse the society; but it will be unable to mask its violence under the forms of the constitution.[5]

History indicates that the Madisonian prescription for reducing the power of majority factions has worked in most cases. Minority factions, however, have proved to be much more of a political problem than Madison or his peers anticipated.

A generation later, Alexis de Tocqueville, a young Frenchman touring the United States, was struck by the great number of associations in the new nation as well as their local and nonideological character: "In no country in the world has the principle of association been more successfully applied to a greater multitude of objects than in America."[6] The associations Tocqueville was describing were not necessarily pressure groups; many sought to influence opinions or performed tasks such as distributing books, caring for the poor, or building hospitals. These groups often served as a substitute for or a supplement to governmental functions. They also performed numerous social functions as well.

Tocqueville saw in this proliferation of associations a check on excessive government growth. Many nonpolitical organizations, in his view, could perform various tasks and thereby reduce the need for more government. Nonetheless, Tocqueville correctly noted the continuing growth of political groups within the country: "At the head of any new undertaking, where in France you find government or in England some territorial magnate, in the United States you are sure to find association."[7]

Both Madison and Tocqueville recognized the principle of political organization, but their concern was whether existing governmental arrangements would successfully countervail group power over time. Theirs was a very different society—dominated by rural, agrarian interests, adhering strictly to laissez-faire economics, and characterized by a very limited franchise of relatively homogeneous voters.

THE FOUNDING FATHERS
OF GROUP THEORY:
BENTLEY AND TRUMAN

Analyzing and evaluating the activities of political interest groups and their contributions to American politics has been a growing preoccupation among social scientists in this century. In 1908, Arthur Bentley perceived the group as the basic element in all political activity:

> We shall have to take all these political groups, and get them stated with their meaning, with their value, with their representative quality. We shall have to get hold of political institutions, legislatures, courts, executive officers, and get them stated as groups and in terms of groups.[8]

For Bentley, groups were not mere sociological curiosities. Rather, they were the stuff of politics, and their influence was pervasive: "When the groups are adequately stated, everything is stated. When I say everything, I mean *everything*."[9] All public policy, according to Bentley, resulted from the continual interaction of competing interests within the political system.

Implicit in Bentley's theory of group-based politics is the concept of modern, democratic government based on competing groups. In focusing on the inevitability of warring factions, as James Madison had, Bentley stressed the virtue inherent in the struggle among the "plurality" of political groups: a balance is established and maintained within the political system. Government's main responsibility, Bentley believed, is to arbitrate and guard the public's interests. One writer summarizes pluralist theory in the following terms:

> Pluralism theory assumes that within the public arena there will be countervailing centers of power within governmental institutions and among outsiders. Competition is implicit in the notion that groups as surrogates of individuals will [represent] the diversity of opinions that might have been possible in the individual decision days of democratic Athens.[10]

Bentley's novel approach to the study of politics and its emphasis on groups rather than on structures of government challenged the conventional wisdom of his day. As a result, the treatises of *The Process of Government* went largely unnoticed and unappreciated.

In the 1950s, David B. Truman resurrected Bentley's thesis of the group basis of politics. Truman's book *The Governmental Process* (1951) restates Bentley's position but utilizes a more analytical base. Like Bentley, Truman sees benefits in the political contributions of groups. In fact, he perceives groups as intrinsic to the political process:

> The behaviors that constitute the process of government cannot be adequately understood apart from groups, especially organized interest groups, groups which are operative at any point in time. Whether we look at an individual citizen, the executive secretary of a trade association, at a political party functionary, at a legislator, administrator, governor, or judge, we cannot describe his participation in the governmental institution, let alone account for it, except in terms of interests with which he affiliates and with which he is confronted.[11]

Groups emerge as the result of what Truman calls environmental disturbances or dislocations. Wars, immigration, depressions, or societal changes emanating from these or other disturbances strain the social equilibrium. Prevailing relationships—among business people, among workers' organizations, between group leaders and followers—are fundamentally disturbed and altered. The rise of new organizations and associations, according to Truman, is to be perceived as an effort to adjust the existing order, and especially those relationships between the private sector and government. For Truman and other proponents of *pluralism*—the view that what happens in American politics is determined primarily by varying combinations of organized interests having access to key policy-making centers—the inevitable expansion of government provides competing groups with the access and influence they need in order to exert countervailing pressures. Truman perceives political interest groups as a "balance wheel" that maintains needed equilibrium in an increasingly complex and fragmented political system. As he sees it,

> the significance among the multiplicity of coordinate points of access to government decisions and the complicated texture of relationships among them is great. This diversity assures various ways for interest groups to participate in the formulation of policy and this variety is a flexible, stabilizing element.[12]

Truman's theoretical contributions are important, not just because of his restatement of Bentley's thesis, but also because of his more orderly and detailed presentation of groups as positive forces in national policy making. A good portion of *The Governmental Process* is devoted to a discussion of the contributions groups make to our democratic process—moderation, stability, and increased public participation.

Publication of *The Governmental Process* stimulated a pluralism–elitism debate over the political efficacy of organized groups in our political system (see Box 1–1). The debate persists to this day, for we cannot prove that our politics are either pluralistic or elitist. As we will see, political influence in one set of circumstances does not necessarily carry over into others. Public officials may respond to business pressures concerning foreign trade but not necessarily to those dealing with the environment. Ethnic or racial groups may be influential in public-housing issues but not in agricultural policies. As David Gerson asserts,

American politics are neither the marketplace of group theory nor the conspiracy of simple elite theories. If America is elitist it is elitist in a pluralistic way, or if pluralistic, then pluralistic in a way that benefits an elite.[13]

BOX 1–1

Pluralism

According to pluralist thought, today's society consists of innumerable groups whose members share common economic, social, religious, racial, ideological, and/or cultural interests. Inevitably, many of these groups organize in order to better influence public policies important to their concerns. Implicit in this arrangement is "government by the people." Democracy is both perpetuated and enhanced by the political activities of all these associations, which represent millions of individuals. The major mechanisms of pluralist democracy are political interest groups and a decentralized governmental structure. Interest groups, reflecting as they do the opinions and aspirations of major segments of our society, serve as surrogates before and linkages to major policy-making bodies and numerous public officials.

A decentralized governmental structure provides ready access for groups to public-policy makers—legislators, jurists, administrators. In these circumstances, public authority is shared by a host of personnel with overlapping authority. Competing interests thus have multiple points of access at which to present their claims. Groups are free to choose the most efficacious level at which to press their claims: national, state, or local. Watchwords of today's pluralism are *access, political decentralization,* and *divided public authority.*

The major consequence of political pluralism, according to its supporters, is a more democratic America. Public policies are largely the result of and in line with the preferences and interests of a majority of the nation's citizens. Political power is limited because most citizens are members of overlapping and frequently conflicting groups or organizations—family, church, occupational, racial, and so on. These interests check each other, and none is consistently dominant. Also, all groups and associations are subject to the constraints of prevailing social values and attitudes. In addition to Truman, other contributors to pluralist thought are Robert Dahl *(Who Governs?)* and Earl Latham *(The Group Basis of Politics)*.

Elitism

In sharp contrast with pluralism, elitism downplays the importance of organized interests in American politics. Rather, it emphasizes a "power elite" that dominates most public-policy making—corporation presidents, affluent families, cabinet secretaries, senior members of Congress, and others. These individuals run the ship of state and influence both the direction and content of public policy—the maintenance of the capitalist system, foreign policy initiatives toward the Soviet Union, and the level of taxes individuals and corporations pay.

The classic treatise on elite theory is C. Wright Mills's *The Power Elite*. Mills perceived that distribution of power in America pyramid-shaped. At the very top is the elite—top-ranking military leaders, corporation executives, the very affluent, and national political figures and celebrities. Below is a middle layer of power brokers that include senior members of Congress, state and local officials, some regional personnel, and a few interest groups. At the bottom of the pyramid are the powerless masses. According to Mills, elites perpetuate the powerlessness of the masses by controlling and manipulating the mass media. Characteristically, the masses are politically apathetic and cynical. Their concerns are immediate and personal. The politically important interest groups, such as labor unions and professional associations, are dominated by their own internal elites. Government, in these circumstances, serves the interests of the power elite. A governmental decision, therefore, to develop a new fighter bomber emanates not from within government but from interaction within the power elite—top Pentagon brass, certain senior members of Congress, and those defense contractors, such as McDonnell Douglas, Boeing, and General Dynamic, that have an economic stake in such a decision.

In sum, elite theorists maintain that only a few organized interests are politically important, and these are subject to their own internal elites. The large majority of existing interest groups, then, are relatively impotent or else serve as surrogates for the power elite.

Gerson goes on to argue that our political system is *elitist* with respect to goals, but *pluralistic* with respect to means. Elites set or limit the agenda of our politics because they dominate our public institutions and a number of our interest groups. Nonetheless, Gerson notes, groups struggle with one another over how government will pursue various parts of the national agenda. (See Box 1-1 and Fig. 1-1.)

But we need to explore other dimensions of group politics before making definitive judgments about the role of organized interests in national policy making. Therefore, in the balance of this chapter we turn to the concepts of group establishment, benefits, and group–party relationships. Examination of these phenomena will help us more accurately assess the expanding role of groups in electoral politics.

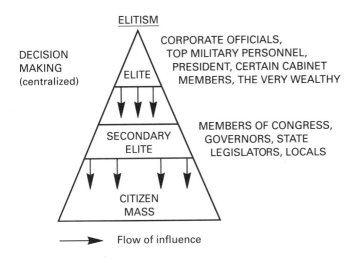

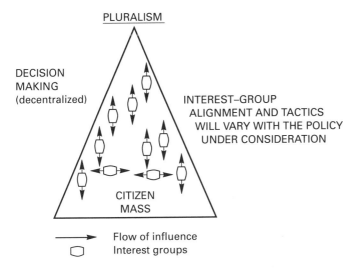

FIGURE 1-1

GROUP FORMATION

Why do people join—or not join—interest groups? Different theories have been proposed. David Truman suggests society's increasing specialization and social differentiation. The industrialization of the American economy over the latter half of the nineteenth century and into the twentieth spawned numerous techno-logical innovations—the radio, the telegraph, the telephone, mass newspapers, the automobile—that radically altered the nation's social and political culture. These advances made it possible for disparate groups from across the nation to recognize their common interests and unite. Additionally, the increasing diversification of the nation's economic base and the increases in social complexity that accompanied industrialization provided interest groups with greater incentives to seek national recourse. Truman's theory of group establishment and proliferation is thus a theory that assumes constant change. Broad economic, technological, or cultural changes alter the status quo, and the subsequent disequilibrium in turn triggers a new wave of groups along with a new political equilibrium.

Truman's bold and intriguing theory has its shortcomings, though. It tends to overlook, as later pages will show, the fact that not all groups emanate from environmental disturbances. The U.S. Chamber of Commerce, for example, was established at the behest of the national government, and Common Cause emerged because of the lack of citizens' organizations dedicated to governmental reform. Additionally, Truman fails to consider the role of group leadership. Interest groups do not automatically emerge because of shifts in public policy; someone must organize those most directly affected.

Economist Mancur Olson offers a different perspective on group formation.[14] He reasons that individuals with common interests do not automatically join organizations addressing their concerns. A major barrier to affiliation is the "free rider" problem: "rational" individuals will not pay to join an organization if they can enjoy the benefits (for example, higher wages) without doing so. Why should white-collar workers join a union if their employer provides them the same benefits that unionized workers have? On the other hand, if the organization offers attractive "selective" benefits—that is, benefits withheld from nonmembers, such as a hospitalization plan, free life insurance, or expanded retirement benefits—they are much more likely to join. Benefits must outweigh the costs of joining.

Olson's theory does not explain all the potential questions relating to organizing.[15] Why, for instance, do members of the Sierra Club and the Wilderness Society seek more general benefits—clean air, clean water, and a safer environment for all—rather than an immediate selective benefit for themselves? Also, Olson downplays the activities of political interest groups—lobbying, propaganda, and involvement in electoral politics—regarding them as by-products of group formation. But these activities are precisely the things that attract people to join the Business Roundtable, the National Association of Realtors, and the National Rifle Association.

What these and other concepts of interest-group formation come down to is that individuals join organizations for a number of reasons—money, prestige, power, personal satisfaction, and other benefits.[17] We each have our own desires, concerns, attitudes, and values, and these affect our organizational choices. This brings us to a discussion of the benefits or incentives interest groups offer to potential members.

GROUP BENEFITS

For groups to exert significant political influence, they must be able to attract and retain dedicated members. Group establishment and member affiliation, though, usually require some kind of inducement. Inducements, of course, must be attractive and generally unavailable to nonmembers. They should also be sufficiently attractive to retain the continued backing of existing members. Unstable or volatile memberships can inhibit organizational performance and ultimately political influence.

Group benefits are either tangible or intangible. A tangible benefit or incentive is one that is real or material—higher wages, better working conditions, expanded retirement benefits, a hospitalization plan, and so on. Intangible benefits are nonmaterial, less direct, and more personal—improved social status, greater professional acceptability, or feelings of gratification.

Benefits can also be classified as selective (divisible) or collective (indivisible, or available to the general public). Money is obviously selective, since it can be used to reward members for various services rendered. Industrial pollution, on the other hand, is collective, or nondivisible, because it affects members and nonmembers alike. Table 1-1 illustrates the kinds of group benefits and their tangibility and divisibility. Let's examine these different benefits in more detail.

Economic Benefits

The most obvious benefits sought by potential and actual group members are economic. In fact, most political interest groups today are those actively seeking to promote the economic well-being of their members. Businesses, trade associations, and labor unions are the most conspicuous in this category.

TABLE 1-1

	Tangible Benefits	Intangible Benefits
Selective (divisible)	Economic: money fringe benefits tax rebates	Solidary: improved status professional acceptance personal satisfaction
Collective (nondivisible)	Policy: antismoking rules handgun controls liberalized abortions	Purposive: clean air and water electoral reforms "good" government ideas

Reprinted with permission of Macmillan Publishing Company from "American Government" 2nd edition by Baker, Pomper and McWilliams, p. 270. Copyright © 1987 by Macmillan Publishing Company.

These and similarly oriented groups offer a range of inducements. Some examples are the wages and fringe benefits offered by the AFL-CIO; the cheaper home heating fuels and insurance that the American Farm Bureau Federation makes available to its members; hospital stipends and practices offered by the American Medical Association (AMA); and discounts on consumer items offered by chain stores to their workers. Access to these and similar benefits are keyed to membership. Economic betterment serves as a strong inducement for affiliation.

Solidary Benefits

A natural result of group affiliation is the establishment of emotional ties across the membership. Associational experiences can contribute to greater self-esteem and self-respect. Involvement in a legislative victory or crucial policy change can provide people with the kind of personal gratification that contributes to continued organizational membership and support. Various officials of the National Association for the Advancement of Colored People (NAACP) feel a sense of accomplishment and satisfaction because of recent victories in public housing, voter rights, and job security. The National Organization for Women (NOW) offers an emotional refuge for hundreds of women who see themselves as second-class citizens because of job discrimination, sexual harassment, or low pay they have experienced. Organizational meetings present opportunities for social interaction and discussion of issues of common concern. Generally, all organizational members will equally share these benefits, by cliques or friendship networks except when cliques or friendship networks prevail. But in no case are such rewards specific; if one is rewarded, all are rewarded.

Purposive Benefits

These are intangible benefits that derive from the satisfaction of having contributed to a worthy cause—cleaning up pollution, eliminating government waste, or supporting a balanced-budget amendment, for example. Purposive benefits, then, flow from demands for some kind of government action or for a policy change that is in the interest of all. By joining the Sierra Club, a person is fulfilling a desire to contribute to a cleaner and safer environment and reduce the continued exploitation of the nation's natural resources. The Common Cause member is helping to bring about reforms that will democratize the governmental process and make it more sensitive to the needs of all citizens. These personal motives are altruistic.

Policy Benefits

Policy rewards are germane to those groups whose concerns go beyond immediate economic or self-gratification. "Man does not live by bread alone" the old adage goes. Many of today's so-called single-issue groups fall into this category—the National Rifle Association (NRA), Handgun Control, Inc., the National Abortion Rights Action League (NARAL), the National Right-to-Life Committee, and the National Committee for an Effective Congress (NCEC), to name just a few. People are attracted to these and similar organizations because they support these groups' goals. NRA members desire easy access to all firearms by all citizens, regardless of marital or economic status, age, or religious preference. The NCEC appeals to those desiring to elect a liberal Congress that will enact liberal social legislation.

Single-issue organizations are nothing new or radical in American politics. Earlier in this century the Anti-Saloon League was ultimately successful in making Prohibition the law. Part of the interest-group explosion, single-issue organizations have also multiplied in recent years because of perceived weaknesses in American political parties. As one commentator has argued, "our parties have atrophied for many of the same reasons [single-issue] groups have arisen: widespread alienation, a perception of governmental unresponsiveness, and the influence of civil rights and anti-war movements."[17] Additionally, political entrepreneurs such as Ralph Nader, Terry Dolan, and Richard Viguerie have organized large numbers of "true believers" of various political stripes who respond to appeals for support and money.[18]

Political groups thus offer several kinds of incentives in order to compete successfully. And they constantly tailor their benefits to attract and retain a body of loyal members. In the next chapter, we will explore a number of other inducements for membership affiliation.

POLITICAL PARTIES AND INTEREST GROUPS: AN EVOLVING RELATIONSHIP

In some ways, our political parties are a conspicuous exception to the general tendency in our society for increasing organizational viability. As organizations, parties have been losing voter support since the mid-1960s.[19] Fewer and fewer individuals describe themselves as "strong" Republicans or "strong" Democrats. Political machines, once prominent in our political history, no longer exist. And holding party office, once a career, is now an avocation of volunteers who can lay claim to needed resources of money, time, and political favors.

These institutional changes are creating opportunities for interest groups to challenge the once-dominant role of political parties in campaign and electoral politics. For example, labor unions, business associations, feminist organizations, and many other groups are compiling and disseminating candidate and issue information to their membership as elections approach. Supplementing these activities are get-out-the-vote drives at the grass-roots level for selected candidates.

Further, more and more organizations are realizing that it is simply not enough to focus only on the more traditional tasks of lobbying, informa-tion dissemination, and endorsements. By borrowing and refining many party techniques—issue development, financing (see Chapter 4), and the furnishing of volunteers—organizations can enhance their leverage with respect to successful candidates. Indeed, the ability of more and more groups to refine and employ "party" strategies testifies to the changing nature of interest group–party relationships.

Finally, as party organizations lose their capacity to control primaries and consistently win general elections, the "military" party of earlier times becomes less relevant. The electoral system used to be predicated on the existence of a body of well-disciplined, loyal troops that went to the polls come rain or shine. And as long as the party leaders could provide the inducements—jobs, money, influence, access—the troops stayed loyal. But then insurgent candidates began to find that they could run on their own and attract enough votes to win occasionally. In the process, the successful candidate became the object of attention of both voters and interest groups, not the party. Once in office, such candidates can act with considerable independence. Organized interests have been quick to exploit the vacuum created by these circumstances.

Interest group–political party relationships are continuing to coalesce. More organizations are devoting increasing amounts of their political and fi-nancial resources to extending their electoral impact generally. Business organi-zations such as the Business–Industry Political Action Committee, the National Association of Realtors, and Associated General Contractors are closely coor-dinating their activities and financial contributions in order to elect Republicans who will support them once in office. And organizations such as the American Federation of Teachers, the International Brotherhood of Electrical Workers, and the National Committee for an Effective Congress are intimately involved in electing or retaining in office sympathetic Democrats. Both sides benefit from this association. Interest groups gain access to key public officials, with some of them being appointed to important public positions. Parties gain needed po-litical support and access to a broad range of organizational resources that are crucial at election time.

SUMMARY

Interest groups are vital elements in contemporary American politics. For a variety of reasons, especially political influence, more and more citizens are joining together. This trend is likely to continue in the 1990s.

There are two major theories of group-based politics. Pluralists argue that political groups are inevitable but make positive contributions to society in general and the political system in particular. Elitists posit that the nation's politics are dominated by private corporations that manipulate public policy making for their own ends. The evidence supports portions of both theories.

All political interest groups, though, face the common problem of attracting and retaining supportive members. Money and voting power can translate into
political influence. Different political organizations emphasize different goals
and incentives. Many are economically motivated; others have noneconomic
concerns—improved social status, feelings of personal satisfaction, favorable
policy ends.

Finally, interest groups and parties have become increasingly intertwined.
Especially in electoral politics, their activities are now virtually indistinguish-
able. This preoccupation with electoral politics will persist for some time. What
will undoubtedly emerge from this set of altered circumstances will be a new
party system in which party functions and responsibilities are quite different
from what they have been since the early 1960s.

NOTES

[1]M. J. Crozier, S. P. Huntington, and J. Watanuki, *The Crisis of Democracy: Report on the
Governability of Democracies to the Trilateral Commission* (New York: New York University Press,
1975), pp. 163–64.

[2]Advisory Commission on Intergovernmental Relations, "The Question of Federalism: Key
Problems," in *State Politics and the New Federalism,* ed. Marilyn Gittell (New York: Longman,
1986), p. 46.

[3]R. G. Kaiser and M. Russell, "A Middle-Class Congress: Haves Over Have-Nots," *Washington Post,* October 15, 1978, p. 1.

[4]*The Federalist,* No. 10.

[5]Ibid.

[6]Alexis de Tocqueville, *Democracy in America* (New York: Colonial Press, 1899), I, 191.

[7]Ibid., II, 114.

[8]Arthur F. Bentley, *The Process of Government* (San Antonio: Principia Press, 1949), p. 210.

[9]Ibid., pp. 208–9.

[10]Carole Greenwald, *Group Power* (New York: Praeger, Co., 1977), p. 305.

[11]David B. Truman, *The Governmental Process,* 2nd ed. (New York: Knopf, 1971), p. 502.

[12]Ibid., p. 519.

[13]G. D. Gerson, *Group Theories of Politics* (Beverly Hills, Calif.: Sage Publications, Inc.,
1978), p. 207.

[14]Mancur Olson, *The Logic of Collective Action* (Cambridge: Harvard University Press,
1965).

[15]For comments on Olson's views, see Terry Moe, *The Organization of Interests* (Chicago:
University of Chicago Press, 1980).

[16]A pioneering study of the benefits offered by groups is found in James Q. Wilson, *Political
Organizations* (New York: Basic Books, 1973).

[17]Jeffery Berry, "Public Interest v. Party Interest," *Society,* 17 (1980), 47.

[18]On this point, see Robert H. Salisbury, "An Exchange Theory of Interest Groups," in
Interest Group Politics in America, ed. Robert H. Salisbury (New York: Harper & Row, Pub., 1970),
pp. 32–67.

[19]On weakening party loyalties, see Alan R. Gitelson, M. Margaret Conway, and Frank B.
Feigert, *American Political Parties: Stability and Change* (Boston: Houghton Mifflin, 1984).

CHAPTER TWO
TODAY'S NEW PLURALISM:
Forces and Actors

OVERVIEW

From the 1960s through the 1970s, the scope of the national government exploded in area after area, from environmental pollution to poverty to the (DE) amelioration of racial and sex discrimination. The list of the actual or potential beneficiaries of these programs is almost limitless. As some writers note, this

> explosion . . . continued almost uninterrupted, during both Republican and Democratic administrations, until slowed by the Reagan Presidency. This accretion of responsibilities, perhaps more than any other single factor, sparked a parallel evolution in the growth of pressure groups which formed around the new government policy initiatives, encouraged by government-provided benefit packages.[1]

Figure 2-1 illustrates this proliferation of groups in the nation's capital. The most significant increase is the result of citizens' organizations multiplying at twice the rate of occupationally based groups.

In this chapter, we will examine a number of forces contributing to the current interest-group universe, analyze several categories of interest groups, and briefly note prevailing democratic and oligarchic tendencies within certain organizations. These tasks are crucial to an understanding of the evolution of today's pressure-group system as well as to any assessment of the contributions by interest groups to the American political system.

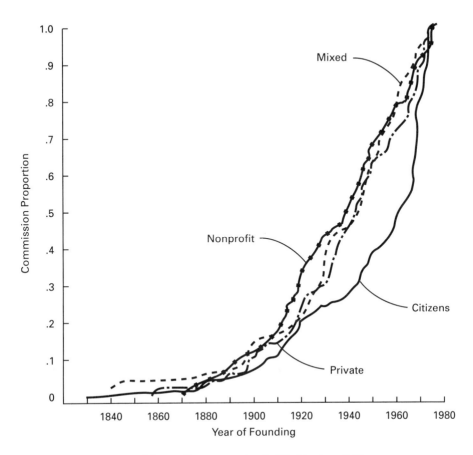

FIGURE 2-1   Growth of Group Representation in Washington, D.C.

Source: Jack L. Walker, "The Origins and Maintenance of Interest Groups in America," *American Political Science Review*, 77 (1983), 395. Used with permission.

WHY THE INTEREST GROUP EXPLOSION?

As with other political phenomena, no single factor can satisfactorily explain the quantum jump in the numbers and types of political interest groups that have emerged since the 1960s. We noted in Chapter 1 that various inducements can stimulate affiliation with these groups. There are a number of other causes of group proliferation, which we can discuss in the context of political, technological, and social changes.

Political Changes

Washington is now more heavily engaged in national policy making than ever before. Take affirmative action, for example. Several agencies are involved in overcoming past discrimination against minorities and women with respect to jobs, pay, promotion, and university admittance. Prior to the 1960s the government's stance on correcting discrimination may best be characterized as "benign neglect." No programs or agencies had responsibilities in this area. Today's affirmative action programs are products of the federal bureaucracy and are administered by it. The Equal Employment Opportunity Commission (EEOC) drafts and enforces regulations prohibiting discrimination on the basis of race, color, sex, religion, or national origin. The U.S. Office of Education has mandated goals for minority admissions to colleges and universities as well as for faculty hiring. The Department of Labor's Office of Federal Contract Compliance requires those firms holding government contracts to comply with EEOC regulations. Federal policies also affect the policies of state and local governments that receive federal funds. Attempts by the Reagan administration, incidentally, to modify or ignore certain affirmative action guidelines were unsuccessful.

Affirmative action is just one of many examples of federal involvement stimulating organizational formation and activity. This new public responsibility, along with that for health and worker safety, inevitably leads to greater concern among citizens. One need not question the wisdom of greater public intervention to understand that it was bound to generate a response among those who are subject to government controls.

Another cause of interest-group growth is the size of the national government, which stimulates the formation of associations concerned with new policies. The 1960s and 1970s saw the establishment of such agencies as the Environmental Protection Agency (EPA), the Office for Civil Rights, the Nuclear Regulatory Agency (NRA), the National Endowment for the Arts (NEA), and the National Transportation Safety Board (NTSB). Quite simply more and more interests are finding their existence affected one way or another as a result of policies emanating from these agencies. One should not be surprised, then, to see labor unions, corporations, farmers, trade associations, and environmentalists increasing their presence in Washington—despite the claims by the Reagan administration that government activity decreased over the 1980s. As one businessman notes,

more and more groups and companies have recognized the increasing size of government involvement. Economically, the government is much more important these days than it was ten years ago. Great Society legislation and environmental and consumer laws have all combined to make companies feel they need to be more active in Washington.[2]

New Political Technology and Communications

Modern, sophisticated technologies also contribute to interest-group formation. Computers and the mass media have made it easier and cheaper to reach both established and incipient constituencies. The computer can develop and almost instantaneously implement massive direct mailings that include interest-group concerns along with appeals for money. In addition, television makes it possible to link up like-minded organizations scattered across the nation. Today's politically oriented organizations are much more technologically sophisticated than their 1950s and 1960s predecessors were.

Social Forces

The American people today are more affluent, more mobile, and better educated than Americans in any previous period. The New Deal, the Fair Deal, and the Great Society have contributed to the nation's relatively high standard of living. These standards are also due in no small part to gains in union bargaining power over the past fifty years. Because of the automobile, mass transit, and government-subsidized freeways, affluent suburbs are a permanent feature of American life. Society's investment in education, initially at the grade-school level, has produced a citizenry far better educated than the citizenry of John F. Kennedy's presidency, just a few decades ago. As a result, we have a society, according to James Q. Wilson, "more and more trained to think in terms of large issues, causes and principles," and it responds to a brand of politics quite different from that of previous years.[3] This spread of affluence and education has contributed to the establishment of a new generation of scientific, professional, and citizen-action groups. The members of these organizations do not require the economic benefits their parents and grandparents did.

Economic background and interest-group membership. Though widespread, group affiliation in the United States is by no means universal. Nor are all segments of society equally organized and equally represented by political organizations. Many individuals are "joiners," but many others are not. As Table 2-1 shows, the frequency of group affiliation correlates with one's economic background.

Group affiliation and its attendant politics remain largely a spectator sport for most adult Americans: Only about 6.5 million of the adult population of 185 million are affiliated with some kind of political organization. Despite this low percentage of citizen participation, group affiliation stimulates activities that often spill over into politics. The more organizations one belongs to, the more likely one is to be motivated to take part in a variety of group pursuits and activities.

TABLE 2-1   Social Class and Interest-Group Membership

Category of People	Percentage Belonging to Interest Groups
All Americans	13%
By income level:	
$25,000 and over	22
$15,000–$24,999	12
Under $15,000	7
By education level:	
College	21
High School	11
Grade School	2

The groups represented in this table have taken positions on such issues as abortion, birth control, environmental protection, gun control, civil rights, tax reduction, generation of nuclear power, homosexual rights, promotion of the free enterprise system, and protection of endangered animal species.

Source: Gallup Poll, *Public Opinion: 1981*, (Wilmington, Delaware: Scholarly Resources, 1982), pp. 177–78. Used with permission.

In general, then, associational life (and its attendant politics) is monopolized by the relatively affluent and *not* by the poor. As Table 2-2 amply demonstrates, in politics as in other aspects of human endeavor, the wealthy thrive while the poor merely survive.

SOME INTEREST-GROUP PROFILES

Having discussed a number of factors in group formation, let us briefly examine some of the groups active in national politics. Through this general overview

TABLE 2-2   Number of Group Memberships by Income

Number of Memberships	$0–3999	$4000–6999	$7000–9999	$10,000–14,999	$15,000–19,999	$20,000–24,999	$25,000 & over
Zero	45.2%	36.4%	30.9%	26.2%	22.1%	20.2%	16.1%
One	30.9	28.9	30.9	27.5	25.7	22.5	20.6
Two	13.9	17.2	17.7	19.2	18.7	18.9	18.0
Three or Four	7.4	13.4	14.5	19.7	22.3	25.6	28.0
Five or More	2.6	4.1	6.1	7.5	11.1	12.7	17.3
Totals*	100.0%	100.0%	100.1%	100.1%	99.9%	99.9%	100.0%
N =	880	924	864	1445	1061	772	995

*Totals may not equal 100% due to rounding.
Source: General Social Survey, 1972–1980.

BOX 2-1   *PUBLIC PERCEPTIONS OF VARIOUS SPECIAL INTERESTS*

Too Much Influence?

The Roper Organization Inc. asked the public in January 1985 whether particular special–interest groups had "too much influence in our society today, or too little influence or about the right amount of influence." Here are the responses.

	Too much	About right	Too little	Don't know
Labor unions	57%	30%	11%	5%
Business and industry organizations	51%	37%	4%	7%
Doctors' organizations	44%	39%	6%	10%
Real estate operators	37%	48%	4%	18%
Military groups	30%	47%	11%	12%
Women's rights organizations	23%	43%	25%	8%
Church groups	22%	44%	29%	6%
Environmental groups	15%	39%	37%	9%
College organizations	14%	54%	16%	15%
Consumer groups	12%	46%	34%	8%
Veterans groups	7%	46%	38%	10%
Farmers groups	6%	25%	60%	8%
Senior citizens groups	4%	33%	58%	5%

Source: *National Journal,* July 13, 1985, p. 1646. Used with permission.

we will gain a better understanding of interest groups and their role in national policy making.

Business

In today's business-government relationships, the following conditions generally prevail:

1. Government decisions affect nearly every management decision made by corporate executives.
2. Business leaders spend more time on government matters each year.
3. Successful business executives must know as much about how government operates as they do about their own corporations.
4. Government not only regulates business and investigates its practices periodically, it also supports it and has become its largest customer.[4]

Government, then, conditions the climate in which business leaders must operate, and its decisions on spending and regulation shape hundreds of business decisions on what is produced and how it is to be produced, distributed, and sold. Governmental decision making is a principal force in today's business affairs.

Given its continuing concern with such issues as public regulation, corporate taxes, and labor legislation, business has traditionally been well organized for political action. In fact, almost every area of industrial and commercial activity within the nation is organized to some degree—oil and gas, new- and used-car dealers, importers and exporters, service industries, coal and steel, and many, many more.

The increasing complexity of legislation in the areas of business taxation, regulation, and international trade has given rise to a new generation of trade associations. Many of these have relatively narrow interests but are determined to get what they want. A typical example is the Fertilizer Institute.

The Fertilizer Institute is an amalgam of chemical and agricultural firms. Its policy focus is quite narrow, and it employs the bulk of its resources in lobbying. Institute representatives are extremely persistent and knowledgeable. Their main strategy consists of frequent and intensive one-on-one contacts with selected legislators or key staff personnel during legislative sessions. Institute lobbyists are known to be articulate and are well respected by Washington officialdom. These qualities have been responsible for legislative victories as well as an exemption for fertilizers from the original Superfund law and from the law as it was reauthorized in 1986.* A former legislative aide explains the Institute's legislative influence by noting that "they're up there [on Capitol Hill] making their case day after day . . . they just wear out their shoe leather."[5]

---

*The 1986 law required the elimination of existing toxic-waste residue and waste dumps in the states.

At the other end of the spectrum are larger organizations that seek to represent business as a whole. One of these is the Business Roundtable, established in the early 1970s. The Roundtable was created, according to one writer,

> to reflect the reallocation of business, human and material resources to political action; new alliances and structures for coordination; [and] the rapid integration of the emerging new information storage, retrieval, and communication technologies in the service of corporate business political advocacy.[6]

The Roundtable's organizers believed that the needs of business were not being adequately met by older, more traditional business associations. The Chamber of Commerce was perceived as not adequately representing big business and as being too "knee-jerk" reactionary and shrill in its perpetual condemnation of governmental regulatory policies. In addition, both the Chamber and the National Association of Manufacturers were viewed as being too slow and cumbersome in their representative processes.

The uniqueness of the Roundtable lies in its commitment to the participation of chief executive officers (CEOs) and in its use of frontline troops, rather than surrogates, in both policy formation and direct lobbying. The Roundtable is a fraternity of powerful and presitgious business leaders that tells "business's side of the story" to legislators, bureaucrats, White House personnel, and other interested public officials. The organization seeks to generate political action from the CEO down through the corporate hierarchy to midlevel executives and employees and outward to stockholders, distributors, and suppliers. An important political advantage in this context is the Roundtable's political access. One writer puts it this way:

> The Business Roundtable almost seems to be a belated recognition of the frequently demonstrated historical principle that royalty always commands more attention, respect, awe, than lesser nobility. Neither the National Association of Manufacturers nor the U.S. Chamber of Commerce can do what a uniquely conceived and specially powered lobby of the largest and most responsible economic interests in the country can achieve.[7]

Unlike the Chamber of Commerce and the National Association of Manufacturers, whose professional staffs wield considerable influence over the agenda and the political direction of their organizations, the Roundtable is run by its members. The major components of the organization are a small executive committee, a somewhat larger policy committee, and task forces (twelve in recent years) that reflect the nation's and the organization's political agendas. The organization's agenda avoids divisive and single-member issues.

Task forces are headed by Roundtable members who coordinate research on issues of common concern and lobby on bills that fall within task force jurisdictions. Close liaison is maintained between task forces and the organization's Washington representatives.

Today, the Roundtable plays a key role in shaping political strategy for big business. Often working with right-wing groups that responsible business people used to shun, Roundtable leaders utilize an arsenal of tactics to undercut their enemies. They frequently advise state and local industry groups opposing citizen initiatives on the ballot. Roundtable leaders also frequently bring CEOs to Washington to lobby—against the establishment of a cabinet-level consumer protection agency, against controls on toxic-waste use, against more stringent clean-air and clean-water legislation, and for labor-reform legislation. In the 1980s the Roundtable sparked millions of dollars of "image advertising," blitzing the country with portrayals of the altruism of corporations and the beleaguered state of the free enterprise system at the hands of public regulation.

Since the late 1970s, business interests have demonstrated a good deal of political adaptability and resiliency. As a reporter for *Fortune* magazine has written, "suddenly business seems to possess all the primary instruments of power—the leadership, the strategy, the supporting troops, the campaign money—and a will to use them."[8] This is certainly the case in electoral politics. Although labor unions pioneered the establishment of political action committees (PACs), business has proved to be a quick learner; its PACs and their spending levels quickly surpassed those of labor (see Chapter 4). The vast wealth of the American business community is being increasingly poured into key congressional races in support of probusiness candidates. Business has also achieved a notable degree of unity and cooperation on a number of economic, social welfare, and labor issues.

ORGANIZED LABOR

The extensive industrialization and commericalization of the nation during the late nineteenth and early twentieth centuries catalyzed worker desires for some kind of industry-wide organization. Growing concerns with wages, grievance procedures, and working conditions led to unionization.

Today the AFL–CIO, with approximately 12.7 million members, is the largest and most authoritative voice of organized labor. Corresponding to many big business lobbies, the federation encompasses over 100 trade unions representing teachers, electricians, plumbers, chemical workers, farm workers, plus a significant number of workers at the state, county, and municipal level. The AFL–CIO maintains a large professional staff at its Washington, D.C., headquarters for disseminating information and guiding members in addition to lobbying. It maintains extensive links with Congress and such relevant departments as Labor, Health and Human Services, and Education. Federation lobbyists are among the most numerous and visible of the lobbyists appearing before our national institutions.

American unions are primarily concerned with the economic benefits that fall to labor—wages, fringe benefits, retirement systems, profit-sharing plans, work conditions, and health-care benefits. Unions typically become politically active when there is a perceived threat to their benefits by government or business. However, the size and the varied makeup of the federation have led it to broaden its concern with benefits beyond the traditional economic ones. It is not unusual, therefore, for the AFL-CIO to push for stronger consumer-protection laws, extended voting rights, health-care benefits, and stringent industrial-pollution controls. Such concerns are taking an increasing share of the federation's resources, and its political linkages are expanding as a result. This trend will undoubtedly continue, given the changing base and aspirations of the American work force.

The significant size of the federation is a mixed blessing. On the one hand, it provides the potential for strong political influence on selected targets. On the other hand, because individual unions pursue their own interests, in the name of organizational flexibility, the federation is frequently divided and its energies fragmented. Divisive internal debates crop up, particularly as traditional labor issues are replaced by new ones—such as affirmative action, free trade versus protectionism, or alleged ties to organized crime.

Presently, most labor unions and the American labor movement in general are on the defensive, politically speaking. There are a number of internal and external reasons for this. First, labor's membership is dwindling (Figure 2–2), and this affects its political clout. Labor is *not* coping well with the effects of deregulation (see Chapter 9) and a rapidly changing economy. Additionally, labor's public image remains tarnished because of a closed, autocratic system of governance contaminated by corruption and racketeering. Nor is labor's

FIGURE 2-2

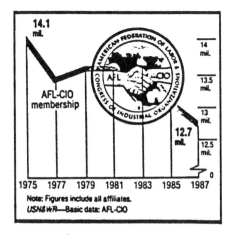

image helped by its relatively late push for minority rights and needs. Finally, there have been sharp reversals in the policies of the National Labor Relations Board.* In short, a general malaise prevails within labor's ranks and leadership with respect to direction and purpose.

These problems are compounded by resurgent business interests that see recent developments as an opportunity for creating a "union-free" environment. A concept of preventative union relations has surfaced even among companies that resisted the antiunion stance currently gaining favor among more and more firms. Unions are finding it increasingly difficult to organize, and even where they are successful, management does not easily concede. Management frequently indulges in delaying tactics both legal and illegal. And business is bringing a new assertiveness to negotiations, demanding more say and possible concessions in terms of job assignments, overtime pay, cost-of-living increases, and the like.

Public sentiment toward unions and their political activities has become less favorable. Fewer and fewer workers affiliate or identify with unions. Many of labor's traditional friends have passed from the political scene, and it has had to strike temporary alliances with other groups. In sum, government sensitivity to, and the political access of, labor are no longer what they once were.

Agriculture

A paradox prevails in agricultural politics. American farmers—the world's most productive—are piling up farm surpluses that are bursting government storage bins and silos. But many American farmers are going broke. Although farm subsidies (government payments to farmers for the production or non-production of certain crops) amount to over $20 billion annually, about 1000 farms are foreclosed each year and many more farmers quit voluntarily.

The situation is really nothing new. For over fifty years, the "farm problem" has consisted of an overabundance of food, which results in low food prices and correspondingly low farm incomes. Many of today's farmers simply cannot survive on an income that does not match the costs of farming. It remains to be seen whether the farm policies of the past fifty years have ameliorated or exacerbated the "farm problem."

Today there are four types of agricultural organizations in terms of policy concerns, quality of membership, and size.[9] From broad to narrow, these types are agrarian protest organizations, multipurpose organizations, single-issue organizations, and single-project organizations (Table 2-3).

Protest organizations desire basic changes in existing agriculture policies—reform of lending institutions (banks and savings and loans), preservation of the

---

*The results of elections held by the NLRB to determine whether workers desire to be union-represented have given unions reason to worry: in 1970 unions won more than half of the elections, in 1975 they won slightly less than half, and by 1982–83 the success rate was down to 40 percent.

TABLE 2-3 A Typology of Contemporary Farm Organizations

Protest Organizations	Multipurpose Organizations	Single-Issue Organizations	Single-Project Organization
American Agriculture Movement	American Farm Bureau Federation	American Farmland Trust	Agriculture Research Institute
Family Farm Movement	National Farmers' Union	National Peanut Growers Group	Farmers for Fairness
North American Farmers' Alliance	National Cotton Council Processors	National Soybean Association	Foundation on Economic Trends
National Catholic Rural Life Conference	American Seed Trade Association	National Food Processors	Environmental Policy Institute

Source: William P. Browne, *Private Interests, Public Policy, and American Agriculture* (Lawrence: University Press of Kansas, 1988). p. 57. Used with permission.

family farm, and an end to the growing dependency on chemicals—and pursue an adversarial style of political participation. These groups are committed to and actively support those issues and ideologies that contributed to their establishment. The American Agricultural Movement (AAM), for example, still refuses to abandon its position of 90 percent-plus parity—a position not strongly supported by other protest groups. Inflexible positions turn off more pragmatic public officials.

Because protest groups lack the organizational stability and personal familiarity that contribute to effective lobbying, their political access to legislative and administrative personnel is generally episodic and limited. Consequently, these organizations frequently depend upon the mass media for the transmission of their policy concerns to public officials. In addition, protest groups provide little, if any, material services, which makes it difficult for them to retain loyal members. As a result, memberships are characteristically small and quixotic, and this limits group activities to little more than protest. Greater opportunities lie in a coalitional politics that will link these organizations with more active groups having broader policy concerns.

As their name implies, *multipurpose organizations* have a range of policy concerns as well as heterogeneous memberships and wider political contacts. In a typical year, it is not unusual for these organizations to address a number of issues, such as agricultural finances, price supports, pesticide regulations, and worker-safety regulations. Unless the organization is well staffed, like the Farm Bureau and the Food Marketing Service, its lobbyists are mainly concerned with reacting to most issues, though they may sometimes be able to modify legislation.

Representatives of these groups maintain contacts with various policy networks, which present opportunities for policy formulation from drafting to implementation. The staffs of multipurpose organizations are experienced, and they frequently contribute to both agenda setting and issue development. Additionally, staffs inform members of new policies and political strategies that are geared to member expectations. Various media are utilized to these ends, such as newsletters, flyers, workshops, and seminars on matters of organizational concern.

Due to their broad, relatively long-term agricultural concerns, multipurpose organizations range across the political spectrum from conservative to liberal, and are so perceived by both legislative and administrative personnel. These perceptions, however, can be modified by a group's orientation on world trade, direct democracy, and disposition of farm surpluses. Given the reactive and generally pragmatic approaches that the representatives of these organizations take on most agricultural issues, members gain a stable and consistent image that coincides with the organizations' political purposes and strategies.

Single-issue organizations consist of more specialized farm interests— dairy, fruit, or soybean farmers, for example. These groups prize their political autonomy and generally avoid encumbering alliances. This strategy allows them to maximize their relatively modest lobbying resources and maintain their organizational image.

Because of their relatively narrow concerns, these organizations establish and maintain close contacts with selected legislative and administrative personnel. Thus, they are able to discuss issues of mutual concern and advance their claims when the situation permits. Of course, not all groups are equal, and groups of this category may not be able to attain the quality of access that they need in order to influence decision making. Or, group contacts may simply not be able to deliver, which can necessitate a shift of emphasis or an effort to gain a structural change in public policy making.

Single-project organizations, as noted in recent literature (see Table 2-3), have more sharply defined and intermediate policy goals than do single-issue organizations. The former groups have an ongoing, comprehensive concern with legislative and/or administrative regulations. Because of the rapid changes in regulatory commodity price levels, the lobbying efforts of these groups are continual.

Influence across the boundaries of these organizations is based primarily on current and accurate information on the issue at hand. Because of the short-term concerns of these organizations, their lobbyists do not rely on personal relationships with numerous public officials. Rather, organizational integrity or policy expertise is the crucial element of success.

It is not unusual for these organizations to hire consultant-lobbyists to expand their political contacts. Occasionally, too, they initiate reports, conferences, or projects and transmit the results to selected individuals who can ultimately influence policy making.

This analysis of farm organizations amply demonstrates how diverse they are—not only in size, structure, and purpose but also in political strategies. Like other organized interests, farm-oriented organizations have expanded greatly since the 1960s. They now include food processors, farm implement dealers, agricultural research foundations and colleges, farm consultants, trade associations, cooperatives, and other groups.

This proliferation of farm groups has resulted in a multifaceted lobby bringing widely varying points of view before national policy makers. This variety militates against any administration forming an overall farm policy. Rather, what frequently occurs is a series of policy skirmishes among various farm interests seeking to divide the available spoils. This, though, is really nothing new. What is new is the range of lobbying tactics that this universe of interests has embraced in order to enhance their political clout. These tactics include greater mobilization of constituent pressure at the grass-roots level, the formation of political action committees and expenditures in behalf of profarm legislators, the use of election consultants, and the establishment of temporary alliances with business, university, or foundation representatives that build goodwill for the future.

The omnibus farm legislation of the 1970s and 1980s involved some complex and diverse compromises and bargaining. Whether concerned with narrow or broad provisions, interest groups negotiated a series of settlements regarding price supports, production controls, social policy, land conservation, and so on. Leading participants were such actors as U.S. Department of Agriculture personnel, members of House and Senate agriculture committees, consumers and other nonagriculturists, and frequently the White House. The agricultural politics of the 1990s will not vary significantly from those of the 1970s and 1980s.

Environmentalism

The environmental movement in the United States emerged suddenly in the midst of political controversy and heightened pressure-group activity in the late 1960s and early 1970s. Voices within the scientific community had been warning of serious environmental abuses by humans:

> All over the world, technological civilization is threatening the elements of nature that are essential to human life, and the values that make it worth living.[10]

> If the present growth trends in world population, industrialization, pollution, food production and resource depletion continue unchanged, the limits of growth on this planet will be reached sometime within the next hundred years.[11]

> If we go on as we are, maintaining the present rate of growth in human population and demanding so much of the environment, we shall inevitably run out of resources and life will cease to exist on the planet[12].

Suddenly humans were perceived as an endangered species, whose very existence was threatened by a materialistic culture, population pressures, technology, and the attendant environmental ravages (Figure 2-3).

Three events in the late 1960s and early 1970s jolted an apathetic public into awareness of the nation's environment—an oil rig blow-out off the California coast near Santa Barbara; the impoundment by public officials of thousands of pounds of DDT-laced silver salmon caught in Wisconsin and Minnesota lakes; and a fire on the sludge-filled Cuyahoga River near Cleveland, Ohio. Environmentalism came to the scene spontaneously fed by these events and the eloquent warnings of Rachel Carson's *Silent Spring*.[13]

The destruction of the nation's land, air, and water, periodically spotlighted by the mass media, led to a huge increase in both the membership base and the organizational diversity of the environmental movement. A number of new organizations—Critical Mass, Environmental Action, League of Conservation Voters, Solar Lobby—committed themselves to a broad range of political activities—demonstrations, lawsuits, electoral endorsements, and dissemination of scientific studies. Quite often, these activities were coordinated with those of older, establishment organizations—the Izaak Walton League, the Wilderness Society, and the Audubon Society. Needless to say, this escalation of political activity caused a number of industries, such as paper mills, oil companies, and

FIGURE 2-3

mining firms, to organize and editorialize in the mass media that they were being unfairly maligned by environmentalists.

The late 1960s and early 1970s saw a huge influx of middle-class activists and volunteers into environmental politics. Not surprisingly, then, the environmental movement is predominantly middle-class. Financially comfortable, many environmentalists are concerned with issues and ideas as opposed to economic benefits. Many college youths were enlisted into environmental politics, and they brought a new vigor and militancy to the movement.

The prevailing political atmosphere during the late 1960s and early 1970s was conducive to the environmental movement's political goals and strategies. The Vietnam war, Watergate, and the civil rights movement mobilized sufficient segments of the middle class to successfully push for greater national responsibility for the environment. Congress subsequently enacted some thirty-five statutes of environmental law—the Clean Air and Clean Water acts, pesticide controls, the safeguarding of endangered species, protection of public drinking water and so on (Box 2-2). The linchpin of this legislation is the National Environment Policy Act (NEPA), establishing the Environmental Protection Agency (EPA). Environmental laws are administered by the EPA in conjunction with similarly named agencies at the state, county, and local level.

BOX 2-2 *MAJOR ENVIRONMENTAL LAWS*

Year	Legislation	Major Provisions
1899	Refuse Act	Restricted dumping of hazardous wastes into navigable streams, lakes, rivers
1948	Water Pollution Control Act	Provided federal assistance to states in establishing water-quality programs
1955	Air Pollution Control Act	Provided federal assistance to states in establishing air-quality programs
1963	Clean Air Act	Authorized federal grants to develop and establish air pollution control programs
1970	National Environmental Protection Act	Established Environmental Protection Agency and required environmental impact statements for major federal projects
1970	Clean Air Act Amendments	Authorized establishment of automobile pollution emission standards
1972	Federal Water Pollution Control Act Amendments	Required companies to obtain permits to discharge pollutants into rivers and lakes
1974	Safe Drinking Water Act	Authorized standards for safe public drinking water
1976	Toxic Substances Control Act	Banned PCBs (polychlorinated biphenyls) and authorized the EPA to require testing of toxic substances
1976	Resource Conservation and Recovery Act	Required EPA to identify hazardous wastes and establish safety standards for their production, transportation, and disposal
1977	Clean Air Act Amendments	Delayed but strengthened automobile-emission and air-quality standards
1980	Comprehensive Environmental Response, Compensation, and Liability Act (Superfund)	Imposed tax on chemical industry for a trust fund to be used in cleaning up abandoned hazardous waste sites
1984	Hazardous and Solid Waste Amendments	Reduced the use of landfills for hazardous wastes and required EPA to act more quickly

Source: Alan Stone and Richard Barke, *Governing the American Republic,* 2nd ed. (New York: St. Martin's Press, 1989), p. 473. Copyright © 1989 by St. Martin's Press, Inc. Reprinted by permission of St. Martin's Press, Incorporated.

Environmental legislation, incidentally, parallels civil rights legislation in that both apply to a wide variety of public and private actions. Also, environmental legislation allows citizen (but in reality interest-group) suits. The Clean Air Act, for example, allows suits over its enforcement: once the EPA makes a decision concerning the type and number of scrubbers necessary for various steel plant exhausts, it may be sued either by the owners of the plant or by environmental interests. The owners, of course, will prefer the cheapest scrubber, whereas concerned environmental organizations will want the cleanest and most efficient scrubbers. Either party may sue if it perceives that the EPA is compromising between cost and cleanliness.

The 1980s saw an escalation in the use of litigation (suits brought before courts for the purpose of changing existing policies) by environmental organizations. (Interest-group litigation will be covered in Chapter 7.) Varying coalitions, including one consisting of the Legal Defense Fund, the Wilderness Society, Population Zero, and the Sierra Club, have instituted suits opposing highway expansion, shopping-center developments, dam and bridge construction, and the erection of high-rise buildings in residential areas. Suits such as these allow policy input by the litigants in the decision. Also, courts can require that federal bureaucrats solicit environmental concerns.

Americans are increasingly concerned about contaminated drinking water and toxic-waste dumps in their neighborhoods. Most believe that the federal government must take the lead in providing solutions. However, citizen participation through political interest groups will ensure that these complex issues are dealt with effectively.

Equal Rights

The struggle for *women's rights* both predates and postdates the black civil rights movement in the 1960s. Precedents for modern feminism are found in the suffrage movement of the late nineteenth and early twentieth centuries, but the present movement grew spontaneously out of the efforts of individual women activists—or feminists—throughout the country. The "women's movement" is defined here as the informal linkage among millions of women to achieve greater social, political, and economic equality with their male counterparts: "make policy, not coffee." A growing awareness and consciousness of existing patterns of sexual discrimination, the lack of public agencies for dealing with women's issues, increased media coverage of the movement, and the establishment of a national commission on women's rights have all been conducive to organizational formation.

The emerging movement spawned groups ranging from formal organizations such as the National Organization for Women (NOW), Federally Employed Women (FEW), Human Rights for Women (HRW), and the National Black Feminist Organization, to a significant number of transitory, amorphous "rap" and "consciousness-raising" groups.[14] NOW was the first nationally organized women's group (1966) concerned with a broad range of issues. A prime purpose of its founders was to create an organization similar to the NAACP that would lobby and litigate for an end to sexual discrimination. Whereas rap and consciousness-raising groups tend to be solidary, NOW is both solidary and purposive. Members of the former organizations gain solidary benefits from their association in sessions concerned with development of self-esteem and self-worth. The problems of individual women are portrayed in these sessions as experiences common to *all* women. NOW, on the other hand, provides both valued relationships and articulation of feminist concerns in post–ERA politics.

The equal rights amendment.   One of the significant issues in feminist politics is the Equal Rights Amendment (ERA). Thus far the ERA has failed to receive state ratification, but it is presently awaiting reconsideration by Congress for resubmission to the states. The issue of ratification has politically energized thousands of women throughout the country, on both sides of the issue. The following brief discussion of the ratification struggle gives further credence to the inevitability of group formation and the increasing involvement of groups in politics at *all* levels of government.

The basic principle of the ERA is to ensure the equality of women with men under the law.[*] Its proponents claim that ratification will open the way for elimination of sexual discrimination emanating from statutory, administrative, and constitutional law; government action; and private-sector action. Under the ERA, national, state, and local governments are committed to ensure equal treatment of the sexes; some 500 to 700 discriminatory state and local laws would be voided.

When Congress passed the ERA in 1972, conditions were generally favorable for its ratification. Most of the nation's political leaders—including the president, most governors, and many state legislators—supported it, as did both major political parties. Within the first year of Congressional passage, twenty-two states ratified—a rate faster than that experienced by most of the eleven successful constitutional amendments in this century. By the end of the second year, the ERA was still ahead of some of these amendments—the Sixteenth (income tax) and the Twenty-second (a two-term limit on presidents). By the fourth year, the ERA had been ratified by 89 percent of the required states. It was at this point that serious, organized opposition to the ERA surfaced in a number of nonratifying states. (See Table 2–4 for a sample of the organizations involved in the ratification struggle).

---

[*]Text of the Equal Rights Amendment:

1. Equality of rights under the law shall not be denied or abridged by the United States or by any State on account of sex.
2. Congress shall have the power to enforce, by appropriate legislation, the provisions of this article.
3. This amendment shall take effect two years after the date of ratification.

TABLE 2-4   Interest Groups Involved in the ERA Struggle

Pro-ERA	Anti-ERA
National Organization for Women (NOW)	John Birch Society
American Association of University Women	Eagle Forum
National Abortion Rights Action League (NARAL)	Daughters of the American Revolution (DAR)
American Jewish Congress	Stop-ERA
American Bar Association (ABA)	Young Americans for Freedom
National Association for the Advancement of Colored People (NAACP)	Christian Crusade
	American Conservative Union (ACU)
state and local ad hocs	state and local ad hocs

The early successes of the pro-ERA forces were due to a number of organizational accomplishments. First, these organizations provided the mechanism for grass-roots mobilization of thousands of women experiencing sexual discrimination. Both NOW and the National Women's Political Caucus (NWPC) provided an emotional refuge for many women perceiving themselves as oppressed.

Second, pro-ERA groups raised needed funding and provided volunteer help at crucial points in the ratification struggle. The League of Women Voters and the Business and Professional Women's Club made telephone calls and conducted fund drives at key junctures of congressional consideration.

Third, pro-ERA organizations broadened their political base. By building coalitions they were able to attract various church-related and occupational groups to the ERA banner—the United Methodist and Presbyterian churches along with a number of Unitarian Universalist associations. A number of labor unions, including the AFL-CIO, also joined the fray, as did agencies, bureaus, and commissions at the national, state, and local levels. These latter supporters issued statements, drafted documents, and prepared legal opinions supporting ratification.

Finally, many "pro" organizations researched and disseminated data documenting the extent of economic discrimination against women, especially with respect to pay. NOW was particularly prominent in publicizing the famous "fifty-nine-cent gap": as of 1980, for every dollar men earned, women earned just 59 cents. This became a powerful symbol of sex discrimination and was effectively exploited.

Anti-ERA forces were essentially group-based and led by Phyllis Schlafly, a political conservative from Illinois. Long known in state Republican party circles, Schlafly wrote and edited the *Phyllis Schlafly Report.* She entered the ERA fray with a strong attack on the ERA in the *Report.* An able organizer, she established Stop-ERA in 1972. This became a large umbrella organization in approximately two dozen states. Claiming about 50,000 members in the mid-

1970s, Stop-ERA consisted mainly of nonworking mothers and housewives who perceived the amendment as a threat to family stability. Schlafly was also involved in the establishment of a number of satellite organizations, such as the National Committee of Endorsers against ERA, comprising congressional wives whose husbands opposed ratification, and AWARE (American Women Already Richly Endowed), ostensibly a national letter-writing committee to pressure state legislators in uncommitted states.

These women's organizations were soon joined by elements of the radical right. The John Birch Society joined the opposition soon after congressional enactment of the ERA in 1972. Others coming aboard soon thereafter included the National States' Rights Party, the Christian Crusade, the Ku Klux Klan, and the Manion Forum Trust Fund. The latter is named after the political conservative Clarence Manion, the controversial former dean of Notre Dame's law school. Helping to offset organized labor's support for ratification were a number of conservative business organizations, such as the National Association of Manufacturers, the American Retail Association, and the Chamber of Commerce.

Just as the ERA opponents' organizational base differed from that of the pro-ERA forces, so did their tactics. Pro-ERA organizations generally utilized traditional lobbying and pressure tactics and sought to appeal to reason and fairness in their arguments. Anti-ERA forces used some of these same techniques but also interjected more symbol manipulation and more radical tactics.[15] They were able to mount an effective countermovement despite a narrower organizational base, less money, and public opinion favoring ratification. Whereas the pro-ERA forces were organized from the top down, the opposition was from the bottom up. Their bottom-up arrangement compensated for the anti-ERA forces' shortcomings and contributed to a more effective lobbying effort.

Schlafly and her allies capably shifted the ratification struggle from the narrow issue of equity to the argument that the ERA represented a broad attack on the American family and its traditional values. Through a barrage of newsletters, speeches, public testimony, and persistent attacks in the mass media, the anti-ERA movement argued that ratification would result in the drafting of large numbers of women into the armed forces, require *all* wives to support a growing number of "freeloading" husbands, and transform all public toilets into unisex horror chambers rife with rape and sodomy.

Opposition forces also linked the controversial abortion issue to the ERA. Pro-ERA values were depicted as essentially value-free; condoning sexual promiscuity, divorce, and where broken homes are the *rule,* not the exception. The rhetoric in these matters was meant to startle and shock. Additionally, most pro-ERA women were portrayed as lesbians, radicals, and atheistic bitches.

Finally, ERA opponents orchestrated an effective direct-mail campaign to selected state legislators. Most letters were handwritten, contained emotional and religious phraseology, and predicted dire consequences for the future of the American family if the ERA passed. Letters were also sent to many out-of-state legislators as well—a traditional "no-no" in American politics. Further, Schlafly's allies and supporters stalked the capitals of the uncommitted states disseminating literature, lobbying, and effectively testifying against the ERA whenever they could. As one state legislator notes,

> the Stop-ERA forces were much better organized and did a better job lobbying. The pro-ERA forces are only visible when there is going to be a vote. . . . The Stop-ERA, Phyllis Schlafly's group, is there all the time, . . . getting to know the legislators, developing a relationship with them, not necessarily harassing them, but constantly reminding them of their presence, maybe even talking to them about other issues, establishing that personal relationship.[16]

Despite a three-year extension, the ERA was not ratified by the required number of states. Several factors were involved in its defeat. One, public support did *not* increase over time. In some states, support for the amendment actually declined. Two, ratification was hurt by the infusion of other issues into the struggle—abortion, the drafting of women into the armed forces, and changing sex roles. These issues broadened the opposition. Third, state legislators interpreted the ERA as a device for further national intrusion into state affairs. Many state legislators believed that under the ERA the U.S. Supreme Court and other federal judges would impose standards of conduct between the sexes and thus displace the traditional role of the states.

The ERA struggle amply demonstrates that a relatively vocal minority can prevail over a better-funded and publicly supported majority. The greater organizational zeal and dedication of Schlafly and her allies allowed them to carry the day. Second, status quo groups, such as Stop-ERA, can frustrate the drive of groups seeking basic policy changes. Because the amendment process requires near consensus, opponents of the ERA or any other amendment have only to create enough public doubt about the effects of the amendment to prevent a consensus from forming. Finally, movement organizations, by their very nature, are diverse. Some forces within the women's movement were more concerned with ideological purity, others promoted separatism, and still others favored pragmatism. Given the number of individuals and groups involved and the complexity of the issue at hand, this was inevitable. Trying to legislate a broad principle through the amendment process is difficult at best.

The Public Interest

A relatively new force in interest-group politics is the *public interest movement,* which consists of a wide range of interests—research centers, public interest law firms, citizens' lobbies, and numerous state and local community organizations.[17] Examples are Common Cause, the Consumer Federation of America, Public Citizen, the Citizen/Labor Energy Coalition, and the League of Women Voters.

The characteristics and political objectives of these organizations will be briefly noted here, and then discussed in detail in Chapter 8. The public interest movement, incidentally, does not represent anything radically new. Progressives, muckrakers, and other turn-of-the-century reformers demanded a number of governmental reforms aimed at democratizing the political system—electoral primaries, broader application of a civil service system, a shorter ballot, and nonpartisan elections.

Latter-day public interest groups are also pursuing governmental reform. These organizations view public regulation of the economy today as deficient and ineffective. Only through greater public participation can the prevailing imbalance favoring private interest be corrected. "Captured" or co-opted agencies must be sensitized to the welfare of all and not just the powerful few.

The goals of public interest groups are uniquely attractive. What public official, for instance, would publicly oppose a call for more honest and open government, or more public participation before state utility commissions, or less contamination or defoliation of the environment? To be sure, these organizations differ on how best to achieve these and similar ends, but society as a whole finds their objectives generally attractive.

Another unique aspect of public interest groups is that a number of them are entrepreneurial—established and led by an activist founder, such as Norman Lear (People of the American Way), Ralph Nader (Public Citizen), and John Gardner (Common Cause) (see Box 2-3). These individuals have impressive organizing abilities and can create organizations for the expression of citizens' interests. Without such people many potential interests would not be heard. Entrepreneurs are links in a series of exchanges between group members and the political system. Leaders provide such services as programs, political direction, and issue articulation. In return for these and other services, the leaders receive the rewards of officeholding—staff, prestige, visibility, and decision-making discretion. For their support of organizational demands, public officials gain political backing, campaign funding, and votes in future elections.

This brief analysis of interest groups and their incentives and goals illustrates their breadth and depth. No one organization or combination thereof is representative of all the rest. The atomization of our national politics will continue as growing numbers of citizens are drawn into politics. According to James Rosenau, more Americans are "mobilizable" now than ever before.[18]

ARE ORGANIZATIONS OLIGARCHIC OR DEMOCRATIC?

How democratically are important organizational decisions made? Should the organizational leadership, for example, follow its own dictates, or should it merely reflect what it perceives to be the desires of the rank and file? What is the degree of organizational democracy?

Earlier in this century, Robert Michels, an Italian-Swiss sociologist study-ing the degree of democracy in large organizations, theorized that an "iron law of oligarchy" prevailed in most of them.[19] Michels saw a division between the leadership and the rank and file. This occurs because the leadership monop-olizes the organization's financial resources, its internal communications, and other devices of control. Growing accustomed to the amenities of power—high salaries, large staffs, the solidary benefits of prestige and interaction with pub-lic officials—the leadership becomes increasingly complacent. Therefore, any strong criticism or dissenting views from the general membership are viewed as threats.

For their part, Michels states, the rank and file are generally indifferent to and uninformed about most organizational business. The general membership gladly relinquishes most of its responsibilities to the organization's officers. As a result, control of the organization comes to reside in the hands of an unresponsive oligarchy that utilizes the organization for its own ends. One must keep Michels's theory in proper perspective, however: his observations were made early in this century, when large, voluntary organizations were fewer and less diverse.[20]

What is the situation today in political interest groups? Thus far no study has answered this question definitively. There are variations from organization to organization. John L. Lewis, founder and former president of the United Mine Workers (UMW), ran that organization virtually as a dictator during the 1930s, 1940s, and 1950s. His strong, authoritative personality made him almost unquestioned in union matters. Since his death, and despite a good deal of controversy within the UMW over its control, the union is much more democratically administered today.

In contrast, the Teamsters Union has been plagued by charges of racke-teering, corruption, and misuse of office by a number of its presidents—Dave Beck, Jimmy Hoffa, Roy Williams, and Jackie Presser. U.S. Senate investiga-tions of these and related charges led to the imprisonment of Beck, Hoffa, and Williams. These allegations and convictions led in turn to a series of dissident movements within the union during the 1970s and 1980s seeking unsuccess-fully to purge corrupt officials. Late in the Reagan administration, plans were drawn up by the Justice Department to place the union under government su-pervision.

To many outsiders, the Southern Christian Leadership Conference (SCLC) seemed little more than a one-man show orchestrated by Martin Luther King, Jr. Unlike the NAACP and the Congress of Racial Equality (CORE), the SCLC was not democratically structured. The annual conventions and twice-yearly board meetings had little to do with policy making; in practice, these were merely ratifying conventions for King's proposals. His popularity, charisma, and fund-raising abilities made him virtually unassailable within the conference. Actually, King did delegate authority within the organization, if only for his distaste for administration and his realization that he did not have

BOX 2-3 *THREE POLITICAL ENTREPRENEURS*

Photo courtesy Common Cause. Used with permission.

John Gardner: Citizen Activist

John Gardner is the founder and former president of Common Cause. After service in

Photo courtesy AP/Wide World.

Norman Lear: Public Activist

Norman Lear is the producer of such popular television shows as "All in the Family," "San-

Photo courtesy UPI/Bettmann Newsphotos.

Ralph Nader: Consumer Advocate

As a young attorney, Ralph Nader took on the Detroit automobile industry because of its overpriced but shoddy products. Nader's book *Unsafe at Any Speed* gave great impetus to a national consumer movement. His name is synonymous with seat belts, model recalls, and public safety issues generally. Nader was instrumental in the passage of the 1967 Wholesome Meat Act, which established federal inspection standards for slaughterhouses and processing plants. He started the Public Interest Research Group (PIRG) in 1970, which fights in communities and on campuses in twenty-six states for consumer and political reform. The following year, he founded Public Citizen, a consumer lobbying group. By the end of 1986, Nader had established two dozen consumer organizations, which he helps fund through speaking fees. During the Reagan administration, Nader's consumer groups launched investigations of the nuclear power industry, the postal service, and the insurance industry. He targeted the vast power of giant corporations as the enemy of recent decades. He publicly criticized President Reagan for "providing a government of General Motors, by Exxon, for Du Pont."

ford and Son," and "Maude." He has fought racial and sexual discrimination in the theater and in society as a whole. He has been president of the California Civil Liberties Union and serves on the Board of Directors of the National Women's Political Caucus, a fundraising organization for women candidates running for public office. Lear also established and serves on the board of directors of the People of the American Way. This liberal organization was established to oppose the New Right in American politics—a coalition of conservatives and religious fundamentalists. Lear views the latter and their activities as threats to our basic political freedoms of speech, press, and religion.

World War II, Gardner joined the Carnegie Foundation and was responsible for a number of large grants to Harvard University for research on the Soviet Union and Africa. Later, he was chosen by President Lyndon Johnson to be secretary of Health, Education and Welfare. He served only briefly, resigning because of what he saw as the deleterious effect of the Vietnam war on our national priorities and the budget. With seed money from wealthy friends and acquaintances, he sent out 200,000 letters in August 1970, asking recipients to join him in "common cause" to bring politics out of "smoke-filled" rooms. Receiving a good response, he established Common Cause as a "citizens' lobby." In the years that followed, the organization achieved a number of reforms aimed at streamlining various congressional procedures. Common Cause also lobbied for an end to the Vietnam war, against the building of the B-1 bomber, and for an extension of the vote to eighteen-year-olds. Gardner eventually left the organization to join the Urban Coalition.

all the answers. As one writer comments, "King did not hand down his decisions from an Olympian height; after consulting with trusted advisors outside
SCLC, he hammered them out with his colleagues."[21]

The existence or absence of organizational democracy does not depend
solely on leader–member relationships. The presence or absence of various
organizational mechanisms and internal procedures also have some bearing.
One of these mechanisms is the annual meeting or convention, where member
delegates convene and discuss policy. The substance of annual meetings varies,
of course, among organizations. Farm Bureau Federation meetings have not
involved serious policy discussions, and challenges to the federation's leadership
are rare. The same can be said, in large part, of the annual AFL–CIO meetings
when George Meany was at the helm. Incumbent AFL–CIO president Lane
Kirkland, on the other hand, is willing to entertain a wider discussion of union
policies and member participation.

American Medical Association meetings in recent times have produced
lively discussions leading to policy changes. The association's House of Delegates voted to require that the organization's $1.4 million in tobacco stocks
be eliminated from the pension fund. Presently the organization is discussing
whether to go on record as opposing cigarette advertising in the popular media.

Membership polling can give the organization's leadership valuable feedback on issues of general concern. Each year, Common Cause asks its members to rank a dozen or so issues—inflation, unemployment, crime, women's
issues, foreign policy, and so on—in terms of importance (see Box 2-4). The
energies and resources of the organization are then concentrated on the top
five or six issues. The Chamber of Commerce also periodically polls its members on salient issues. The results are made known to the general membership
as well as congressional incumbents having high concentrations of Chamber
members in their districts. Other organizations periodically poll through their
newsletters or trade magazines.

BOX 2-4 *MEMBERSHIP POLLING*

1987 CC Issues Poll

More than 57,248 members, or 25 percent of Common Cause's membership,
responded to the 1987 Issues Poll. As they have in recent years, members expressed
great concern over special interest influence in Congress, nuclear arms control and
defense spending. In addition, similar concerns were expressed about the
government's budget deficit.

Poll results showed strong membership approval of the organization's current
issues agenda. 97 percent agreed that the organization should continue to place
major emphasis on improving government integrity and accountability through
support of campaign finance reform, conflict of interest regulation, and disclosure of
lobbying activity. 90 percent agreed that CC should continue to place emphasis on

nuclear arms control. 92 percent indicated that the effort to protect and enhance civil rights should continue to be an important issue for CC. Finally, 93 percent agreed that the federal budget process and the federal deficit should continue to be an important issue for Common Cause.

The results of the poll were:

Question 1. The federal budget deficit is projected to be $160 to $180 billion next year, absent any changes in current tax and spending policies. Please indicate your views on the following questions related to the federal budget.

1. Do you believe the federal government's budget deficits are:
    86.6% Very serious   9.9 Somewhat serious   0.6 Not very serious   0.5 Not sure

2. Please indicate which, if any, of the following options you would favor as part of a comprehensive effort to reduce the budget deficit:
    a. Cut defense spending
        78.5% Strongly favor   17.1 Favor   2.5 Oppose   0.7 Strongly oppose
    b. Reduce Social Security cost of living increases
        4.4% Strongly favor   18.1 Favor   45.0 Oppose   28.0 Strongly oppose
    c. Require those who are not poor to pay taxes on a greater share of Social Security benefits
        18.1 Strongly favor   43.9 Favor   24.8 Oppose   8.1 Strongly oppose
    d. Reduce Medicare, student loans and other federal entitlement programs in which a large share of the benefits go to the middle class
        3.8% Strongly favor   18.4 Favor   50.2 Oppose   22.5 Strongly oppose
    e. Make across the board spending cuts in all non-defense programs except those which are targeted to serve low income citizens
        7.7% Strongly favor   26.9 Favor   42.4 Oppose   17.0 Strongly oppose
    f. Establish a consumption tax, such as a value added tax or a national sales tax
        8.7% Strongly favor   31.1 Favor   32.8 Oppose   20.0 Strongly oppose
    g. Impose an energy tax
        12.7% Strongly favor 36.8 Favor   31.2 Oppose   8.5 Strongly oppose
    h. Raise taxes for upper-income individuals
        36.9% Strongly favor 42.6 Favor   12.8 Oppose   3.2 Strongly oppose

3. Given the present state of the economy, efforts to reduce the deficit should be deferred.
    1.8% Strongly agree   4.0 Agree   48.4 Disagree   42.8 Strongly disagree

Question 2. Listed below are a number of statements about the role of the federal government in general and with respect to selected domestic policy issues. Please indicate the extent to which you agree or disagree with the following statements:

1. The trend toward diminishing the role of the federal government and leaving more responsibilities to the states should be continued.
    7.4% Strongly agree   25.1 Agree   45.9 Disagree   16.8 Strongly disagree

2. Given the present federal deficit situation, the federal government should not take on costly new domestic policy initiatives.
    11.1% Strongly agree   38.3 Agree   36.2 Disagree   7.7 Strongly disagree

3. The federal government should make greater efforts to protect the safety and health of the public in such areas as the environment, working conditions and consumer products.
    46.2% Strongly agree   42.9 Agree   7.6 Disagree   1.0 Strongly disagree

4. The federal government should increase expenditures designed to help the poor get jobs and move out of poverty permanently.
    45.6% Strongly agree   42.0 Agree   8.2 Disagree   1.3 Strongly disagree

5. The federal government should increase its efforts to combat teenage pregnancy.
    35.9% Strongly agree   38.8 Agree   18.0 Disagree   2.9 Strongly disagree

6. The federal government should do more to protect U.S. business from the competition of foreign imports.
    9.7% Strongly agree   26.5 Agree   45.8 Disagree   10.5 Strongly disagree

7. The federal government should do more to help American industry modernize and compete effectively, but should not embark on a protectionist trade policy.
    26.3% Strongly agree   54.3 Agree   12.1 Disagree   2.1 Strongly disagree

8. Poverty is a national problem and aid to the poor should be primarily a responsibility of the federal government, rather than of states and localities.
    25.8% Strongly agree   41.0 Agree   23.7 Disagree   4.2 Strongly disagree

9. Education—and efforts to upgrade public schools—should be primarily a state and local, rather than national, responsibility.
    12.9% Strongly agree   37.4 Agree   32.9 Disagree   12.7 Strongly disagree

10. The federal government should encourage broader drug testing in the work place and should require drug testing for federal employees.
    12.0% Strongly agree   27.0 Agree   34.1 Disagree   21.1 Strongly disagree

11. The federal government should make AIDS research and prevention a greater priority.
    37.1% Strongly agree   48.4 Agree   9.7 Disagree   1.5 Strongly disagree

12. The Senate is doing an inadequate job of exercising its constitutional responsibility to review and approve federal judicial nominations.
    31.4% Strongly agree   38.7 Agree   16.1 Disagree   2.6 Strongly disagree

Question 3. Please indicate your reaction to each of the following statements about national security and nuclear arms control.

1. It is more important to develop the president's Strategic Defense Initiative— popularly known as the Star Wars program—than to negotiate a nuclear arms control agreement.
    2.9% Strongly agree   3.4 Agree   15.4 Disagree   75.9 Strongly disagree

2. The U.S. needs to strengthen conventional (non-nuclear) forces to deter the Soviet Union and allow us to reduce our reliance on nuclear weapons.
    20.0% Strongly agree   45.8 Agree   18.2 Disagree   7.1 Strongly disagree

3. The U.S. should continue to abide by the terms of the unratified SALT II treaty so long as the Soviets do likewise.
    61.5% Strongly agree   33.0 Agree   2.0 Disagree   0.7 Strongly disagree

4. The U.S. should impose a moratorium on nuclear weapons testing so long as the Soviets do likewise.
    65.5% Strongly agree   27.3 Agree   3.3 Disagree   1.3 Strongly disagree

5. Congress's decision in 1985 to limit to 50 the number of MX missiles that can be deployed should be reversed to permit deployment of a greater number of missiles.
    3.1% Strongly agree   4.9 Agree   27.3 Disagree   58.1 Strongly disagree

6. U.S. involvement in the shipment of arms to Iran and the diversion of funds to the contras could have been prevented in Congress had properly exercised its oversight responsibilities.
    23.6% Strongly agree   29.7 Agree   28.2 Disagree   6.4 Strongly disagree

7. The U.S. should work to establish closer ties with Iran.
    4.1% Strongly agree   34.9 Agree   36.9 Disagree   12.6 Strongly disagree

8. The U.S. should not negotiate with terrorists or states sponsoring terrorism for the release of U.S. hostages.
    48.8% Strongly agree   30.1 Agree   6.9 Disagree   3.3 Strongly disagree

9. Congress needs to play a greater role in decisions to involve U.S. military personnel in conflicts or hostile situations abroad.
    55.3% Strongly agree   30.8 Agree   6.9 Disagree   3.3 Strongly disagree

10. The U.S. should continue to provide assistance to the contras in their fight against the Sandinista government in Nicaragua.
    4.7% Strongly agree   7.4 Agree   21.4 Disagree   61.5 Strongly disagree

Question 4. Please indicate your views regarding the appropriate role for Common Cause in the areas described below.

1. Supporting comprehensive campaign finance reform in order to reduce the influence of special interest PACs and protect the integrity of the electoral process should continue to be a major emphasis for Common Cause.
    79.3% Strongly agree   17.4 Agree   0.8 Disagree   0.7 Strongly disagree

2. Supporting ethics and conflict of interest regulations, lobby disclosure laws and similar measures in order to improve government accountability, integrity and openness should continue to be a major emphasis for Common Cause.
    78.7% Strongly agree   19.1 Agree   0.3 Disagree   0.1 Strongly disagree

3. Supporting nuclear arms control agreements and opposing destabilizing weapons programs, such as the MX missile and Star Wars, should continue to be a major emphasis for Common Cause.
    68.8% Strongly agree   20.1 Agree   5.8 Disagree   2.3 Strongly disagree

4. Protecting and enhancing civil rights should continue to be an important issue for Common Cause.
    59.3% Strongly agree   32.6 Agree   4.9 Disagree   0.9 Strongly disagree

5. The federal budget process and the federal deficit should continue to be an important issue for Common Cause.
    62.9% Strongly agree   30.8 Agree   3.3 Disagree   0.6 Strongly disagree

6. Common Cause is taking on too many issues and should begin to cut back.
    3.4% Strongly agree   13.5 Agree   53.0 Disagree   14.7 Strongly disagree

Source: *Common Cause Magazine*, 1987. Used with permission.

1988 CC Issues Poll

More than 56,000 members, or 19 percent of Common Cause's membership, responded to the 1988 Issues Poll. As they have in recent years, members expressed great concern over special interest influence in Congress, nuclear arms control and defense spending. In addition, similar concerns were expressed about the government's budget deficit.

Poll results showed strong approval of the organization's current issues agenda: 99 percent of those responding believe that campaign finance reform should continue to be a priority of Common Cause; 99 percent also agree that supporting ethics in government should continue to be a major emphasis of the organization. Ninety-two percent expressed approval of emphasis on nuclear arms control and similar issues. Ninety-four percent approved emphasis on civil rights protection. And 97 percent agree that the problems of the federal budget process and the federal deficit are issues Common Cause should continue to work on.

The results of the poll were:

I. The Federal Budget

1. Do you believe the federal government's budget deficits are:
    90.5% Very serious   8.4 Somewhat serious   0.6 Not very serious   0.5 Not sure

2. Would you approve or disapprove of these ways to reduce the deficit:

	% Approve	% Disapprove
a. Reduce social security cost-of-living increases	31.5	68.5
b. Reduce Medicare payments to doctors and hospitals	39.9	60.1
c. Reduce Medicare benefits to those at higher income levels	75.0	25.0
d. Reduce entitlement programs that primarily benefit the middle class	65.0	35.0
e. Make major defense spending cutbacks	88.4	11.6
f. Make major domestic spending cutbacks, except programs benefiting low income persons	56.4	43.6

3. Raising Taxes is another way of reducing the deficit. What do you think of the following revenue proposals?

   a. Establish a consumption tax, such as a value added tax or a national sales tax.
       13.5% Strongly favor   35.3 Favor   28.7 Oppose   22.4 Strongly oppose

   b. Impose an energy tax.
       16.9% Strongly favor   42.6 Favor   29.2 Oppose   11.3 Strongly oppose

   c. Raise taxes for middle income individuals.
       4.6% Strongly favor   26.9 Favor   47.4 Oppose   21.1 Strongly oppose

   d. Raise taxes for upper income individuals.
       48.6% Strongly favor   36.3 Favor   11.2 Oppose   3.9 Strongly oppose

   e. Raise excise taxes on alcohol and cigarettes.
       58.3% Strongly favor   33.1 Favor   6.5 Oppose   2.1 Strongly oppose

   f. Require those who are not poor to pay taxes on a greater share of social
security benefits.

24.5% Strongly favor   42.9 Favor   23.3 Oppose   9.2 Strongly oppose

4. Given the current economic conditions, do you agree major reductions need to
be made in the federal budget?

46.6% Strongly agree   43.0 Agree   9.1 Disagree   1.4 Strongly disagree

5. Would you say the national economy is in good shape, fair shape or poor
shape?

8.2% Good   54.3 Fair   37.5 Poor

6. Which one of the following factors do you feel was *most* responsible for the
sharp drop in the stock market last October?

   a. Wall Street speculators who kept driving up the price of stocks 31.6%
   b. The failure of the federal government to reduce the deficit   21.4
   c. Computerized trading of stocks   21.3
   d. Rising interest rates   0.5
   e. Large trade deficit   3.5
   f. Not sure   21.7

7. As a result of economic conditions, do you agree or disagree that the following
events will happen in the next year?

	% Agree	% Disagree
a. Prices will go up much faster	43.6	56.4
b. Unemployment will increase	67.9	32.1
c. Interest rates will climb	57.6	42.4
d. You will be a more cautious consumer	79.2	20.8
e. The country will enter a recession	56.9	43.1
f. The economy will continue to look much the same	58.0	42.0

II. Please indicate your level of concern about each of the following problems.

	Very highly concerned	Highly concerned	Moderately concerned	Not concerned
1. Quality of education	56.6	32.0	10.5	0.8
2. Escalation of nuclear arms race	54.0	25.6	17.4	3.0
3. Poverty	42.8	35.2	20.4	1.7
4. Spreading AIDS epidemic	40.0	34.6	23.0	2.4
5. Unemployment	26.7	36.3	32.9	4.1
6. Too much secrecy in government	42.0	31.5	22.6	3.9
7. Waste and mismanagement in government programs	50.1	31.9	16.5	1.5
8. Environmental pollution	51.1	33.3	14.4	1.2
9. Declining international competitiveness of U.S. business	32.5	39.3	25.1	3.1
10. Continued recession in farm economy	22.8	37.6	34.5	5.1

11.	Availability of child day care and after-school care	23.5	32.9	35.0	8.6
12.	Drug and alcohol abuse	34.6	35.9	26.1	3.4
13.	Housing the homeless	34.7	37.4	25.4	2.6
14.	Protecting consumers on products and services	21.1	36.3	37.8	4.8
15.	Teenage pregnancy	24.2	36.6	34.5	4.7

III. Domestic Policy Issues

(A) Please indicate the extent to which you agree or disagree with the following statements:

1. Given the present federal deficit situation the federal government should not take on costly new domestic policy initiatives.
   19.8% Strongly agree   41.0 Agree   33.0 Disagree   6.3 Strongly disagree

2. The federal government has failed to support adequately efforts to educate the general population about the dangers of AIDS.
   25.9% Strongly agree   43.9 Agree   27.1 Disagree   3.1 Strongly disagree

3. Education—and efforts to upgrade public schools—should be primarily a state and local, rather than national, responsibility.
   14.2% Strongly agree   32.5 Agree   35.8 Disagree   17.4 Strongly disagree

4. The federal government should encourage broader drug testing in the work place and should require drug testing for federal employees.
   12.6% Strongly agree   28.6 Agree   37.0 Disagree   21.8 Strongly disagree

5. The press has gone too far in focusing on the private lives of public officials.
   12.4% Strongly agree   39.2 Agree   38.2 Disagree   10.2 Strongly disagree

6. There were many government programs created in the 1960s to try to improve conditions for poor people in this country. Do you think these programs generally made things better, made things worse, or do you think that they didn't have much impact one way or the other?
   55.1% Made better   8.1 Made worse   36.7 Little impact

7. In recent years, there have been many cases of alleged ethical improprieties by Administration officials. Do you think this problem is worse now, about the same, or not as bad as in past Administrations?
   78.9% Worse   18.9 About the same   2.2 Not as bad

(B) Following are some institutions in this country. As far as people running these institutions are concerned, would you say you have a great deal of confidence in them, only some, or hardly any?

		Great deal	Only some	Hardly any
a.	Business	18.9%	64.3%	16.8%
b.	Organized labor	5.7	60.7	33.6
c.	The press	26.0	60.3	13.7
d.	U.S. Supreme Court	41.0	51.2	7.7
e.	The military	12.7	49.3	38.0
f.	U.S. Congress	13.1	65.5	21.4
g.	State government	11.8	68.9	19.2
h.	Local government	13.7	66.0	20.3
i.	Federal government	4.3	64.3	31.5

IV. **Please indicate your reaction to each of the following statements about national security and nuclear arms control.**

1. President Reagan's Strategic Defense Initiative—popularly known as the Star Wars program—should progress from the research stage into actual deployment.
    3.5% Strongly agree   7.5 Agree   21.5 Disagree   67.5 Strongly disagree

2. The United States needs to strengthen conventional (non-nuclear) forces to deter the Soviet Union and allow us to reduce our reliance on nuclear weapons.
    15.8% Strongly agree   47.8 Agree   24.7 Disagree   11.8 Strongly disagree

3. An agreement to reduce strategic nuclear weapons by 50% would be a historic step forward in reducing the risk of nuclear war.
    47.3% Strongly agree   45.8 Agree   5.6 Disagree   1.3 Strongly disagree

4. The Iran-contra affair could have been prevented if Congress had properly exercised its oversight responsibilities.
    20.5% Strongly agree   32.3 Agree   38.3 Disagree   8.9 Strongly disagree

5. The Iran-contra affair was not a result of a failure of the system but a problem of the people who were running that system.
    51.2% Strongly agree   35.5 Agree   9.0 Disagree   4.3 Strongly disagree

6. There was no serious problem disclosed by the Iran-contra affair.
    5.2% Strongly agree   4.7 Agree   19.0 Disagree   71.0 Strongly disagree

7. Congress needs to play a greater role in decisions to involve U.S. military personnel in conflicts or hostile situations abroad.
    49.4% Strongly agree   38.1 Agree   8.5 Disagree   4.0 Strongly disagree

8. Efforts to restore democracy in Nicaragua are best addressed through the regional peace process rather than U.S. military aid to the contras.
    74.0% Strongly agree   20.5 Agree   3.8 Disagree   1.7 Strongly disagree

V. **Please indicate your views regarding the appropriate role for Common Cause in the areas described below.**

1. Supporting comprehensive campaign finance reform in order to reduce the influence of special interest PACs and protect the integrity of the electoral process should continue to be a major emphasis for Common Cause.
    79.5% Strongly agree   19.6 Agree   0.7 Disagree   0.2 Strongly disagree

2. Supporting ethics and conflict of interest regulations, lobby disclosure laws and similar measures in order to improve government accountability, integrity and openness should continue to be a major emphasis for Common Cause.
    80.9% Strongly agree   18.5 Agree   0.4 Disagree   0.1 Strongly disagree

3. Supporting nuclear arms control agreements and opposing destabilizing weapons programs such as the MX missile and Star Wars should continue to be a major emphasis for Common Cause.
    67.6% Strongly agree   24.1 Agree   6.2 Disagree   2.2 Strongly disagree

4. Protecting and enhancing civil rights should continue to be an important issue for Common Cause.
    59.1% Strongly agree   35.2 Agree   4.7 Disagree   1.0 Strongly disagree

5. The federal budget process and the federal deficit should continue to be important issues for Common Cause.
    66.8% Strongly agree   30.3 Agree   2.4 Disagree   0.5 Strongly disagree

Source: *Common Cause Magazine,* 1988. Used with permission.

Is internal democracy a general prerequisite for all interest groups? Not necessarily. Some exceptions would be organizations with relatively small memberships (500 or less), single-issue groups that are highly cohesive, and organizations that periodically solicit donors but lack permanent members.

SUMMARY

The interest-group universe is significantly different today from what it was just thirty years ago. Social and technological changes within the nation are giving rise to a new set of politically active organizations. Older, more established interests are being increasingly challenged by these new organizations, which pursue essentially noneconomic goals. Collectively, these changes are broadening the national political agenda.

Group formation is highly complex. At times, economic self-interest is the root stimulus. But immediate gratification is only one of several explanations for interest-group formation today. Individuals may also come together because they strongly identify with organizational objectives. Additionally, group strategies in shaping and articulating issues—for example, the pro- and anti-ERA arguments—may attract (or repel) potential members.

Finally, government itself contributes not only to the establishment of interest groups but to their variety as well. Government programs stimulate organizational growth among recipients as well as nonrecipients. This ongoing atomization of national politics looks like it will continue for years to come.

NOTES

[1]R. C. Sachs, J. E. Center, and T. M. Neal, "Congress and Pressure Groups: Lobbying in a Modern Democracy," quoted in *The Transformation in American Politics: Implications for Federalism* (Washington, D.C.: Advisory Commission in Intergovernmental Relations, 1986), p. 229.

[2]Quoted in K. L. Schlozman and J. T. Tierney, "More of the Same: Washington Pressure Group Activity in a Decade of Change," *Journal of Politics* (1983), Vol. 45, p. 367.

[3]James Q. Wilson, *The Amateur Democrat* (Chicago: University of Chicago Press, 1966), pp. vii–ix. Paperback edition.

[4]See A. L. Fritschler and Bernard H. Ross, *Business Regulations and Government Decision Making* (Cambridge, Mass.: Winthrop, 1980).

[5]Linda G. Stuntz, quoted in the *National Journal*, 27 (1987), p. 1708.

[6]Michael Pertschuk, *Revolt Against Regulation: The Rise and Pause of the Consumer Movement* (Berkeley: University of California Press, 1982), p. 57.

[7]Albro Martin, in a letter to the editor of the *Harvard Business Review*, July–August 1981, p. 110.

[8]Walter Guzzardi, Jr., "To Win in Washington," *Fortune*, March 27, 1978, p. 53.

[9]William P. Browne, *Private Interests, Public Policy, and American Agriculture* (Lawrence: University of Kansas Press, 1988).

[10]Rene Dubos, "The Human Landscape," *Bulletin of Atomic Scientists*, Vol. 25 (1970), 31.

[11]Donella H. Meadow et al., *The Limits of Growth* (New York: Universe Books, 1972), p. 143.

[12]Arthur Bourne, *Pollute and Be Damned* (London: Dent & Sons, 1972), p. 198.

[13]Rachel Carson, *Silent Spring* (Boston: Houghton Mifflin, 1962). Carson's book was updated by Frank Graham, *Since Silent Spring* (Boston: Houghton Mifflin, 1972).

[14]See Ann C. Costain, "The Struggle for a National Women's Lobby: Organizing a Diffuse Interest," *Western Political Quarterly,* 33 (1980), 110-13.

[15]Certain issues can evoke strong emotions that in turn can play a major role in determining individual behavior. A leading writer on this phenomenon of *political symbolism* is Murray Edelman. See, for example, his *Symbolic Uses of Politics* (Urbana: University of Illinois Press, 1964).

[16]Quoted in Jane J. Mansbridge, *Why We Lost the ERA* (Chicago: University of Chicago Press, 1986), p. 159.

[17]See Jeffery M. Berry, *Lobbying for the People* (Princeton, N.J.: Princeton University Press, 1977); and Jeffrey M. Berry, *The Interest Group Society* (Boston: Little, Brown, 1984).

[18]James Rosenau, *Citizenship between Elections* (New York: Free Press, 1974).

[19]Robert Michels, *Political Parties,* trans. Eden and Cedar Paul (New York: Free Press, 1985).

[20]For an analysis of Michels's theory, see Maurice Duverger, *Political Parties* (New York: John Wiley, 1963).

[21]Adam Fairclough, "The Southern Christian Leadership Conference and the Second Reconstruction, 1957-1973," *South Atlantic Quarterly,* 80 (1981), 181.

CHAPTER THREE
LOBBYISTS AND LOBBYING:
Professionalization
of the Art of Persuasion

A GROWING PROFESSION

When Michael Deaver, deputy chief of staff during the first Reagan administration, resigned to establish his own consulting firm (Michael K. Deaver and Associates), he joined a growing army of former elected and appointed public officials marketing their political expertise and contacts. He in effect became a lobbyist. Lobbying has been a growth industry in Washington, especially since the early 1970s. AFL–CIO lobbyist Ray Denison, referring to a prestigious downtown corridor of glass-and-marble office buildings housing dozens of lobbyists, proclaims, "Lobbying is a healthy and growing business. All you have to do is look at K Street to see the monuments to that fact."[1] No one knows for sure just how many lobbyists are presently trying to influence Congress and the bureaucracy or how much money they are spending.

To better comprehend the business of political influence and persuasion, we must first become familiar with the kinds of lobbyists and techniques they use. Both vary from organization to organization. Lobbying is quite different today from what it was just a generation ago. Then, a few lobbyists were lawyers, others were public-relations experts, some crunched numbers, some twisted arms, others raised money, and still others conjured strategies for other lobbyists to pursue.

Today lobbying is much more professional. Many more private attorneys and law firms are available to organizations. A new type of lobbying organization has emerged, and the revolving-door syndrome (to be discussed later in the chapter) is a fact of life. These changes, coupled with an everbroadening

"LOBBIES"

FIGURE 3-1

Source: Dick Lochner Editorial cartoon *U.S. News & World Report,* September 19, 1983, p. 63. Reprinted by permission of Tribune Media Services.

array of lobbying techniques, require closer examination if we are to appreciate the complexities of modern lobbying. In this chapter we analyze lobbyists and lobbying firms along with the numerous techniques of influence that prevail in group politics today.

We must keep in mind that lobbying serves several purposes. It is not just a technique for gaining legislative support or other institutional approval for some objective—a policy shift, a judicial ruling, or the modification or passage of a law. Lobbying is also employed to *reinforce* support for established policy, or it can be used to activate allies for *defensive* purposes—to oppose a policy shift and maintain the political status quo.

AN OVERVIEW OF THE LOBBYIST

Lobbyists perform the dual role of organizational representative and spokesperson. They represent their clients in various public forums and articulate their policy preferences. There is no "typical" lobbyist: some come from private firms, others have public experience at the state level, and others have been involved

FIGURE 3-2

"Manipulating the US government . . . legally. Be a lobbyist!" by Jeff Danziger. *The Christian Science Monitor* (4/28/86). Copyright © 1986 TCSPS. Reprinted with permission.

in national policies, some are former corporate executives, some have headed public agencies at the state and local level, and still others have worked on Capitol Hill (discussed more fully later in the chapter).[2]

Most organizations that seek to influence public policies consider a good lobbyist indispensable. "Good lobbyists" fall into a number of categories. However, most effective lobbyists tend to be in the latter stages of their careers. They have already attained a high level of prestige and success in some other profession—business, law, education, or some area of public service—and have become lobbyists in the second or third stage of their careers. They also tend to be middle- or upper-class WASP males. They are comfortable in high government circles because their socioeconomic background is similar to that of congressional and administrative personnel. This shared background provides a basis for common social, economic, and political perceptions.

But background isn't everything. More and more groups consider it crucial to be represented by lobbyists who not only can gain access to—and the confidence of—key policy makers, but have the requisite bargaining and technical skills as well. Lobbyists are diplomats for their organizations, but they must also be knowledgeable information brokers and negotiators. They may be called upon by legislators, bureaucrats, or White House personnel to provide technical data or clarify an issue of concern to the organization they represent, and their ability to adapt to a variety of situations and strategic shifts is an important attribute. Some cardinal rules for a successful lobbyist would read like this:

1. Be pleasant and inoffensive.
2. Convince the official that it is important for him or her to listen.
3. Be personally convinced.
4. Be well prepared and well informed.
5. Be succinct, well organized, and direct.
6. Use the soft sell.
7. Always leave a short written summary of the case.

THE LOBBYING ESTABLISHMENT

We now turn to some of the most specific elements of Washington's lobbying establishment. These lobbyists and lobbying firms make up the nucleus of that establishment. Although there is no "typical" lobbyist, some types of lobbyists share common characteristics and purposes.

Former Legislative and Administrative Personnel

An increasing number of former senators, such as J. William Fulbright, Robert Taft, Jr., Frank Moss, Thomas Kuchel, and George Smathers, have become lobbyists both on Capitol Hill and before federal agencies. The same can be said for former House members Dan Kykendall, John O'Hara, Carter Manasco, John McCollister, and many others.[3]

Besides being very knowledgeable about the legislative process, these individuals have advantages other lobbyists do not. They know how to pitch their appeals, showing an awareness of members' districts and their political makeup. They also have access to the floor of the House or Senate, the members' gymnasium, and the dining room. Such privileges help former members of Congress maintain their status within the congressional fraternity and obtain favors for their clients. This kind of access, of course, does not guarantee success, but it can be extremely helpful. Most incumbent members of Congress are sympathetic to the requests of former colleagues.

Virtually the same advantages can accrue to former agency and especially White House personnel (Box 3–1). The latter can contact friends and energize networks extremely helpful to clients. As Edward Rollins, former White House aide to President Reagan, states,

> I've got many, many friends who are all through the agencies and equally important, I don't have many enemies. . . . I tell my clients I can get your case moved to the top of the pile.[4]

This kind of political clout is a crucial ingredient in the battle for influence. It opens doors and allows clients' claims to be heard at high policy-making levels. The prestige and directness of these contacts are significant assets in today's group struggle.

Lawyer Lobbyists

This is the largest element of establishment lobbying. The growing complexity and specialization of legislation passing through Congress today has increased the need for legal expertise.* Hundreds of specialized law firms and private attorneys have become involved in the political process. On behalf of their clients, they have become influential in areas ranging from the air we breathe and the food and drugs we consume to the cars we drive and the amount of taxes we pay. The political consequences of these lobbies' influence touch virtually all Americans:

> what the social Philadelphia lawyer was two generations ago and the financial Wall Street lawyer one generation ago, Washington lawyers are today—as the locus of public power shifts from pedigree, to money, to politics. They are to all lawyers and citizens what the heart is to the body; by dint of central location and essential function, both are the reigning organs of their respective body politic. In short, Washington lawyers are the most powerful people in the country today.[5]

---

* Legal training is *not* a prerequisite for lobbying success. Nonlawyer lobbyists can be just as effective as their attorney counterparts. Legal advice and assistance is readily available to all lobbyists, from their own organizations, from law firms, or through contacts with public and private attorneys.

BOX 3-1 *LIFE AFTER WORKING IN THE WHITE HOUSE*

Life After Working in the White House

They don't always like to be called lobbyists. "I'm a lawyer," proclaimed Clark M. Clifford, once special counsel to President Truman and now senior partner at the Washington law firm of Clifford & Warnke. Clifford handles clients' work at regulatory agencies but not, he says, at the White House or on Capitol Hill. "I've been in government in a number of Administrations and then [I go] back to the law," he said. "In the mind of some, that makes me a lobbyist. I'm a little sensitive about that."

Not everyone is, though. There's been no shortage of people who've left the White House to become lobbyists, lawyers who dabble in government, public relations experts or political consultants. Here's a list of some of them with their White House titles and current positions.

Reagan White House

Michael K. Deaver, deputy chief of staff; Michael K. Deaver and Associates, president

Edward J. Rollins, assistant to the President for political and governmental affairs; Russo, Watts & Rollins Inc., managing partner

Lyn Nofziger, assistant to the President for political affairs; Nofziger & Bragg Communications, partner

Kenneth M. Duberstein, assistant to the President for legislative affairs; Timmons and Co. Inc., vice president

M. B. Oglesby, assistant to the President for legislative affairs; Bill Hecht and Associates, vice chairman

Richard V. Allen, assistant to the President for national security affairs; Richard V. Allen Co., president

Lee Atwater, deputy assistant to the President for political affairs; Black, Manafort, Stone & Atwater, partner

James W. Cicconi, special assistant to the President and special assistant to the chief of staff; Akin, Gump, Strauss, Hauer & Feld, senior associate

David L. Swanson, special assistant to the President for legislative affairs; Craft & Loesch, executive director, legislative and regulatory affairs

Wayne H. Valis, special assistant to the President for business liaison; Valis Associates, president

Robert Bonitati, special assistant to the President for labor relations; The Kamber Group, vice president

Sheila Tate, First Lady's press secretary; Burson-Marsteller, senior vice president

Peter B. Teeley, Vice President's press secretary; Peter B. Teeley & Associates, president

Joseph W. Canzeri, assistant to the President and assistant to the deputy chief of staff; Canzeri Co., president

Frank J. Donatelli, deputy assistant to the President for public liaison; Patton, Boggs & Blow, partner

Carter White House

Stuart E. Eizenstat, assistant to the President for domestic affairs; Powell, Goldstein, Frazer & Murphy, partner

Anne Wexler, assistant to the President for public liaison; Wexler, Reynolds, Harrison & Schule Inc., chairman

William H. Cable, deputy assistant to the President for congressional liaison; Timmons and Co. Inc., vice president

James C. Free, special assistant to the President for congressional liaison; Charls E. Walker Associates, senior associate

David M. Rubenstein, deputy assistant to the President for domestic affairs and policy; Shaw, Pittman, Potts & Trowbridge, partner

Danny C. Tate, deputy assistant to the President for legislative affairs; Camp, Carmouche, Barsh, Hunter, Gray, Hoffman & Gill, partner

Gretchen Poston, social secretary; Washington Inc., partner

Nixon and Ford White House

William E. Timmons, assistant to the President (for congressional relations); Timmons and Co. Inc., chairman of executive committee

Tom C. Korologos, deputy assistant to the President (legislative affairs); Timmons and Co. Inc., president

Leonard Garment, special counsel, assistant to the President; Dickstein, Shapiro & Morin, partner

Nixon White House

Ronald L. Ziegler, press secretary; National Association of Truck Stop Operators, president

John P. Sears, deputy counsel to the President; Law Offices of John P. Sears

Johnson White House

Joseph A. Califano Jr., special assistant to the President; Dewey, Ballantine, Bushby, Palmer & Wood, partner

Harry C. McPherson Jr., special assistant to the President and counsel; Verner, Liipfert, Bernhard, McPherson & Hand Chartered, partner

Kennedy White House

Frederick G. Dutton, special assistant to the President; Dutton & Dutton P.C., president

Truman White House

Clark M. Clifford, special counsel to the President; Clifford & Warnke, partner

Duberstein

Rubenstein

Sears

Califano

Source: *National Journal,* May 3, 1986, p. 105. Used with permission.

These individuals know "the ins and outs" of policy making, and who the influentials are. They use their contacts to cut through red tape and apply direct pressure to those important to their clients' interests. The proliferation and increased specialization of these Washington lobbyists and law firms can be inferred from the public listings in Box 3-2.

A relatively new addition to Washington's evolving lobbying establishment is the "mega-firm"—a jack-of-all-trades organization offering a range of services. Mega-firms have come about because a number of elite lobbying organizations have seen fit to expand their services in an increasingly competitive market. Lobbying services are offered to prospective clients cafeteria-style. The client organization chooses those services best meeting its needs; it does not have to look elsewhere. Some of Washington's leading mega-firms and their range of services are shown in Box 3-3.

For some organizations, the mega-firm is the way to go. A coalition of over 100 health-policy groups requiring a range of services found their needs met by a mega-firm. As Box 3-3 shows, coalitions or large corporations needing a number of services—public relations, grass-roots lobbying, media strategies, and political consulting, for example—can receive all of them in one location. Mega-firms can also provide selected services and contacts for groups newly arrived on the Washington scene. Some mega-firm personnel have likely served in administrative or other government capacities that enhance lobbying access. Finally, mega-firms can provide important political knowhow to client groups that have marginal lobbying concerns.

Mega-firms do have drawbacks, however. The cost of their services may be too high for small firms and organizations. Mega-firms may be slow in responding to client needs because of internal management complexities. Is bigger necessarily better? Large staffs, big payrolls, and swank offices do not inevitably lead to political influence. For the time being, though, the mega-firm represents a further refinement in Washington's lobbying establishment. More time is needed to judge its effectiveness.

A unique aspect of lobbying is the interchange of public and private personnel, more commonly known as the *revolving-door syndrome.* Recent decades have witnessed more and more government employees leaving for similar positions in private industry—Environmental Protection Agency lawyers leaving for private firms concentrating in administrative and regulatory law; Securities and Exchange Commission personnel taking jobs in brokerage and bond houses; and Department of Justice lawyers taking positions in regulated industries. The extent of this shift of personnel can be seen in Table 3-1.

The combined administrative experience and knowledge of former public-sector employees are invaluable to interests that are subject to regulation by these lobbyists' former agencies. The "regulator" thus becomes the representative of the "regulated." This persistent drain of talent to "the other side" often places government at a disadvantage in its regulatory proceedings with special-interest organizations.

BOX 3-2 *A SAMPLE OF WASHINGTON REPRESENTATIVES*

WASHINGTON REPRESENTATIVES

GRISKIVICH, Peter
V. President, Motor Truck Mfrs. Division, Motor Vehicle Manufacturers Ass'n of the United States
Suite 1000, 1620 Eye St., N.W., Washington, DC 20006
Telephone: (202) 775-2700

GRKAVAC, Olga
Manager, Government Relations, ADAPSO, the Computer Software & Services Industry Ass'n
1300 North 17th St. Suite 300, Arlington, VA 22209
Telephone: (703) 522-5055
Registered as lobbyist at U.S. Congress.
Background: Also responsible for the ADAPSO PAC.

GROAH, William J.
Technical Director, Hardwood Plywood Manufacturers Ass'n
1825 Michael Faraday Dr., Reston, VA 22090
Telephone: (703) 435-2900
Background: Also represents the Formaldehyde Task Force Fund.

GROFF, James B.
Exec. Director, Nat'l Ass'n of Water Companies
Suite 1212, 1725 K St., N.W., Washington, DC 20006
Telephone: (202) 833-8383
Background: Served for over 24 years in the Civil Engineer Corps, U.S. Navy, retiring as a Captain.

GROMAN, Hazel A.
Editor, Wetlands Newsletter, Nat'l Wetlands Technical Council
1616 P St., N.W., Washington, DC 20036
Telephone: (202) 328-5150

GRONER, Isaac N.
Cole and Groner, P. C.
1615 L St., N.W., Suite 970, Washington, DC 20036-5602
Telephone: (202) 331-8888
Background: Law Clerk to Chief Justice Vinson 1948-50; Dep't of Justice 1950-51; Chief Counsel, Wage Stabilization Board 1951-53.
Clients:
Nat'l Ass'n of Postmasters of the U.S.

GRONINGER, James N.
Senior Gov't Relations Director, Independent Petroleum Ass'n of America
1101 16th St., N.W., Washington, DC 20036
Telephone: (202) 857-4704
Registered as lobbyist at U.S. Congress.

GROOM, Beverly L.
Federal Legislative Representative, American Council of Life Insurance
1001 Pennsylvania Ave., N.W., Washington, DC 20004-2599
Telephone: (202) 624-2159
Registered as lobbyist at U.S. Congress.

GROOM AND NORDBERG
1701 Pennsylvania Ave., N.W., Suite 1200, Washington, DC 20006
Telephone: (202) 857-0620
Members of firm representing listed organizations:
Groom, Theodore R.
Harding, Robert D.
Background: Assistant to Rep. Charles A. Halleck, Office of Minority Leader, House of Representatives, 1963-67. Attorney, Securities and Exchange Commission, 1967-68. Special Assistant to the Secretary for Congressional Affairs, HEW, 1970-71.
Holmes, Peter E.
Howell, Elizabeth C.
Background: Legislative Affairs Consultant, Groom and Nordberg.
Nordberg, Carl A., Jr.
Schiffbauer, William G.
Background: Legislative Affairs Consultant, Groom and Nordberg.
Clients:
Ad Hoc PFIC Group *(Peter E. Holmes, Carl A. Nordberg, Jr.)*
American Petrofina, Inc.
American Petroleum Institute
Bankers Life Co. *(Theodore R. Groom, Robert B. Harding)*
Baxter Internat'l, Inc. *(Robert B. Harding, Carl A. Nordberg, Jr.)*

Colorado-Ute Electric Ass'n *(Robert B. Harding)*
John Hancock Mutual Life Insurance Co. *(Theodore R. Groom, Robert B. Harding)*
Minnesota Mutual Life Insurance Co. *(Theodore R. Groom, Robert B. Harding)*
New York City Teachers Retirement System
Ocean Drilling and Exploration Co. *(Robert B. Harding, Carl A. Nordberg, Jr.)*
Phillips Petroleum Co. *(Robert B. Harding, Carl A. Nordberg, Jr.)*
Physicians Mutual Insurance Co.
Prudential-Bache Securities, Inc. *(Elizabeth C. Howell)*
Prudential Insurance Co. of America *(Theodore R. Groom, Robert B. Harding)*
Puerto Rico, U.S.A. Foundation *(Carl A. Nordberg, Jr.)*
Reading and Bates Corp. *(Robert B. Harding, Carl A. Nordberg, Jr.)*
Southern California Edison Co. *(Robert B. Harding)*
Union Texas Petroleum *(Robert B. Harding)*

GROOM, Theodore R.
Groom and Nordberg
1701 Pennsylvania Ave., N.W., Suite 1200, Washington, DC 20006
Telephone: (202) 857-0620
Registered as lobbyist at U.S. Congress.
Clients:
Bankers Life Co.
John Hancock Mutual Life Insurance Co.
Minnesota Mutual Life Insurance Co.
Prudential Insurance Co. of America

GROSS, Richard A.
Foley, Hoag and Eliot
1615 L St., N.W., Suite 950, Washington, DC 20036
Telephone: (202) 785-8800
Registered as lobbyist at U.S. Congress.
Background: Exec. Director, U.S. Consumer Product Safety Commission, 1979-81.
Clients:
Massaro Properties, Inc.

GROSSI, Ralph E.
President, American Farmland Trust
1920 N St., N.W., Suite 400, Washington, DC 20036
Telephone: (202) 659-5170

GROSSMAN AND FLASK
1101 14th St., N.W., Washington, DC 20005
Telephone: (202) 842-4840
Members of firm representing listed organizations:
Flask, Jon T.
Background: Trial Attorney, Office of Chief Counsel, Internal Revenue Service, 1971-75.
Grossman, Robert D., Jr.
Background: Senior Trial Attorney, Office of Chief Counsel, Internal Revenue Service, 1971-75.
Clients:
Internat'l Business Machines Corp. *(Robert D. Grossman, Jr.)*

GROSSMAN, Jerome, Jr.
Treasurer, PEACE PAC
100 Maryland Ave., N.E., Washington, DC 20002
Telephone: (202) 543-4100
Registered as lobbyist at U.S. Congress.

GROSSMAN, Robert D., Jr.
Grossman and Flask
1101 14th St., N.W., Washington, DC 20005
Telephone: (202) 842-4840
Background: Senior Trial Attorney, Office of Chief Counsel, Internal Revenue Service, 1971-75.
Clients:
Internat'l Business Machines Corp.

GROSVENOR, Gilbert M.
President & Chairman of the Board, Nat'l Geographic Soc.
1145 17th St., N.W., Washington, DC 20036
Telephone: (202) 857-7000

GROTON, H. Page
Legislative Director & Internat'l V.P., Internat'l Brotherhood of Boilermakers, Iron Shipbuilders, Blacksmiths, Forgers and Helpers
400 First St., N.W., Suite 814, Washington, DC 20001

GROUNDWATER, John
Public Relations & Marketing Director, Soc. of Industrial and Office Realtors
777 14th St., N.W., Washington, DC 20005
Telephone: (202) 383-1150

GROVE, JASKIEWICZ, GILLIAM AND COBERT
Suite 501, 1730 M St., N.W., Washington, DC 20036
Telephone: (202) 296-2900
Members of firm representing listed organizations:
Calderwood, James A.
Background: Trial Attorney, Department of Justice, Antitrust Division, 1970-73. Special Assistant U.S. Attorney for the District of Columbia, 1973. Trial Attorney and Senior Trial Attorney, Department of Justice, Antitrust Division, 1974-78.
Cobert, Ronald N.
Background: General Counsel, American Institute for Shippers' Ass'ns.
Danas, Andrew M.
Jaskiewicz, Leonard A.
Clients:
American Institute for Shippers' Ass'ns *(Ronald N. Cobert)*
Canadian Trucking Ass'n
Intermodal Transportation Ass'n *(Leonard A. Jaskiewicz)*
Internat'l Shipping Ass'n, Inc. *(Andrew M. Danas)*
Interstate Carriers Conference *(Leonard A. Jaskiewicz)*
Nat'l Ass'n of Shippers' Agents *(Ronald N. Cobert)*
Soc. of Glass Decorators *(James A. Calderwood)*
Streamline Shippers Ass'n *(Andrew M. Danas)*
United Van Lines, Inc. *(James A. Calderwood)*
WSSA Intermodal Services, Inc. *(Andrew M. Danas)*

GROVE, Jon P., CAE
Exec. Vice President, American Soc. of Ass'n Executives
1575 Eye St., N.W., Washington, DC 20005
Telephone: (202) 626-2723

GROVE, V. P.
V. President, Congressional Affairs, Oshkosh Truck Corp.
Suite 1018, 4660 Kenmore Ave., Alexandria, VA 22304
Telephone: (703) 823-9778

GROVE, William A., Jr.
Division Mgr., Congressional Relations, Chesapeake and Potomac Telephone Co.
1710 H St., N.W., Washington, DC 20006
Telephone: (202) 392-1905
Background: Serves as Vice Chairman and Administrator, Chesapeake and Potomac Telephone Co. Federal Political Action Committee.

GRUBER, Elliot
Director, Government Division, United Jewish Appeal Federation of Greater Washington
7900 Wisconsin Ave., Bethesda, MD 20814-3698
Telephone: (301) 652-6480

GRUENINGER, Antoinette
Manager, Public Relations, Center for Media and Public Affairs
2101 L St., N.W., Suite 505, Washington, DC 20037
Telephone: (202) 223-2942

GRUMBLY, Thomas P.
President, Clean Sites, Inc.
1199 North Fairfax St., Alexandria, VA 22314
Telephone: (703) 683-8522

GRUPENHOFF, John T.
Grupenhoff, Maldonado and Forrester
10,000 Falls Road, Suite 300, Potomac, MD 20854
Telephone: (301) 983-9773
Registered as lobbyist at U.S. Congress.
Clients:
American Academy of Dermatology
American Academy of Otolaryngology-Head and Neck Surgery
American Ass'n of Clinical Urologists
American Soc. for Gastrointestinal Endoscopy
American Soc. of Clinical Oncology
American Urological Ass'n
Cooley's Anemia Foundation

Source: *Washington Representatives,* Washington, D.C.: Columbia Books, 1987. Reprinted with permission of Columbia Books, Washington, D.C.

The revolving-door syndrome is most prevalent between defense contractors and the Pentagon. A study of this interaction noted that approximately 1600 Pentagon civilian employees (GS-13 or above) moved directly to defense-related industries between 1977 and 1979. Many of these were en-

BOX 3-3 *MEGA-FIRMS*

Selling a Variety of Power Options

	Law	Washington lobbying	Grass-roots lobbying	Coalition building	Public relations	Media strategies	Advertising	Av/media production	Direct mail	Economic consulting	Management consulting	Political consulting	Political fund raising	Opinion polling	Issues monitoring	Event planning
Arnold & Porter, law: Apco Associates, lobbying and consulting subsidiary; the Secura Group, financial consulting affiliate	●	●	●	●	●	●				●	●		●		●	●
Black Manafort Stone & Kelly Public Affairs Co., lobbying: Campaign Consultants Inc. (formerly Black Manafort Stone & Atwater), political consultants; National Media Inc., media production and placement	●	●	●	●	●	●	●	●		●	●	●	●		●	●
Burson-Marsteller, public relations (parent company—Young & Rubicam Inc., advertising agency): Rogers Merchandising, direct-marketing subsidiary; Cohn & Wolfe Inc., PR subsidiary	●	●	●	●	●	●	●	●						●	●	●
Hill and Knowlton Inc., public relations (parent company—JWT Group, advertising): Strategic Information Research Corp., opinion polling subsidiary	●	●	●	●	●		●	●			●	●	●	●	●	●
The Kamber Group, communications	●	●	●	●	●	●	●	●			●	●			●	●
Ogilvy & Mather Public Affairs (parent company—the Ogilvy Group, advertising): Targeted Communications, direct-mail affiliate; Charls E. Walker Associates Inc., partly owned lobbying affiliate	●	●	●	●	●	●	●	●	●	●	●				●	●

BLACK, MANAFORT, STONE & KELLY Public Affairs Company

Burson·Marsteller

A R N O L D & P O R T E R

Ogilvy & Mather K

HILL AND KNOWLTON

THE KAMBER GROUP

Source: *National Journal,* March 21, 1987, p. 662. Used with permission.

TABLE 3-1   The Revolving Door

Percentage of organizations in which a professional on staff of Washington office has previously worked in the federal government

	Corporations	Trade associations	Unions	Citizens' groups	All organizations
Federal government	90%	97%	65%	82%	86%
Executive branch	60	63	31	55	52
White House	8	15	6	10	9
Congress	46	63	31	30	46

Source: Table from *Organized Interests and American Democracy*, Kay L. Schlozman & John T. Tierney. (New York: Harper & Row, Pub., 1986), p. 269. Copyright © 1986 by Kay Lehman Schlozman and John T. Tierney. Reprinted by permission of Harper & Row, Publishers, Inc.

gineers and technicians, but a good number were knowledgeable in weapons procurement, government relations, or planning for future weapons systems.[6] These individuals possess not only technical expertise but political expertise as well—information on and access to policy making. This expertise can create a network in a community of common interests and shared assumptions. As Harmon Zeigler has noted,

> ideally, one sure way for an interest group to guarantee close ties with an agency is to play a part in the selection of its personnel. Generally unsuccessful in their efforts to influence the electoral process, interest groups have had more luck in the appointment of administrative personnel. The acknowledgement that the interest group and the government agency will work together in a common area of interest of less concern to a more general public perhaps establishes more credibility.[7]

Some very important benefits are exchanged through the movement of personnel. Defense interests gain insights into defense or space plans, access to key officials in the Pentagon and other agencies dealing with security matters, personnel with an intimate knowledge of both sides of weapons contracting, and an increased ability to develop successful government relations strategies. For its part, the government gains technically trained and knowledgeable individuals for weapons development and marketing, along with useful insights into the defense industry's way of doing business with the government.

LOBBYING STRATEGIES

Before we can draw any meaningful conclusions about the role of lobbyists in policy making, we need to examine the various strategies groups use to maximize their influence. Lobbyists and their organizations want results, and they direct their efforts accordingly. A combination of methods deemed appropriate for the circumstances and within the resources of the organization will be employed. The focuses of major lobbying efforts are key points where decisions are made and policy is implemented. Group politics are dynamic, not static. A legislative defeat, for example, can lead to stepped-up administrative pressures or alternate approaches at the state or local level. The process continues indefinitely until an acceptable decision is achieved.

Direct and Indirect Lobbying

Generally speaking, lobbying strategies are either direct or indirect. *Direct lobbying* consists in bringing organizational representatives into direct contact with public officials. Consulting with legislators or their staffs, presenting committee testimony, presenting research, and interacting with agency personnel are all forms of direct lobbying. *Indirect lobbying* consists of more circuitous methods of influencing policy makers. For example, lobbyists can pressure public officials by generating support or opposition at the congressional district level. They can also launch mass media campaigns or establish opposition groups. Figure 3-3 illustrates a number of ways in which lobbyists can exert direct or indirect pressure on Congress.

Direct lobbying includes a range of approaches (some of which are covered in greater detail in subsequent chapters). These channels are *not* necessarily open to all lobbies, and they are more open to some groups than to others. Well-established organizations such as the American Farm Bureau, the Business Roundtable, and the National Rifle Association are more likely to utilize the approaches just mentioned than are, say, a small consumer organization, representatives of itinerant farm workers, or a coalition of nonsmokers. An informal hierarchy of group acceptability prevails, as we noted in Chapter 2.

In the legislative setting, the most crucial stage of lobbying is at the committee or subcommittee level. Except in the case of highly controversial issues, committee and subcommittee decisions are generally upheld by the entire chamber. The lobbyist provides the committee and its staff with extensive background and technical information on the issue at hand, legislative language for the proposed bill or amendments to it, and lists of potential witnesses in case of further hearings.

During the "mark-up" sessions, where the bill is put together line by line, there are additional opportunities for lobbyists and committee personnel to interact—additional language changes and/or the adoption of compromise language. Sunshine laws and recent congressional rules change require that these sessions be relatively open. In addition, congressional votes on amendments and sponsors are matters of public record, which makes it easy for groups and lobbyists to monitor a situation and apply pressure when and where it will be most effective.

Unorthodox forms of lobbying include organizational bribery and personal threats. Both occur, but they are not very common and they involve

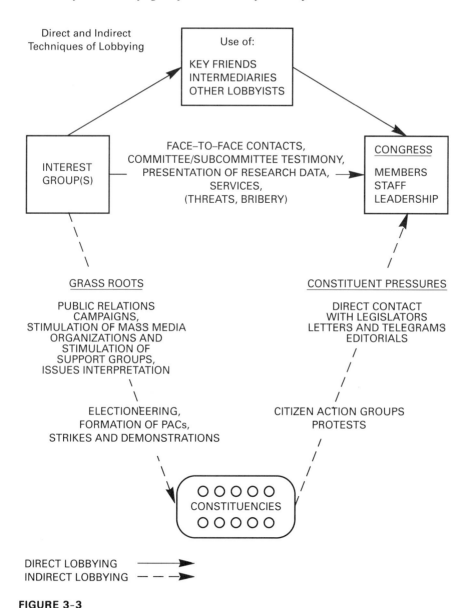

FIGURE 3-3

Direct and Indirect Techniques of Lobbying Congress

political risks. Because of the huge amounts of money involved, bribery is frequent in the awarding of defense contracts. In June 1988, for example, an FBI investigation was launched into alleged procurement fraud and bribery at the Pentagon. A former senior research official in the Navy Department was charged with bribing Pentagon personnel in order to obtain inside information in behalf of his employer, McDonnell Douglas. This lobbyist was seeking information on pending bids for the development of overseas sales of war planes as well as classified information on the Navy's new Advanced Technical Aircraft.[8] Two weeks later, hearings before the House Armed Services Committee disclosed a network of Pentagon officials, weapons contractors, and lobbyists seeking to rig bidding on eighty-five defense contracts worth tens of billions of dollars. Pentagon personnel were to gain monetary benefits while the defense contractors were to be awarded huge contracts at an agreed-upon bid.[9]

During the final stages of the ERA struggle, the National Organization for Women threatened legislators from unratified states with electoral defeat if they voted against the amendment. Similarly, the National Rifle Association has periodically threatened legislators with electoral defeat if they vote for gun-control legislation.

Direct lobbying can involve providing services as well as making requests. Lobbies can assist overburdened legislators in a number of important ways—drafting legislation, providing background material for public statements and speeches, generating data, devising strategies, and serving as liaison to other groups. Providing these services to legislators and administrative personnel can make them "look good" to their constituents. Thus, persistent group demands on policy makers can be partially offset by offers of group resources when they can be of help.

A wide range of *indirect* techniques have been perfected by Washington's lobbyist establishment. Given the increased turnover of legislative personnel and a weak party system, Congress is less tied to tradition, more easily swayed by public opinion, and more open to petitions by organized interests. Today, labor unions, business associations, environmentalists, and public interest groups each have an indirect, grass-roots network to back up their Washington lobby. For organizations lacking such networks, ample help is available from professional lobbying firms.

Prevailing grass-roots methods, as noted in Figure 3-3, include various kinds of communication between legislators and their home districts—letter writing or call-in campaigns, legislative visits to local establishments, and cultivation of supportive relationships with state and local newspapers and radio and television stations. Exploitation of these relationships for political ends is *not* new; what *is* new is the growing sophistication and magnitude of these contacts.

Ideally, the essence of grass-roots pressure lies in generating pressures that have the appearance of spontaneity: a "ground swell" of public opinion or widespread expressions of "public concern" over an issue possess a certain legitimacy that orchestrated pressures lack. Usually, home-district pressures do *not* spring spontaneously from the constituencies; this is a political fact of life.

Rather, genuine grass-roots pressures are enhanced by special interests, public relations firms, or, to a lesser degree, by business firms or a local labor union. Modern technologies offer lobbyists and their organizations abundant opportunities to activate specific constituencies at virtually a moment's notice. The computer has made citizens activation easier and less expensive. For example, mass mailings using computerized mailing lists can target a specific social or economic group overnight. As a result, organizations spanning the political spectrum can address appeals to, solicit money from, and endorse positions on issues of concern to their constituencies. See Box 3-4A to 3-4C for some examples.

Active use of the mass media—magazines, newspapers, radio, and particularly television—can expand the national audience available to group claims. A media campaign can be used for either offensive or defensive purposes. The National Organization for Women orchestrated a last-ditch lobbying offensive in the late 1970s and early 1980s to spur ratification of the Equal Rights Amendment. Over two dozen women's magazines included ads urging their readers to pressure legislators in uncommitted states to support the amendment. Examples of these pro-ERA appeals are shown in Box 3-5A to 3-5B. During the oil crunch of the mid-1970s, major oil companies such as Texaco, Exxon, and Shell initiated a series of television ads disclaiming any blame for the domestic oil shortage.

Political scientist Nelson Polsby believes that television has been a boon to some of the newer political interest groups. It has

> meant a rise in the influence of groups with, oddly enough, few or no members but good public relations—examples would be various offshoots of Ralph Nader's operations—in comparison with groups having large membership—trade unions are an obvious example—but no particular skill at feeding the mass media the sorts of things they like to process.[10]

Group utilization of the media may also involve "goodwill" campaigns. These are not concerned with a specific threat or target but are designed to mold a favorable public image of the organization. Oil companies, insurance firms, defense contractors, and others spend a good deal of money portraying themselves as "public-spirited" groups who are concerned with consumers' and the nation's welfare. These campaigns usually invoke traditional American values or the importance of preserving the nation's noble past. The maintenance of a favorable public image will provide the organization with a political resource to exploit in time of need. The following ad in Box 3-6 was part of a goodwill campaign.

The final dimension of indirect lobbying we want to examine is *electioneering,* whereby groups elect their friends and supporters to public office. Interest groups are inextricably linked to the electoral process. Though primar-

BOX 3–4A *CONSTITUENCY ACTIVATION*

"Forty years ago I had a back-alley abortion. I almost died from it."

If you wonder whether legal abortion is a good idea, ask any woman who survived an illegal one.

She'll tell you how painful, dirty, humiliating, and horribly dangerous a back-alley abortion was.

But despite the incredible risks, millions of American women had abortions before they were legalized nationwide in 1973. An untold number were maimed for life. Thousands were literally slaughtered, packed off bleeding and infected to die in abject terror.

Today the threat to women's lives and health no longer comes from abortion. It comes from those who want to outlaw it. People who argue that abortions should be banned—even if the result will be

as horrifying as it was in the past.

This increasingly vocal and violent minority will stop at nothing. They've resorted to harassment, physical threats, and even bombings. They're attacking the Constitution. And they're pressuring lawmakers to make abortion illegal again—for all women. Regardless of circumstances. Even if her life or health is endangered. Even if she's a victim of rape or incest. Even if she's too young to be a mother.

Speak out now. Use the coupon below. Or they just might succeed in turning back the clock to when women had no choice. But the back-alley.

The decision is yours.

☐ I've written my representatives in Congress to tell them I support: the need for abortion by preventing unwanted pregnancy; and keeping safe and legal abortion a choice for all women.

☐ Here's my tax-deductible contribution in support of all Planned Parenthood activities and programs: ☐ $25 ☐ $35 ☐ $50 ☐ $75 ☐ $150 ☐ $500 or: $_____

NAME _____

STREET·CITY·ZIP _____

 **Planned Parenthood®**
Federation of America, Inc.

810 Seventh Avenue
New York, New York 10019

This ad was paid for with private contributions. © Copyright 1985

Source: Reprinted by permission Planned Parenthood Federation of America.

BOX 3–4B

ATTENTION IMMIGRATION REFORM ADVOCATES:

YOUR CONGRESSMAN MUST GET THIS MESSAGE

This is how to do it! Call Western Union's Toll Free Number: 1-800-325-6000. Ask for operator 9042

Call the number above and tell the operator you want to send the above Mailgram to your Congressman. The operator will provide you with the name and address of your Congressman: The cost is only $4.00 and will be charged to your phone bill.

Your Congressman
U.S. House of Representatives
Washington, D.C. 20515

Please support the Immigration Reform bill, H.R. 3810. American jobs and social services must be protected for American citizens and legal immigrants. Let's control our borders and stop illegal immigration.

The vote of every member of the House is crucial if we are to see immigration reform legislation pass this year. Congress is scheduled to adjourn in October. If the bill is not passed by then it will die! Let your Congressman know that you think passage of a *strong* bill, without destructive loopholes, is important to the future of our country.

FAIR favors Employer Sanctions. H.R. 3810 will make it illegal to hire an illegal alien. Jobs are the magnet that draw illegal aliens to the United States. We won't stem the flow of illegal immigrants until we make it illegal for employers to knowingly hire illegal aliens.

FAIR supports Verification of Employment Eligibility which requires employers to verify that *all* new employees have proper work documents.

FAIR favors additional funding for INS Enforcement and Services. The Immigration and Naturalization Service can't do its job without adequate manpower and equipment. H.R. 3810 would give them the money they need to control our borders.

FAIR opposes Amnesty for illegal aliens in the United States. We will fight to delete amnesty and resist any effort to expand the excessive amnesty now in the bill.

FAIR opposes the provision proposed by agricultural interests. We will fight this provision that will grant immediate permanent resident status to any illegal alien who worked sixty days in agriculture last year and that will allow countless additional agricultural workers to be brought into the United States.

DO YOUR PART TO STOP ILLEGAL IMMIGRATION!

See other side for detailed provisions of H.R. 3810

Federation for American Immigration Reform

1424 16th Street, N.W., Suite 701, Washington, DC 20036

BOX 3–4C

BULLSEYE

Brazil is the latest country seeking to sell hundreds of thousands of tons of subsidized steel slabs to an American steel company for finishing into steel products. The slabs would replace steel made in America, further reduce our steelmaking capacity and throw out of work additional thousands of steel industry suppliers, steelworkers, and service employees in steel towns.

However, a Brazilian government representative said Brazil is "... being cautious and is still waiting to see the outcome of a similar deal between United States Steel Corporation and British Steel Corporation."

In earlier statements we warned the American public that if British Steel is allowed to annually ship 3 million tons of subsidized steel to U.S. Steel's Fairless Works, there would be a flood of cheaper deals from Brazil, Korea, and other countries.

Already, Brazil is negotiating with Wheeling-Pittsburgh Steel to ship raw steel slabs to Steubenville, Ohio. The Steubenville Works has just installed brand new "state-of-the-art" equipment to make its own slabs. Workers there have taken deep cuts in pay and benefits to help their company modernize.

Still, Wheeling-Pittsburgh officials say, the Brazilian steel would be far cheaper. Steubenville's inland location, modern equipment, and substantially lower labor costs are all overcome by the Brazilian government's subsidy to its new steel industry.

What is happening in the steel industry is a dramatic example of the problem of international targeting of selected industries.

Through targeting, a government gives preferred treatment to a chosen industry—subsidizing its development in many ways until its products can be dumped on foreign markets at prices far below the true cost of production.

Because of our high consumption and lack of a national industrial policy, the United States is a sitting duck for these practices. Look at what has been targeted:

COMPUTERIZED MACHINE TOOLS: Japan's share of this market in the United States has increased from 5% to 50% since 1976. 24,000 American jobs have been lost.

AIRBUS: Western European countries targeted the world commercial aircraft market in the early 1970's with the creation of a joint venture called Airbus Industries—which now accounts for half of the free world market for widebodied aircraft. This rapid market penetration contributed to Lockheed's decision to stop production of the L1011, with a loss of 4,000 jobs.

Private American business firms and workers cannot compete against the governments of foreign countries. Some American industries are simply disappearing. Others are falling far behind their subsidized foreign competitors.

Today we are faced with the very real threat of losing America's steel independence. If we do, much of our military power and economic base will also be lost.

Tomorrow, it could be *your* industry. It could be *your* job.

USA

Brazil Joins Britain In Attack On USA's Steel Independence

UNITED STEELWORKERS OF AMERICA
Lloyd McBride, President
Five Gateway Center
Pittsburgh, Pennsylvania 15222

Source: Used with permission of United Steelworkers of America. *Iron Age,* 1983.

BOX 3-5A   *MEDIA APPEALS*

GETTING**DOWN**

As of this month, the Equal Rights Amendment has been ratified by thirty-five states. In order for the Amendment to become law ratification is needed by three more states by June 30, 1982. I happen to be a supporter of the Equal Rights Amendment and am urging those of you who live in states where ERA has not been ratified to get out and help build support for it as well as vote for it yourselves.

I know that there is much more that needs to be done to secure our Civil Rights, to bring full equality of opportunity to our people. And I know that we need every bit of ammunition that we can muster to that end. ERA is but another means. It does not take the place of the Civil Rights laws that we struggled to achieve, it merely stands beside them helping to bolster the cause of Human Rights in this country. What does it say? *1. Equality of rights under the law shall not be denied or abridged by the United States or by any state on account of sex. 2. The congress shall have the power to enforce, by appropriate legislation, the provisions of this article. 3. This amendment shall take effect two years after the date of ratification.*

I know that there are people who will say that this is not a Black woman's issue, yet they are wrong. In the world that we live in any restriction of our rights is our concern. In fact anyone who wishes to tell me that because I'm a woman I can't pursue my life's course as I see fit or who seeks to narrow my choices and horizons based on my sex is an enemy of freedom. And I did not stand up for my rights as a Black person in America to be told that I have to sit down because I'm a woman.

The women's movement is a fact of life—all around this world women are moving to redress grievances, to address issues and concerns that directly effect their lives, to help create whole healthy nondiscriminatory societies. As women of color we know the toll injustice takes. We know the need for child care, the need for equal pay and increased mobility in the work force. We know we need to be able to do and be more if we as a people are to survive and thrive tomorrow. The women's movement can and should be used by us for us. We can make the movement more responsive to the people, only when we bring the people and their concerns to the movement, and come not to follow but to lead. ERA can be a beginning so seize the time!

Marcia Ann Gillespie

EDITOR-IN-CHIEF

BOX 3–5B

1. Equality of rights under the law shall not be denied or abridged by the United States or by any State on account of sex.

2. The Congress shall have the power to enforce, by appropriate legislation, the provisions of this article.

3. This amendment shall take effect two years after the date of ratification.

It's hard to see what is so controversial about the simple text of the Equal Rights Amendment. Still, it has been more than 50 years since such a constitutional amendment was first proposed, and over seven years since Congress submitted the above articles to the states for ratification before the deadline date of March 22, 1979.

Proponents of the legislation won a major victory last year when the deadline was extended to June 30, 1982. But much remains to be done if the amendment is to be approved by that date—instead of being put to rest while over 800 federal statutes and thousands of state laws, which openly discriminate on the basis of sex, remain in effect. (These estimations are from a recent report by the U.S. Civil Rights Commission.)

Such discrimination persists largely because unrestricted coverage of equal protection, which the Fourteenth Amendment has afforded minorities, corporations and certain religious sects,

has never been extended to women. The Supreme Court has traditionally held that sex discrimination is not comparable to other kinds of discrimination: a Justice reaffirmed this distinction as recently as 1978, as a supporting point in the controversial Bakke case.

It is true that 35 of the requisite 38 states have already ratified ERA. Or to put it another way, only a dozen votes of individual state legislators block national passage of the amendment. But ground has been lost even as ground is gained: Three states have rescinded ratification of the amendment—Nebraska, Tennessee and Idaho. However, the legality of these rescindments is in question, and similar efforts to rescind have been overturned in 10 states.

The major thrust of public action for ERA's passage should now be directed at the legislators in the 15 states that have not ratified the amendment: Alabama, Arizona, Arkansas, Florida, Georgia, Illinois, Louisiana, Mississippi, Mis-

souri, Nevada, North Carolina, Oklahoma, South Carolina, Utah and Virginia. (In Florida and Illinois, ratification was narrowly defeated, so public pressure there is expected to make a critical difference.)

If you live in a state that has already ratified, you might send a letter or telegram to your governor, asking him to speak with the governor of an uncommitted state. Remember that mail is always most effective when it is sent to one's own elected representatives rather than to politicians in another state.

The state legislators seated in the 1979-1980 session will be the same people as last time, so they can be expected to simply repeat their votes concerning ERA—unless the public induces them to change their minds. Many of these legislators will come up for reelection later in 1980, so they will be more sensitive to their constituents' opinions on controversial topics.

—KATIE LEISHMAN

Many organizations with local chapters and offices are spearheading the effort to insure ERA's passage. You may want to work with such a group or to simply stay informed about ERA's progress. To find an active organization in your area, here are some groups to contact:

AFL/CIO
815 16th Street
Washington, D.C. 20006

American Association of University Women
2401 Virginia Avenue, N.W.
Washington, D.C. 20006

B'nai B'rith Women
1640 Rhode Island Avenue, N.W.
Washington, D.C. 20036

Common Cause
2030 M Street, N.W.
Washington, D.C. 20036

Girl Scouts of the U.S.A.
2133 Wisconsin Avenue, N.W.
Washington, D.C. 20007

Gray Panthers
711 Eighth Street, N.W.
Washington, D.C. 20001

Leadership Conference on Civil Rights
2027 Massachusetts Avenue, N.W.
Washington, D.C. 20036

League of Women Voters
1730 M Street, N.W.
Washington, D.C. 20036

NAACP
1790 Broadway
New York, N.Y. 10019

National Center for Voluntary Action
1214 16th Street
Washington, D.C. 20036

National Organization for Women
425 13th Street, N.W.
Washington, D.C. 20004

Young Women's Christian Association
1649 K Street, N.W.
Washington, D.C. 20006

If you haven't time to volunteer, your support in the form of a donation would be an important part of the effort. Send your check to:

ERA America
1525 M Street, N.W.
Washington, D.C. 20036

ERA America also has a coalition in each state, which you may want to join.   ■

Source: "ERA: Where We Stand" by Katie Leishman, *Working Mother Magazine*, Nov., 1979, p. 20. Used with permission.

BOX 3–6

One of a series of messages in support of a brighter future for America.

HOORAY FOR THE YANKEE PEDDLER

The Yankee Peddler was America's first entrepreneur.

He'd load his wagon with his wares and drive around selling them to folks in the neighborhoods. It's an honorable tradition.

Today — in a variety of forms — the Yankee Peddler has millions of lineal descendants. They're called independent contractors.

They are people who are self-employed.

Self-employed men and women have been the backbone of American society from its earliest beginnings.

As everyone knows, self-employment is the earning of one's living directly from one's own profession or business rather than as an employee of another. It's the right to be your own boss.

Self-employed people include writers, doctors, lawyers, waiters and waitresses, realtors and real estate agents, artists, direct sellers, plumbers, electricians, carpenters, and all independent contractors in a wide range of other entrepreneurial endeavors.

Being self-made, self-reliant, and self-employed — just like the Yankee Peddler — are all parts of the fabric of the American dream.

It is simply people creating jobs for themselves.

If every American created his or her own business or profession — no matter how small — billions of revenue dollars would be generated to help lift our sagging economy.

That is something the federal government, including the Internal Revenue Service, should be actively encouraging and promoting.

It's a "back-to-basics" idea.

Everyone has a skill. Why not offer that skill for trade or recompense?

Let's bring back the Yankee Peddlers.

Amway

Amway Corporation, Ada, MI 49355

ily concerned with policy formulation, they are becoming increasingly involved in elections. Labor unions, business associations, ideological organizations, veterans, and feminists are pursuing a growing number of electoral activities. This deepening involvement serves two purposes: group support is a partial inducement for a candidate to back the group's policy objectives, and it ensures that sympathetic officials remain in office.

An increasing range of techniques are being employed by more and more organizations in order to provide campaign assistance. These include endorsements, assistance in voter registration, get-out-the-vote drives, dissemination of campaign literature, and of course financial contributions (see Chapter 4). Group support through any of these techniques can be crucial in helping elect or reelect legislative or administrative candidates.

Organized labor pioneered the concept of establishing significant support systems for selected candidates. The AFL-CIO's Committee on Political Education (COPE) is the modern prototype of the political action committee.[11] COPE screens candidates for the federation membership, advising who is to be supported and who is not. These decisions are made on the basis of labor issues more than on the basis of a candidate's party. Although labor has traditionally worked for Democratic legislative and administrative candidates and against Republicans, it maintains some autonomy from both parties. Labor leaders at various levels within the federation plan for upcoming elections by concentrating union efforts and resources on key races. The money and manpower poured into these races derives from union memberships throughout the federation.

A more specialized and sophisticated organization closely tied to the national electoral process is the National Committee for an Effective Congress (NCEC).* Established by national Democrats to elect liberal candidates to Congress, this organization offers a range of technical and financial assistance to candidates in selected congressional districts across the country (see Box 3-7A and 3-7B).

In the general election of 1988, the NCEC endorses eighty-five candidates, twenty-one in the Senate and sixty-four in the House. These candidates received varying degrees of financial assistance, help in fund raising, and technical assistance in planning, organizing, and managing their campaigns. The NCEC also contracted with other candidates for polling services, voter targeting, and media consulting.

In off years, the NCEC conducts a broad range of research—congressional district composition, preelection strategies for selected races, polling, and so on. The organization has also intensively studied various industries' (particularly oil and gas) political contributions and their main beneficiaries. Staff research for key candidates focuses on basic issues, speech materials,

*The NCEC was founded in 1948 by Senator Harley Kilgore, D-W. Va., Eleanor Roosevelt, and Maurice Rosenblatt. In that year, the NCEC supported six underdog liberal candidates, including Hubert Humphrey, and all six were elected.

BOX 3-7A *ELECTIONEERING*

NCEC MEDIA MARKET TARGETING ...

Because campaigns allocate more and more of their budgets to radio and television advertising, the NCEC has developed a sophisticated media buying analysis which assures that a candidate's message reaches the most persuadable element of the electorate with maximum impact and minimum cost.

For example, when a campaign needs to reach working women,

NCEC's media market analysis identifies the precise geographic concentration of this demographic group.

The success of our media program in 1986 convinced us to provide every progressive candidate in 1988 with a media market analysis covering a high to low range media budget.

This NCEC Election Update will

examine the high price of television media in Ohio and Florida. The outcome of the Senate races in these two states will, in large measure, be determined by the success or failure of each candidate's media campaign. Our analyses of the various markets contain breakdowns of the audiences in terms of expected vote, persuadability and Democratic performance, as well as approximate price quotations for 30 seconds of prime time air-play.

OHIO

Democratic Incumbent:

Howard Metzenbaum

Republican Challenger:

George Voinovich,
        Mayor of Cleveland

Although Ohio has 12 in-state media markets, many of its markets overlap and most of the state's population can be reached by purchasing air time in the three largest media markets: Cincinnati, which covers the southern portion of the state; Cleveland, which covers the north; and Columbus, which covers the middle.

Metzenbaum's strength in the Democratic north is being undermined by Voinovich, and it now looks as though this race will be decided in traditionally conservative southern Ohio. In order to reach the voters in this part of the state, Metzenbaum will need to buy substantial blocks of media time in the Columbus and Cincinnati markets.

CINCINNATI		CLEVELAND		COLUMBUS	
TV Households:	1,495,100	TV Households:	2,506,000	TV Households:	1,448,800
Expected Vote:	576,801	Expected Vote:	1,525,464	Expected Vote:	639,175
Persuadable Vote:	88,084	Persuadable Vote:	199,286	Persuadable Vote:	92,304
Persuasion Percent:	15.3%	Persuasion Percent:	13.1%	Persuasion Percent:	14.4%
Democratic Performance: 46.9%		Democratic Performance: 61.4%		Democratic Performance: 48.8%	
Network Affiliates:		Network Affiliates:		Network Affiliates:	
WLWT (NBC)		WKYC (NBC)		WCMH (NBC)	
Cost of 30 seconds during		Cost of 30 seconds during		Cost of 30 seconds during	
"LA Law":	$4,200.00	"The Cosby Show":	$6,000.00	"The Cosby Show":	$4,200.00
WCPO (CBS)		WJW (CBS)		WBNS (CBS)	
Cost of 30 seconds during		Cost of 30 seconds during		Cost of 30 seconds during	
"60 Minutes":	$2,200.00	"60 Minutes":	$3,700.00	"60 Minutes":	$2,400.00
WKRC (ABC)		WEWS (ABC)		WSYX (ABC)	
Cost of 30 seconds during		Cost of 30 seconds during		Cost of 30 seconds during	
"Moonlighting":	$2,700.00	"Moonlighting":	$2,500.00	"Moonlighting":	$3,500.00

Source: Used with permission of National Committee for an Effective Congress.

BOX 3–7B

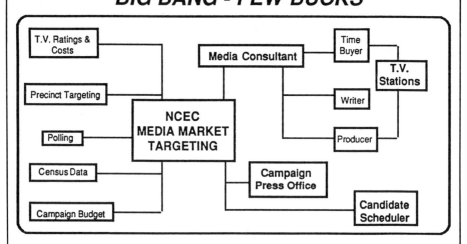

NCEC MEDIA MARKET TARGETING:

"BIG BANG - FEW BUCKS"

This diagram shows the impact of NCEC Media Market Targeting. By constructing a complex data–base of television ratings, market costs, polling and census data and precinct electoral targeting, the NCEC provides progressive campaigns with the tools to reach the most crucial segments of the electorate at the minimum cost.

FIGHT THE RIGHT. WRITE A CHECK.

Source: Used with permission of National Committee for an Effective Congress.

and data on opponents' voting records. The NCEC is generally recognized as one of the largest and most effective campaign-assistance organizations in the country.

The favorable track record of the NCEC stimulated political conservatives to establish the Committee for the Survival of a Free Congress (CSFC) in the mid-1970s. The Committee functions in conjunction with the Free Congress Research and Education Foundation, a conservative think tank engaged in policy research and voter education.[*] The organization has approximately 60,000

[*]The CSFC is directed by Paul M. Weyrich, who is also president of the Free Congress Research and Education Foundation.

contributors. Since 1980 the Committee has shifted its emphasis to campaign organization and candidate training at the precinct level. Though claiming to be bipartisan, the Committee maintains a very conservative position on such issues as abortion, homosexuality, the free enterprise system, and a balanced budget. The overwhelming majority of candidates it endorses are Republicans. As part of the nation's New Right, the CSFC is more strident and dogmatic in its public positions than earlier conservative organizations.

The Committee has a very sophisticated system for providing campaign assistance to those it endorses. As part of an ongoing information-gathering process, it stockpiles political data on which judgments are subsequently made about which candidates to endorse, what kinds of campaigns the organization will be involved in, and what the chances are for conservative victories. The data also help to identify vulnerable liberal candidates and to recruit conservative challengers. Selected challengers are required to attend various seminars dealing with precinct organization and campaigning. Upon election, new members backed by the CSFC receive a general orientation and assistance in staffing their Washington and home-state offices. Recipients of CSFC electoral support include former senators Paula Hawkins and Jeremiah Denton and incumbent Steven Symms. The same pattern of support is also extended to candidates for the House.

The CSFC publishes extensively, dealing with such topics of organizational concern as legislative apportionment, political action committees, judicial activism, public school curricula, and lobbying. Additionally, periodic conferences are held to provide up-to-date information on political lobbying and issue development. Other conferences have dealt with fund raising, volunteer recruitment, grass-roots organizing, and coalition building. In late 1981, the affiliated Research and Education Foundation convened a two-day conference to open up a broader dialogue among the invited business leaders, social-issue advocates, and academicians. The main purpose of the event was to dispel growing public misconceptions among social advocates on the Committee's position on abortion, the women's movement, and gun-control legislation.

The CSFC has supported approximately 100 successful conservative candidates. So, it is widely recognized as one of the more effective New Right groups. Writer Alan Ehrehalt offers this assessment:

> When a dozen or so active New Right PAC's meet around a luncheon table each Monday afternoon to compare notes, each group has its say. But the CSFC has the most notes to compare. As often as not, the other[s] follow its lead.[12]

A CASE STUDY

Having examined direct and indirect lobbying techniques, let us now see how they are put into play. In late 1982 and early 1983, a combination of banks and savings and loan institutions mounted a massive lobbying campaign directed at

Congress. At issue was a bill to repeal taxes on interest and dividends awarded by lending institutions. Under a new law, which was not yet in effect, institutions paying interest or dividends were to withhold 10 percent of those payments for transfer to the IRS. According to U.S. Treasury Department estimates, some $23 billion would be collected over six years, beginning in 1983.

Banks and S&Ls supported repeal of the withholding legislation. They developed a series of technical arguments to the effect that the costs and other difficulties of compliance made the new law unworkable. Their complaints focused on start-up costs for administering the plan, recruitment and training of additional personnel, and difficulties in informing clients of how the legislation would affect them.

While preparing to comply with the law, concerned associations such as the American Bankers Association, the League of Savings Institutions, and the National Association of Credit Unions began intensive lobbying efforts aimed at repeal. A well-orchestrated direct and grass-roots campaign aimed at repeal was led by the American Bankers Association with the support of dozens of independent banks, brokerage houses, and credit unions.

The lobbying efforts of the banking coalition involved both direct and indirect approaches. Direct methods included increased visibility and legislative pressures and contacts on Capitol Hill. The grass-roots campaign galvanized thousands of institutional customers into political action. The consensus of those orchestrating this effort was that Congress simply could not withstand these pressures and would be forced to repeal the withholding law.

A key ingredient in the grass-roots effort was a "statement stuffer" developed by the League of Savings Institutions. More than 75 million of these kits were eventually distributed to customers, savings and loan institutions, banks, and credit unions. The kits provided the tools to mobilize customer and shareholder support for the repeal campaign, and material for local media campaigns. Included in the kits were prewritten advertising copy, sample letters to stockholders and members of Congress, speech material, press releases, and even sample feature articles and editorials for local newspapers backing the coalition's position. An extraordinarily sophisticated lobbying device, the kit included materials targeted to specific audiences—areas with high unemployment and areas with a concentration of senior citizens, for example. Some samples of this voluminous packet are featured in Box 3-8.

The grass-roots effort paid off by activating a significant number of banking and credit union customers. The resulting flood of mail pushed the average number of letters, postcards, and mailgrams handled by the House post office from a daily average of 250,000 to about 650,000. The Senate post office experienced a similar surge. The final vote in the two chambers testifies to the success of the banking lobby's repeal campaign in the face of strong administration opposition—382 to 41 in the House and 86 to 4 in the Senate. Robert Dole, chairman of the Senate Finance Committee and a direct participant in the repeal legislation, characterized the bank lobbying as the most massive campaign in history to intimidate the Congress. . . . If you've got enough money and send in enough mail, you'll probably get results.[13]

In late July 1983, Congress accepted a conference report repealing the 1982 Tax Act's requirement that depository institutions withhold 10 percent of depositors' interest.

BOX 3-8   *A GRASS-ROOTS LOBBYING CAMPAIGN*

Industrywide Grassroots Effort to Repeal the 10% Withholding Tax on Savings Interest

Objectives

The fundamental objective is to generate widespread and heavy grassroots mail from bank depositors and stockholders to Congress urging repeal of the 10 percent withholding tax on savings interest before it becomes effective July 1, 1983.

The repeal effort has several other very important objectives, each of which carries significant depositor and stockholder relations benefits for participating banks, which are:

1. To alert your bank's depositors and stockholders about this new law which, it is safe to assume, most do not know exists.

2. To explain clearly that it is the Federal government—*and not your bank*—that wants to begin withholding interest earned on their savings and their dividends next July 1.

3. To inform depositors and stockholders that your bank strongly opposes this 10 percent withholding tax and that, *on their behalf,* your bank is working vigorously to bring about Congressional repeal of the law.

4. To make your depositors fully aware that the Federal law also requires money market funds, credit unions, corporations that pay dividends, etc., to withhold 10 percent from their customer earnings.

The Repeal Plan

The plan is geared to produce heavy depositor and stockholder write-ins to Congress during January, February and March 1983, with some spillover into April probable.

However, it is assumed that many, if not most, depositors would not know who their elected Federal officials are, or might resist sitting down and writing "repeal withholding" letters. Thus an alternative is offered: Fill-in postcards, which you can make available in the offices of your bank. Each bank can collect these postcards in bank lobby "ballot boxes" and then deliver the postcards to the appropriate Representative, *or* they can participate in a coordinated delivery of the postcards through their state association.

What This Kit Contains

This Repeal kit contains the public relations and advertising material that you will need to help mobilize your customers to fight for the repeal of the 10 percent withholding tax on savings.

An order form is attached for stuffers to be used in a direct mail campaign—they can either be placed in the 1099 statements you send to your depositors or in their regular bank statements.

Please read the attached information "How To Use This Kit" and then look over the kit itself. Do not hesitate to call on the ABA if you need any additional information or have any questions about the kit.

Note: Amounts spent for grassroots lobbying are not deductible business expenses for Federal income tax purposes.

How To Use This Kit

The 10% Withholding on Savings Kit you have in front of you contains the following items:

1. *An Information Sheet* that outlines some of the consumer issues raised by the 10 percent withholding tax. This sheet should be distributed to your bank's own public relations and advertising departments for developing their campaigns.

2. *Questions and answers* about specific provisions of the 10 percent withholding tax. These can be distributed to your employees to help them answer customer questions, to the media, to customers themselves and as background when you give speeches or talks.

3. *A sample postcard/ballot* for your customers to fill in at your bank. These postcard/ballots should be printed locally and placed in your bank lobby. Once your customer has filled it in, he or she can put it in a "ballot box" in the bank lobby. These postcard/ballots will then be personally delivered to the Congressional representative whose district your bank is in.

4. *A sample letter to bank stockholders.* This should be retyped on your chief executive officer's stationery and sent to each bank stockholder.

5. *Three sample letters to Congress*—one from a banker, a consumer and a senior citizen. These letters are suggestions only, but on all of them, be sure to ask your Congressional representatives to inform you of *their* positions, so your concern will truly register.

6. *Two sample letters to the editor.* In any grassroots campaign, it is essential that the media know how concerned the public is. Letters to the editor are very effective. Included here are sample letters from a banker and a customer.

7. *A logo sheet.* This contains "10% Withholding on Savings" logos in six different sizes. Working with your local printer, you can use these on your news release paper, the sample ballot/postcard, your bank letterhead and in your public advertising and direct mail campaigns.

8. *A speech,* "The Government Wants a Piece of Our Savings." This speech spells out in detail just where the problems lie in savings withholding and what kind of solution—repeal—should be adopted by our elected officials. You may use the speech any way you like. It may be delivered as is or in a modified version. You may also choose to use it as a source document. The speech is about 15–20 minutes long.

9. *A sample news release* to be distributed to your local media when the speech is given. The release highlights all of the important points made in the speech. Please be sure to complete the speech by filling in the blanks to reflect the time, place and the name and title of the person who gave the speech. It should be retyped on your bank's letterhead.

10. *A speech insert detailing problems senior citizens* will have if 10 percent withholding goes into effect. You should substitute the insert for page 4 of the main speech and use it whenever you speak to a group that is made up or involved with senior citizens.

11. *A sample news release to go with the senior citizen speech,* highlighting the important points made in the speech. Again, please retype it on your bank's letterhead, with the appropriate time, place and speaker's name filled in and distribute it to your local media when the speech is given.

12. *A speech insert dealing with problems the unemployed will have* if 10 percent withholding becomes effective. You should substitute this insert for page 4 of the main speech.

13. *A sample news release to go with the unemployed speech,* highlighting the important points made in the speech. Besides releasing it when the speech is given, your bank should also consider releasing it when your area's unemployment figures are announced. Again, it should be retyped on your bank's letterhead with the blanks filled in.

14. *An op-ed (or banker's editorial) article,* "Withholding: A Bad Law." This should be retyped on your bank's letterhead and sent with a personal note to your newspaper's editor.

15. *A sample news feature article* discussing the problems senior citizens will have if 10 percent withholding goes into effect. This should be distributed to your local media and could also go into your bank's magazine or newsletter.

This may look like a lot of material—and it is. But in order to repeal this bad law, Congress is going to have to be convinced that the public insists that it be done.

By involving your customers, you will be accomplishing two important objectives—

You will get the message to Congress that there is a mandate for repeal.

And, if Congress fails to act, your customers will blame the Congress, not the banks.

1982. Used with permission of American Bankers Association.

SUMMARY

Lobbying is much more professional and sophisticated today than it used to be, and the lobbying profession has lost much of its stigma of a century ago. Recalling those days, one writer states that

> between 1865 and 1885 the concept of government by all the people, so movingly reaffirmed by Abraham Lincoln, almost went into eclipse. Special interest pressure and corruption in government mounted to dizzy heights. Popular government was threatened as never before in this country.[14]

Present-day lobbyists perform indispensable jobs for dozens of public officials and many citizens. These include informing legislative and administrative personnel about important problems and issues, stimulating public debate, and providing decision makers with political intelligence on supporters and opponents of pending legislation or rules changes. To perform these tasks, lobbyists are developing and refining strategies of influence. Our national policy makers therefore face a growing army of lobbyists employing a widening range of pressure tactics.

The type of lobbyist employed and techniques he or she uses still depends, of course, on the group and its policy objectives. For example, a consortium of oil companies seeking tax benefits will employ the traditional methods of approaching key members of Congress on that body's tax-writing committees. The consortium's relatively narrow concerns and established access will require a minimal lobbying effort. On the other hand, a public interest group desiring a change in national election laws will mount a grass roots campaign to arouse its members to inundate Congress with pressure mail. The political goals of the latter group are broader and thus will require a significant lobbying effort.

Today's technologies, particularly in the realms of the mass media and computers, are a boon to lobbies and lobbyists. It is now easier and less expensive for groups to energize existing and incipient constituencies. These and other technologies enhance group competitiveness. Thus, new organizations can begin to effectively compete more quickly than was possible fifteen or twenty years ago. Though affluence and prestige enhance lobbying success, effective use of modern communications is becoming increasingly important.

NOTES

[1]Quoted in *U.S. News & World Report,* June 17, 1985, p. 31.

[2]The first systematic study of lobbyists was that of Lester Milbrath, *The Washington Lobbyist* (Chicago: Rand McNally, 1963).

[3]For an excellent analysis of many current Washington lobbyists, see "The Influence Industry," *National Journal,* 17 (September 14, 1985).

[4]Quoted in *National Journal,* 18 (May 3, 1986), p. 1052.

[5]Mark Green, *The Other Government: The Unseen Power of Washington Lawyers* (New York: Viking, 1975), p. 4.

[6]For an in-depth analysis of the extensive linkage between defense-related industries and the Pentagon, see Gordon Adams, *The Politics of Defense Contracting: The Iron Triangle,* (New Brunswick, N.J.: Transaction Books, 1981).

[7]Harmon Zeigler and Wayne Peak, *Interest Groups in American Society,* 2nd ed. (Englewood Cliffs, N.J.: Prentice-Hall, 1972), p. 169.

[8]Congressional Quarterly *Weekly Report,* 46 (June 18, 1988), 1696.

[9]Congressional Quarterly *Weekly Report,* 46 (July 2, 1988), 1814.

[10]Nelson Polsby, "Prospects for Pluralism in the American Federal System: Trends in Unofficial Public-Sector Intermediation," quoted in *The Transformation in American Politics: Implications for Federalism* (Washington, D.C.: Advisory Council on Intergovernmental Relations, 1986), p. 231.

[11]See Harry Holloway, "Interest Groups in the Postpartisan Era: The Political Machine of the AFL-CIO," *Political Science Quarterly,* 94 (1979), 117–33.

[12]Quoted in the Congressional Quarterly *Weekly Report,* 40 (May 1, 1982), 1027.

[13]Quoted in the Congressional Quarterly *Weekly Report,* 41 (March 21, 1983), 491.

[14]James Deakin, *The Lobbyists* (Washington, D.C.: Public Affairs Press, 1966), p. 67.

CHAPTER FOUR
PACs AMERICANA:
The Bucks Start Here

AN ORIENTATION

The nationalization of pressure group politics during the 1970s was accompanied by a unique development in campaign finance. In 1972, for example, all congressional candidates spent a total of $77 million in their campaigns; four years later the total was up to $115.5 million, and by 1986 the total was approaching $500 million—an increase of almost 500 percent since 1972. The figure remains sizable even when we allow for the increase of the price index over the same period—165 percent—and even when we correct for inflation—125 percent.

By and large, the major contributor to this significant increase in campaign spending is the political action committee (PAC).[1] PACs are political organizations that specialize in aggregating resources with which to affect the outcomes of political elections. PACs are altering traditional methods of campaign financing as well as the nature of interest group participation in national elections. Congressional legislation, such as the Federal Election Campaign Act (FECA), regulations issued by the Federal Election Commission, Supreme Court decisions, and actions by individual campaigners themselves have all contributed to the emergence of this organizational phenomenon. Recent technological developments, such as survey research (for example, polling data), computer data bases for information and analysis, professionalized fund raising, and strategic planning and scheduling, have also played a role.

In this chapter we will explore the emerging role of PACs by focusing on their establishment and growth, their patterns of campaign fund raising and spending, the controversy over their perceived impact on congressional legislation, and their current political status. We can thereby attain a more sophisticated understanding of this new organizational phenomenon and its contribution to our electoral system.

THE LEGISLATIVE BASIS
OF PACS

In recent years, growing numbers of individuals and reform organizations have expressed concerns about the connection of private contributions to congressional and presidential candidates and the decisions of those candidates once they are in office. The possibility of undue influence of money from large corporations or labor unions is a constant problem. In fact, this concern drives the current debate over the role of PACs in political races. Efforts to legislate and regulate campaign expenditures have been made for more than half a century, but they have not been successful.[2] Additionally, enforcement of existing legislation has been half-hearted at best.

In the early 1970s, as a result of growing public agitation over rising campaign costs and candidate expenditures, legislation was finally enacted. The Federal Election Campaign Act of 1971 was the first overhaul of federal campaign legislation since the 1925 Corrupt Practices Act. The 1971 law was amended in 1974, 1976, and 1979. The 1974 amendments were in response to public revelations before the Senate Watergate investigating committee. These hearings revealed that in 1972 millions of dollars of illegal and "laundered" cash contributions from private corporations and individuals had made their way to the Committee to Re-elect the President (CREEP).

The FECA as amended

defines campaign contributions and expenditures;

establishes contribution limits for individuals, political parties, and political action committees;

establishes the Federal Election Commission (FEC) to administer the law, issue regulations, and receive reports;

sets expenditure limits for parties and presidential candidates accepting public funding; and

sets requirements for reporting (disclosing) sources and amounts of campaign contributions and expenditures.

The 1971 Revenue Act provides for the public funding of presidential campaigns through a one-dollar check-off on federal income tax returns. (By the mid-1980s, 27 percent of taxpayers were using the check-off option.) Publicly funded presidential candidates cannot accept private contributions for the general election campaign.

AFFILIATED AND
NONAFFILIATED PACS

Affiliated PACs are political committees created by such organizations as labor unions, business and professional organizations, and cooperatives and corporations without stock. These PACs solicit contributions and disburse money to candidates of their choice. Such PACs are restricted to internal solicitations—that is, solicitations of management, the rank and file, and families, and not the general public. Examples are the political action committee of the American Bankers' Association (BANKPAC), American Gas Association (GASPAC), and American Health Care Association (AHCAPAC). About 80 percent of PACs are of the affiliated type. *Nonaffiliated PACs* are totally independent in terms of fund raising and spending. These PACs are not subject to the restrictions binding affiliated PACs; they can solicit the general public. Examples of organizations with these PACs are Americans for Democratic Action (ADA/PAC), the National Abortion Rights Action League (NARALPAC), and Life Amendment (LAPAC). These organizations use direct-mail solicitations for the bulk of their fund raising.

THE DEVELOPMENT
OF PACS

The first modern political action committee was organized by the Congress of Industrial Organizations (CIO) in 1943. This was followed by the American Federation of Labor's PAC, established in 1947. Other unions followed suit in the 1950s and 1960s.* These early PACs set the present pattern of channeling contributions into separate accounts (rather than the union treasury) so that they would be clearly distinguishable as political contributions.

While the unions were establishing PACs, corporations were active in political campaigns in their own ways. Most frequently, corporate executives and their families made personal contributions. Under the law, corporations were forbidden to contribute to political campaigns. But the Senate Watergate hearings disclosed numerous violations of the law by private corporations during the 1972 presidential campaign. American Airlines, Braniff Airways, Gulf Oil, and others were found guilty of illegal contributions and fined.

The Federal Election Campaign Act of 1971 allowed the establishment of affiliated PACs by unions and corporations. The number of these PACs was slow to increase, however, until passage of the 1974 amendment to the FECA. Part of the initial slow growth in PACs is attributable to the reluctance of corporations. Many had genuine concerns about the legality of

---

*There were about forty national labor union PACs, along with numerous state and local affiliates, when Congress passed campaign reform legislation in 1971.

holding government contracts, establishing PACs with corporate funds. The 1974 amendment sufficiently modified the earlier law to enable unions and corporations with government contracts to establish PACs and begin soliciting their members.

When the 1971 law took effect, there were 113 PACs. As Figure 4-1 shows, the number of PACs has climbed consistently in recent years, from approximately 1000 in 1977 to slightly over 4000 in the late 1980s. Yearly increases have averaged about 23 percent, but that rate is slowing now.

Figure 4-1 also shows that different types of PACs demonstrate different growth patterns. The most spectacular long-term growth is among corporate PACs—close to 295 percent over eleven years. By contrast, labor PACs have grown at a more sluggish pace of 11 percent over the same period.

Subsequent amendments to the FECA led to marked increases in the number of business-related and other PACs. Another factor in PAC growth was an advisory opinion issued by the Federal Election Commission in 1975. At issue was whether the Sun Oil Company's political action committee could solicit campaign contributions from its employees. The FEC advised that these solicitations were legitimate under existing legislation. This opinion permitted a corporation to establish multiple PACs as long as it used a payroll deduction

FIGURE 4-1   Political Action Committees

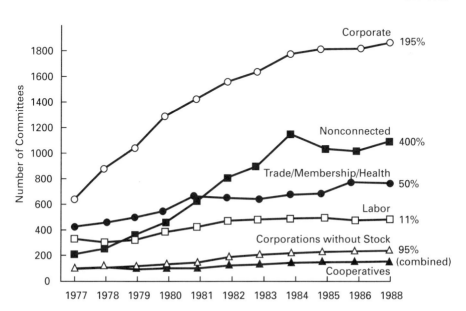

Source: Federal Election Commission.

system. Contributions had to be voluntary, however, and no reprisals were to be taken against recalcitrant employees.* The SunPAC opinion was a key element in the expansion of corporate electoral activity. Now the tremendous organizational and financial resources of corporations became available to probusiness candidates throughout the country.

One other important development was the Supreme Court's 1976 decision in *Buckley* v. *Valeo*.[3] In this landmark ruling, the Court held that 1974 FECA amendment limits on candidates' contributions to their own campaigns, limits on campaign expenditures by candidates, and limits on independent committee expenditures were all restrictions of the First Amendment right of free speech and therefore unconstitutional. The Court did, however, uphold the law's aggregate-expenditure limits for presidential candidates accepting public financing and also left in place the FEC's limits on contributions from individuals and groups to federal candidates, political committees, and political parties.†

The Court's ruling on independent expenditures—that campaign expenditures made independently of a candidate or of his or her committees, without collusion, consultation, or cooperation, cannot be limited by law—opened the way for widespread independent spending by nonaffiliated PACs (and individuals). Because of this decision, nonaffiliated PACs today account for a lion's share of independent expenditures in political campaigns.[4] The *Buckley* decision is important not only in and of itself but also in the atmosphere of official approval it created for the portions of the law it left untouched.

The nation now finds itself in an ironic situation. Reformers of the early 1970s originally intended to regulate campaign contributions, control spiraling campaign costs, and eliminate undue influences from special interests by encouraging more individual donors. Yet, almost the reverse has happened. There are now between 4000 and 4500 PACs, and their role is growing rather than diminishing. Political action committees are the "bastard children" of FECA legislation: they were not planned for, and their consequences were totally unanticipated. As Frank Sorauf concludes,

> So, the single issue or single configuration of issues is replacing in part the broad, all-encompassing political parties, and the new activism is more selective and less partisan. Combined with the decline of the parties' role in campaigns, this new style of politics increasingly produces candidates who, . . . organize their own campaigns, assembling the resources and directing their spending. All in all, the new campaign politics fits the PACs like the proverbial glove.[5]

---

*The 1976 amendments to the FECA wrote into law some of the provisions of the SunPAC advisory opinion: Corporations without stock and membership organizations could establish their own PACs; contributions had to be voluntary, with no reprisals; corporate, union, and association officials could decide how the money was to be collected and spent.

†An important by-product of publicly funded presidential campaigns—that candidates cannot accept PAC contributions—leaves a lot of "interested money" available for congressional races. The ever-increasing costs of campaigning virtually force candidates to seek PAC money. Also, today's electorate is more indifferent to party exhortations for campaign contributions.

Whatever the reasons for their inception, PACs represent the institutionalization of campaign reforms of the 1970s.

INTERNAL OPERATIONS
OF PACS

PACs demonstrate a wide variety of structures and modes of operation. To understand how affiliated and nonaffiliated PACs allocate money, we need a general overview of these internal structures and processes.

An affiliated PAC is, of course, subject to the political preferences of its sponsoring organization. For example, if a private corporation established a PAC, the corporation pays for the PAC's operations, monitors the PAC's allocative decisions, and provides overall guidance and direction. In practice, this means the establishment of a PAC governing board drawn from the corporate hierarchy. This board is generally representative of the corporation's operation units—a plant, a department, a subsidiary. Labor unions and associational PACs are generally headed by locally elected officials who meet periodically with member representatives.

PAC boards are relatively autonomous. They depend a good deal on the permanent staff that runs the day-to-day business while collecting and evaluating candidate information, state electoral data, and federal regulations pertaining to PAC operations.

Unaffiliated or independent PACs are governed quite differently. No board or other organizational governance exists. Many unaffiliated PACs have a single person or a coterie of insiders calling the shots, with virtually no peer review. Many independent PACs are founded and maintained by a single, energetic entrepreneur. Some examples are the late Terry Dolan's National Conservative Political Action Committee (NCPAC), Paul Weyrich's Committee for the Survival of a Free Congress (CSFC), and Paul Brown's Life Amendment Political Action Committee (LAPAC). Frank Sorauf characterizes these committees as "extension[s] of the ego or persona of one individual."[6] The political goals of these organizations reflect the homogeneous policy and/or ideological preferences of their founders and leaders.

WHY DO PEOPLE
CONTRIBUTE?

The evidence suggests that the motivations of those who donate to PACs are more than merely political. PACs allow these individuals to make personal contributions at a "reduced" cost and to achieve nonpolitical side benefits as well.[7] Some of the reduced costs are as follows:

The donor is saved the annoyance of repeated campaign solicitations.

Decision costs are reduced or eliminated because the donor does not have to collect information on various candidates and agonize over a choice. The donor escapes responsibility for the final allocative decision.

The nonpolitical side benefits are these:

The donor contributes to professional or workplace solidarity.
The donor's image or reputation for social responsibility is enhanced.
The organizationally loyal donor enjoys the benefits of promoting the interests of the parent organization, if there is one.

Sorauf concludes that PACs serve as low-cost vehicles for the marginally active desiring to fulfill their political obligations.

To what extent do donors influence PAC decision making? Are there avenues for donors to exert some authority? Donor contributions, as a PAC's chief resource, do represent an avenue for influence. A small number of labor PACs and approximately 35 percent of corporate PACs allow donors to *earmark*, or designate, the candidates to receive their contributions. Less than 20 percent of donors, however, choose to earmark. PACs do not encourage this practice, although most affiliated PACs do actively solicit recommendations from their memberships. PAC managers and allocation committees *do* heed these recommendations, whether they agree with them or not. In the words of a PAC manager for United Technologies, "We frequently find people urging us to support an incumbent or challenger whose philosophy may not be in accord with our long range objectives."[8] Sometimes, a PAC may contribute to both sides in a campaign in order to honor donor wishes. Thus, the political realities of the moment may require a conservative PAC to contribute to a liberal member of Congress because a number of its donors want access to that person later on.

Unaffiliated PACs do not engage in earmarking. Their donors are not bound by a common profession or workplace, nor are they loyal to any sponsoring organization. Also, there are virtually no leader–member contacts— no newsletter, annual report, or periodic meetings. The only linkage is a computer printout. It is not at all surprising, then, that unaffiliated donors have no say in allocative decisions. It is also not surprising to find that these PACs make considerably larger candidate donations than their affiliated counterparts. The former have fewer organizational pressures and restraints that could inhibit support for a candidate.

Exiting (terminating one's PAC affiliation and contributions) is an option by which donors can exert their preferences. Donors drop out of PAC activities for both political and nonpolitical reasons. *Nonpolitical* reasons include death, retirement, career changes, and bad economic times that reduce one's income. *Political* reasons could be heightened donor interest in partisan elections, candidate or party concerns transcending PAC concerns, or the waning of the excitement or novelty of electoral concerns. All of these can affect allocative decision making within PACs.

Membership attrition affects both types of PACs. Donor restiveness and exiting can be addressed by periodic appeals to donor loyalties, demonstrations of political efficacy by reference to the percentages of past electoral "victories," and anticipation by the PAC leadership of shifts in the political perceptions and loyalties of donors.

These strategies are more applicable to affiliated than to unaffiliated PACs. Sponsoring organizations serve as symbols of continuity as well as stabilizing forces for donor interests. Lines of accountability run from the PAC directors to the sponsoring officials, who define PAC concerns and political orientations. As a result, the PAC is mandated to carry out its mission in terms of the collective benefits of sponsors *and* donors. This mandate strengthens cohesion and reduces donor exiting tendencies.

PAC CONTRIBUTIONS AND SPENDING PATTERNS

PACs differ significantly in whom they contribute to. Many prefer incumbents over challengers, others prefer conservatives over liberals, and others prefer probusiness candidates over those sympathetic to organized labor. In this section, we will examine patterns of PAC spending, criteria in gaining PAC support, and some of the big spenders among today's PACs.

Like PACs themselves, the money they spend has proliferated since the late 1970s. As these Federal Election Commission data show, PAC contributions to congressional candidates almost quadrupled in ten years:

Election Cycle	PAC Contributions
1977–78	$35,100,000
1979–80	55,217,291
1981–82	83,620,190
1983–84	106,826,888
1985–86	129,301,111

Breaking the data down, we find that officeholders, as opposed to challengers, are the favored conduits for PAC dollars:

Election Cycle	PAC Contributions	Incumbents	Challengers	% to Incumbents
1979–80	$55,217,291	$33,538,721	$14,483,562	60.6
1981–82	83,620,190	55,024,361	16,182,510	66.3
1983–84	106,826,887	75,628,488	18,531,700	70.7
1985–86	129,301,111	89,301,428	18,403,156	82.9

Although incumbents consistently receive more PAC funds, Michael J. Malbin and Thomas W. Skladony attribute this to "candidate seriousness" rather than to incumbency per se:

> A candidate's seriousness—that is, his or her chance of winning—continues to be a better predictor of fund raising than incumbency, challenger or open-seat status.[9]

Federal Election Commission data also show that Democratic candidates receive more PAC money than their Republican counterparts:

Election Cycle	PAC Contributions	Democrats	Republicans	% to Democrats
1979–80	$55,217,291	$28,895,741	$26,221,794	52.1
1981–82	83,620,190	45,414,812	38,183,268	54.3
1983–84	106,826,877	61,327,984	45,775,403	57.8
1985–86	129,301,111	79,923,748	56,411,023	56.4

Two factors contribute to this partisan imbalance. First, though corporate and trade association PACs lean Republican, they prefer to "share the wealth" and contribute to both parties. On the other hand, labor PACs contribute almost exclusively to Democratic candidates, as demonstrated in Table 4–1.

Second, the relationship between party label and PAC money is not as strong as it is between incumbency and contributions. As we have noted, PACs prefer incumbents with as established record of electability. Because of their numerical dominance in Congress since 1976, Democrats have enjoyed a wide edge in PAC money over their Republican challengers.*

It is not surprising that the increasing levels of PAC contributions are given with definite purposes in mind. Business, trade, and labor PAC contributions manifest themselves in different ways. Sometimes they are concentrated in the membership of certain key committees, at other times they are used to reward certain members of Congress for "correct voting" on a variety of litmus-test issues, and sometimes they are used simply to maintain access to certain legislators.

Defense-related PACs, for example, contribute heavily to legislators on the armed services committees in both the House and the Senate as well as to members of the respective defense appropriations subcommittees. Table 4–2 shows PAC contributions to these committees and subcommittees for 1985–86.

---

*In the 1986 elections, for example, of the $43.3 million contributed by PACs in races where a Democratic incumbent was seeking reelection, the incumbents received $41.1 million (94.7 percent) while their Republican challengers received $2.3 million (5.3 percent). Conversely, of the $31.1 million given by PACs in races where the Republican was the incumbent, the incumbents received $24.7 million (79.4 percent) while their Democratic rivals received $6.4 million (20.6 percent).

TABLE 4-1 PAC Contributions to Congressional Candidates in General Elections by Type of PAC and by Party (in millions of dollars), 1974–1984

	1974		1976		1978		1980		1982		1984	
	D	R	D	R	D	R	D	R	D	R	D	R
Labor	$5.4 95%	$.4 5%	$7.2 97%	$.2 3%	$8.3 93%	$.5 6%	$11.5 93%	$.8 7%	$19.1 95%	$1.1 5%	$23.7 94%	$1.3 5%
Corporate	$.9 38%	$1.4 58%	$2.9 43%	$3.8 57%	$3.1 34%	$6.0 66%	$6.3 35%	$11.8 65%	$9.4 34%	$18.1 66%	$13.9 38%	$22.2 61%
Trade/Membership/ Health	$.5 28%	$1.3 72%	$1.0 38%	$1.6 62%	$4.4 42%	$6.2 59%	$6.5 43%	$8.5 57%	$9.3 43%	$12.5 57%	$13.3 49%	$13.5 50%
Nonconnected	$.3 48%	$.3 52%	$.6 45%	$.7 55%	$.5 23%	$1.7 77%	$1.3 29%	$3.2 71%	$5.5 51%	$5.2 49%	$7.8 53%	$6.8 46%

Source: Federal Election Commission.

TABLE 4-2   PAC Contributions to Members of Congressional Committees
with Defense-Related Jurisdiction, 1985-86

Senate Armed Services Committee			
Alan Dixon (D–Ill.)	$90,690	John Spratt Jr. (D–S.C.)	8,300
John Glenn (D–Ohio)	80,750	Frank McCloskey (D–Ind.)	11,200
Tim Wirth (D–Colo.)	23,800	Solomon Ortiz (D–Tex.)	11,900
Richard Shelby (D–Ala.)	43,750	George Darden (D–Ga.)	26,125
		Tommy Robinson (D–Ark.)	24,600
Dan Quayle (R–Ind.)	147,852	Albert Bustamante (D–Tex.)	12,600
Steve Symms (R–Idaho)	125,460	Barbara Boxer (D–Calif.)	650
John McCain (R–Ariz.)	119,370	George Hochbrueckner (D–N.Y.)	2,000
Senate Defense Appropriations		Joseph Brennan (D–Maine)	3,700
Subcommittee		Owen Pickett (D–Va.)	1,500
Daniel Inouye (D–Hawaii)	52,000		
Ernest Hollings (D–S.C.)	83,524	William Dickinson (R–Ala.)	88,250
Patrick Leahy (D–Vt.)	20,825	Floyd Spence (R–S.C.)	31,550
		Robert Badham (R–Calif.)	64,750
Jake Garn (R–Utah)	83,285	Bob Stump (R–Ariz.)	22,300
Robert Kasten (R–Wis.)	117,713	James Courter (R–N.J.)	19,280
Alfonse D'Amato (R–N.Y.)	83,900	Larry Hopkins (R–Ky.)	21,400
Warren Rudman (R–N.H.)	2,500	Robert Davis (R–Mich.)	28,050
		Duncan Hunter (R–Calif.)	29,080
House Armed Services Committee		David Martin (R–N.Y.)	16,700
Les Aspin (D–Wis.), chairman	51,825	John Kasich (R–Ohio)	17,100
Melvin Price (D–Ill.)	21,750	Lynn Martin (R–Ill.)	21,650
Charles Bennett (D–Fla.)	19,250	Herbert Bateman (R–Va.)	28,850
Samuel Stratton (D–N.Y.)	28,000	Mac Sweeney (R–Tex.)	27,450
Bill Nichols (D–Ala.)	22,250	Andy Ireland (R–Fla.)	18,150
Dan Daniel (D–Va.)	33,225	James Hansen (R–Utah)	23,800
Sonny Montgomery (D–Miss.)	9,675	John Rowland (R–Conn.)	9,925
Ron Dellums (D–Calif.)	3,620	Curt Weldon (R–Pa.)	16,150
Patricia Schroeder (D–Colo.)	3,000	John Kyl (R–Ariz.)	12,649
Beverly Byron (D–Md.)	37,375	Arthur Ravenel Jr. (R–S.C.)	7,000
Nicholas Mavroules (D–Mass.)	22,175	Jack Davis (R–Ill.)	6,900
Earl Hutto (D–Fla.)	13,250		
Ike Skelton (D–Mo.)	21,550	*House Defense Appropriations*	
Marvin Leath (D–Tex.)	35,750	*Subcommittee*	
Dave McCurdy (D–Okla.)	42,000	Bill Chappell (D–Fla.), chairman	82,500
Thomas Foglietta (D–Pa.)	6,750	John Murtha (D–Pa.)	68,000
Roy Dyson (D–Md.)	38,700	Norman Dicks (D–Wash.)	42,500
Dennis Hertel (D–Mich.)	12,650	Charles Wilson (D–Tex.)	62,850
Marilyn Lloyd (D–Tenn.)	36,750	Bill Hefner (D–N.C.)	51,250
Norman Sisisky (D–Va.)	12,000	Les AuCoin (D–Ore.)	33,650
Richard Ray (D–Ga.)	30,325	Martin Sabo (D–Minn.)	16,640
		Joseph McDade (R–Pa.)	61,000
		C. W. (Bill) Young (R–Fla.)	28,980
		Clarence Miller (R–Ohio)	14,500
		Robert Livingston (R–La.)	8,000

SOURCE: Federal Election Commission.

The PACs of such defense-related industries as General Dynamics, Rockwell International, Lockheed, Boeing, Martin Marietta, LTV, and General Motors contribute during election cycles and at other times in order to maintain access to and visibility with these lawmakers. The same holds with other PACs and other congressional committees, the ultimate objective being to influence the content of legislation.

Negative Spending

Although most PACs promote the financial fortunes of selected candidates, some independent PACs indulge in "negative" campaigning—that is, in defeating certain candidates. Terry Dolan, for example, founder and former head of the National Conservative Political Action Committee (NCPAC), once asserted, "A group like ours could lie through its teeth, and the candidate it helps stays clean."[10] Dolan, the master of the sensational or controversial phrase, was referring to nonaffiliated PACs such as his and their freedom under the law to spend huge sums of money to defeat candidates.* As Table 4-3 shows, about 80 percent of the funds spent by unaffiliated PACs in the 1981–82 election cycle were negative. Certainly a lot of money was spent in this fashion in 1980, and it contributed to the defeats of such Senate liberals as George McGovern, Birch Bayh, and Frank Church.

Negative campaigning raises some important questions concerning our electoral process. Many independent PACs operate on the personal whim

*Senators who have been recent targets of negative campaigning include Edward Kennedy of Massachusetts, Paul Sarbanes of Maryland, Robert Byrd of West Virginia, and Lowell Weicker of Connecticut. Representatives Dan Rostenkowski of Illinois, Robert Edgard of Ohio, and former Representative Jim Wright of Texas have also experienced negative campaigning.

TABLE 4-3   Committees Reporting Largest Independent Expenditures, 1981-82

Political Committee	Spending for Candidates	Spending against Candidates
National Conservative Political Action Committee	$137,724	$3,039,490
Citizens Organized to Replace Kennedy	0	416,678
Fund for a Conservative Majority	0	388,399
Life Amendment Political Action Committee	36,455	219,055
NRA Political Victory Fund	232,350	477
American Medical Association PAC	211,624	0
Realtors PAC	188,060	0
Progressive PAC	8,090	134,795
Independent Action, Inc.	0	132,920
League of Conservation Voters	129,163	0

Source: Federal Election Commission.

of the entrepreneur rather than as the result of a consensus. This means less accountability, because internal mechanisms for discussion and consensus building do not exist. There are few opportunities for donors to inform the leadership of their preferences. Finally, negative campaigning could in the long run add to voter alienation and cynicism toward issues and candidates.

ALLOCATING PAC MONEY

Deciding which candidates to support—and how much money to give—is a subjective process within each PAC. Most PACs base these judgments on criteria relevant to their own interests. However, this does not preclude using information from other sources, such as other PACs, national political parties, and government reports. In spite of unique concerns, a general list of PAC criteria would include the following:

INCUMBENTS

1. What is the candidate's voting record on issues of concern to the organization?
2. What are the candidate's committee or subcommittee assignments?
3. What are the characteristics of the candidate's district? Does it have business facilities? Labor unions? Is it urban or rural? What is the prevailing level of partisanship?
4. What is the candidate's attitude toward the organization and its legislative goals?
5. How much money does the candidate need?

CHALLENGERS

1. Who is the campaign manager? (Experienced? Effective?)
2. What is the campaign budget, and how much has been raised?
3. Who is doing the campaign polling, and what are the latest results?
4. Does the challenger have a reasonable chance of defeating the incumbent?
5. What is the candidate's first choice for a committee assignment? (This must be compatible with the organization's legislative goals.)
6. What are the candidate's views on at least three issues of importance to the association?

The preoccupation of PACs with committee and subcommittee assignments is natural. Committees and subcommittees draft legislation having important consequences for interests throughout the country. BreadPAC, for example, represents 350 allied bakers in the nation, including such large companies as Rainbow, Colonial, and Wonder. A disproportionate amount of BreadPAC's contributions go to personnel on the House and Senate Agriculture committees, which have jurisdiction over commodity prices (wheat, barley, corn), loan rates, sugar legislation, and other agriculture-related issues affecting the baking industry; the House Interstate and Foreign Commerce committees and the Senate Energy Committee, which have control over energy legislation, particularly as it pertains to natural-gas and motor-fuels policy and sodium-labeling legislation; and the House Administration and Senate Rules committees, which have jurisdiction over campaign financing. In selecting individuals for campaign contributions, BreadPAC seeks candidates from either party who are, or who will be, sympathetic to and influential in formulating those agricultural and energy policies of concern to the general membership.

Ideologically oriented (liberal and conservative) PACs publish periodic "report cards" or "issue ratings" on members of Congress.[11] The Right-to-Life PAC, the National Christian Action Coalition, and the Committee for the Survival of a Free Congress (CSFC) regularly engage in ratings. Ratings involve "passing" or "failing" grades on a series of votes—for example, on a nuclear moratorium, a cap on food-stamp expenditures, curbs on the use of public funds for abortions, and broad cuts in social programs in order to increase defense spending.

A "passing" grade on a series of votes enhances the eligibility of a legislator for contributions by the evaluating organization. Congressional challengers, who have no voting record to rate, receive a questionnaire addressing issues of concern to the PAC's sponsoring organization. Or challengers may be quizzed at party caucuses or conventions on issues ranging from federal aid to education, to collective bargaining, to nuclear disarmament, to tuition tax credits for parents. PACs want to ensure that their contributions go to those candidates most compatible with their organizational interests.

PAC MONEY AND CONGRESSIONAL VOTING

A number of factors determine a legislator's vote on a bill—party affiliation, interest group pressures, constituency preferences, presidential initiatives, as well as the legislator's own perceptions. What about PAC money? Does it follow votes, or do votes follow it? Rather than *buying* votes, are PACs merely *rewarding* their friends? Do PACs just want access to certain legislators? Is Congress increasingly "up for sale"? To answer these and related questions, we need to look more closely at the possible linkage between legislators' votes and their receipt of PAC money.

A growing number of studies are investigating this question. Through sophisticated techniques such as multivariate analysis and regression analysis, it is possible to examine certain independent variables beyond those of party, constituency, or ideology that affect voting decisions. James B. Kau and Paul Rubin, examining patterns of congressional voting on seven bills, did find that labor PAC contributions appeared to have more impact on voting than did corporate PAC contributions.[12] An examination by Common Cause found PAC contributions correlated positively with voting patterns on Senate and House environmental committees. Those members voting *for* weakening clean air leg-islation received an average of fifteen times more money in PAC contributions than those voting *against* weakening amendments. Kirk R. Brown, using multiple regression techniques, isolated the effects of PAC contributions on two 1982 legislative bills.* In both cases, Brown found a strong relationship between vot-ing patterns and PAC contributions. He states in the conclusion of his study,

> Campaign contributions *have* an effect on voting that is independent of ideology, party, and previous voting record. For a congressman who is at margin between supporting and opposing a bill, a contribution of $5,000 can increase the prob-ability of voting for the PAC's position by as much as 20%. In the example of the professionals' exemption bill, it is clear that campaign contributions by doctors and dentists secured the House passage of the legislation.[13]

It appears from this evidence that PAC money does influence legislation on occasion. When the issue is narrow and hidden from public view, political contributions appear to buy influence. Brown's study notes the influence of PAC money in the *early stages* of bill formation. Intensive media scrutiny in the latter stages of bill formation, though, generated opposition strong enough to neutralize earlier PAC advantages. Conversely, when many groups are involved in legislation, as is the case with a farm bill, consumer protection, or environmental standards, it is less likely that one set of interests will dominate the others. Concentrations of PAC money can be crucial, but usually only in limited situations and over a short period. A final point: PACs will use their assets as a lobbying tool in certain situations. Representative Les Aspin (D–Wisc.) explains:

> There are various degrees of being for a bill—co-sponsoring it, or fighting for it in committee, in debate, on the floor, or in a leadership role on the floor. PAC funds can determine a member's intensity as well as position.[14]

Like everything else, PAC money and congressional voting must be kept in perspective. Political parties and interest groups also win some and lose some. Recent attempts to weaken clean-air legislation, the establishment of a consumer agency, and common situs picketing all failed in Congress despite a lot of PAC money. Party affiliation, constituency pressures, and the constitutional system of checks and balances played a more decisive role.[15] PAC money can buy influence, but only the naive or cynical believe that it *always* buys influence.

---

*A resolution vetoing the Federal Trade Commission's rule that used-car dealers must disclose major defects to prospective buyers, and a bill exempting doctors, lawyers, dentists, and other professionals from the commission's regulations.

PACS AND THE
ELECTORAL PROCESS:
FORCES FOR GOOD
OR FORCES FOR EVIL?

As a result of their growing numbers and affluence, PACs are the focus of a good deal of public debate and controversy today. A recent study by the Center for Research on Business and Social Policy at the University of Texas (Dallas) found that people with negative attitudes toward PACs outnumbered those with positive attitudes by nearly three to one. Certainly, abuses in national elections by business and organized labor have made many citizens wary of political action committees. We need, therefore, to examine some of the charges directed toward PACs if we are to gain a balanced perspective of their role in our electoral system today. We will pursue this task by examining both negative and positive evaluations of PACs.

Journalist Elizabeth Drew believes that the great amounts of money PACs spend on candidates have a corrupting influence that threatens our entire political system (Figure 4-2). Congressmen, according to Drew, are preoccupied with fund raising for the next election and are therefore easy prey

FIGURE 4-2

Etta Hulme's 1982 PAC Man Cartoon. Copyright © 1982 by the Fort Worth Star Telegram. Reprinted by permission of the Fort Worth Star Telegram.

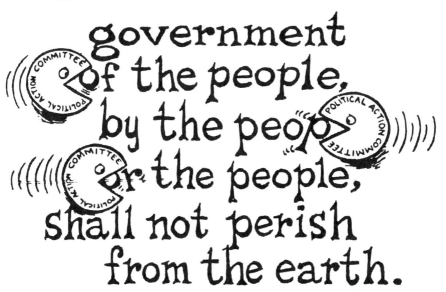

for well-heeled private interests. PAC money not only buys extensive access to lawmakers but also has undue influence on legislation that affects all citizens. This results in

> a corrosion of the system and new kind of squalor—conditions that are well known to those who are in it and to those who deal with it at close range. The public knows that something is very wrong. As the public cynicism gets deeper, the political system gets worse. Until the problem of money is dealt with, the system will not get better.[16]

Drew advocates a number of reforms designed to eliminate the corrupting influence of PAC money—public financing of congressional campaigns, a ban on the purchase of political advertising and the provision of free air time for *all* candidates, and a reimposition of limits on expenditures by independent committees. "The point," she concludes, "is not to try to establish a *perfect* political system but to try to get the system back closer to what it was *intended to be.*"

Fred Wertheimer and Archibald Cox, officers of Common Cause, have "declared war" on PACs and their campaign activities (Box 4-1). Both believe that the very existence and viability of representative government are at stake because of the involvement of so much special interest money in congressional elections.

Cox and Wertheimer are convinced that PAC contributors gain extraordinary access to lawmakers and in turn unwarranted influence over the content of legislation. According to both, legislative decisions made under these conditions are frequently inimical to the public interest.

Common Cause has joined a coalition of other organizations, including the Consumer Federation of America, the League of Women Voters, the American Federation of State, County, and Municipal Employees (AFSCME), and Rural America, calling for reforms in congressional campaign financing. This coalition wants public financing of congressional elections coupled with overall limits on PAC contributions. The adoption of these reforms would restore a greater sense of fairness in congressional races and generate more public confidence in the electoral system.

Edward Roeder, a Washington free-lance journalist, has examined the relationship of PAC money and congressional voting in recent Congresses. His analyses of PAC contributions and regulatory legislation convinces him money "talks." Roeder finds the bulk of oil PAC money going to members of Congress having *direct* influence over oil legislation—members of the House Interstate and Foreign Commerce committees, which have jurisdiction over interstate sales of oil; members of the Interior and Insular Affairs Committee; and senators who sit on the Finance and Energy and Natural Resources committees, which are

BOX 4-1   *COMMON CAUSE TAKES ON THE PACS*

A DECLARATION OF WAR

The time has come to draw the line. Political Action Committees (PACs) have put Congress on the take. And *you're* being taken for a ride. Consider your health: PAC money from doctors helped convince Congress *not* to pass a bill that would help keep your hospital costs from skyrocketing. Consider your protection from fraud: PAC money from auto dealers helped convince Congress *not* to pass a bill that would require used car dealers to tell you what's wrong with the second-hand car you're buying. Consider your savings: PAC money from the dairy industry has helped to convince Congress, year after year, *not* to make needed cuts in dairy subsidies, which artificially inflate the price of the milk, butter and cheese you buy. Consider yourself *mute*. Your voice is being *drowned out* by the ringing of PAC cash registers in Congress.

Senator Robert Dole, Chairman of the Senate tax writing committee, says, "When these PACs give money, they expect something in return other than good government." These are contributions with a purpose—a legislative purpose. And the PAC system works according to the golden rule, says former Congressman Henry Reuss: "Those who have the gold make the rules."

We're not talking about illegal campaign contributions of the sort that ten years ago created a national scandal called Watergate. We're talking about $80 million in campaign contributions that are *perfectly legal,* creating a new national scandal corrupting our democracy. And *that* is a crime.

Unless we change our system for financing Congressional campaigns and change it soon, our representative system of government will be gone. We will be left with a government of, by and for the PACs. We can't let that happen. We *won't* let that happen. Common Cause has declared war —— a war on PACs. Ours has always been a government of, by and for the *people*. We must keep it that way.   Common Cause.

Source: *The New York Times,* February 6, 1983, p. E18. Used with permission of Common Cause.

concerned among other things with the interstate shipment of oil and with oil drilling. Based on his findings, Roeder concludes that

> money in . . . massive concentrations begets power, at least power's close cousin—influence. The ways of influence are often meandering, but one direct and time-honored path is through campaign contributions to those who make policy and pass legislation. Modern and up-to-date as oil companies might be, there is an old-fashioned technique they still use. Indeed, big oil has refined the practice—with care for the law and the companies' public image—and pumped contributions into the U.S. Congress at a rate that has made it the single largest business donor to federal elections.[17]

Roeder contends that PAC money will continue to buy influence until reform legislation is passed freeing members of Congress from their financial vulnerability to special interests.

On the other hand, Michael J. Malbin, an authority on campaign finance legislation, argues that "PAC power" accruing from campaign contributions is greatly exaggerated. Malbin believes that studies documenting the influence of political contributions on congressional voting are "weak and irrelevant" because

> the complicated quantitative methods used by political scientists and economists have failed to separate the modest role of campaign contributions from the much larger lobbying world within which [campaign contributions] are assumed to fit.[18]

Mere acceptance of PAC contributions, according to Malbin, does *not* necessarily mean a candidate, once in office, will conform to the expectations of the contributor.

Malbin is of the opinion that PACs are *positive* forces in elections. Many try to educate, motivate, and involve their members, politically speaking. In this way they will fill a void left by atrophying parties. Malbin advocates increasing the role of parties in order to balance the fragmenting effect of interest groups on congressional elections. This can be accomplished by enacting higher party spending limits while encouraging more state and local party volunteer activities. Malbin also favors public financing of congressional elections, but *without* limits. He reasons that unrestricted public financing will encourage more challengers to run because it will be easier for them to raise money in the early stages of their campaigns. More stringent or punitive regulatory legislation is simply not the answer.

Herbert E. Alexander, director of the Citizens' Research Council, the nation's principal private collection agency for campaign financial data, has a good deal of expertise on political finance and campaign laws. Like Malbin, Alexander views PACs in a positive light. Alexander has analyzed extensive financial data on PAC spending over a ten-year period as well as evaluating a series of criticisms of PACs. He concluded that "PACs have made significant contributions to the political system".[19]

1. PACs increase participation in the political process by encouraging their members and supporters to become politically active.
2. PACs allow individuals to increase the impact of their political activity by providing them with a sense of accomplishment that accompanies taking part in politics with like-minded persons.
3. PACs are mechanisms for political fund raising for different socioeconomic groups. Organized around a specific occupational or social group, a PAC allows its members to participate and contribute with those sharing similar views.
4. PACs have made more money available for political campaigns. By helping candidates pay the rising costs of campaigning, PACs are helping ensure to broader communication of the candidates' views to more voters than might be possible otherwise.

Alexander opposes legislation limiting PAC contributions. He believes that most such legislation is unrealistically restrictive and would *not* attain its intended purposes; in fact, it would cause more problems than it would solve. PACs can help their cause, Alexander counsels, by responding to criticisms with specific and accurate information and by articulating the values they bring to the political process. When, for example, critics use simple correlations to demonstrate undue PAC influence on legislative decision making, PACs should respond by presenting the *whole* campaign finance picture rather than merely their own participation. It would also be useful, Alexander adds, to publicize negative correlations demonstrating that in many instances PAC contributions do *not* affect legislative decisions. Curbing PAC relationships with members of Congress will not free these legislators from future legislative dilemmas where they must choose between what will help them remain in office and what will serve the public good.

We can easily see that there is no consensus among informed observers of PACs on the best solution to the "PAC problem." Indeed, as we have noted, it is ironic that PACs were intended to be part of the campaign reforms of the 1970s. Perhaps the reformer was right who noted, "You shouldn't constantly tinker with the system."[20] Further legislation may breed more frustration and cynicism with campaign reform if its intent is not achieved.* Therefore, the status quo will continue.

---

*Dozens of PAC "reform" bills have been introduced in Congress, but none has passed. Legislation with the best chance is a bill by Senator David Boren, D-Okla. If enacted, it would reduce from $5000 to $3000 the amount a PAC could contribute to a candidate in a national election. The bill would also set a ceiling on the total PAC contributions a Senate candidate could receive in a campaign, using a sliding scale based on state population.

FIGURE 4-3

Cartoon by Wasserman. Copyright © 1988 *Boston Globe*. Reprinted by permission of Los Angeles Times Syndicate.

SUMMARY

Barring drastic change, PACs willl remain a significant, though controversial, force in American elections. People in and out of government remain divided over the amount of influence PACs exert in elections. Nonetheless, a rising chorus of critics are demanding public regulation of these proliferating organizations.

Is this growing concern justified? The evidence cited in this chapter is mixed. Individual PACs, or coalitions thereof, *can* be influential when dealing with narrowly focused, complex legislation. Party affiliation, constituency pressures, or presidential intervention will countervail PAC influence. We must also remember that PAC contributions today *represent only about a third of all contributions to candidates,* though this share is growing.

Restrictive legislation will *not* free legislators from voting dilemmas. Members of Congress are subject to pressure from a host of sources, as we

TABLE 4-4 Survey Question: Please Explain How PACs Affect Congressional Operations (by Chamber)

Multiple Responses Allowed	Members			Personal Staff			Committee Staff		
	House	Senate	Total	House	Senate	Total	House	Senate	Total
PACs increase campaign costs, requiring more time spent raising money, meeting people, etc.	24.1%	37.0%	27.2%	15.2%	20.0%	16.4%	25.9%	34.6%	30.2%
PAC contributions get access to members	25.3	29.6	27.2	37.4	53.3	41.0	37.0	26.9	32.1
The large number of PACs promotes diversity on issues	18.4	18.5	18.4	13.3	13.0	13.1	3.7	0.0	1.9
The large number of different PACs balances each other out	8.0	14.8	9.6	2.2	0.0	1.6	7.4	7.7	7.5
Members hold independent views	10.3	7.4	9.6	8.7	6.7	8.2	3.7	3.8	3.8
PACs make it easier to raise money	8.0	3.7	7.0	4.3	0.0	3.3	0.0	0.0	0.0
Current regulations are adequate to prevent abuses	5.7	0.0	4.4	0.0	0.0	0.0	0.0	0.0	0.0
PACs have made members more parochial	1.1	0.0	0.09	4.3	0.0	3.3	0.0	4.0	1.9
Other	18.4	14.8	17.5	0.0	0.0	0.0	3.7	0.0	1.9
n =	87.0	27.0	114.0	37.0	24.0	61.0	27.0	26.0	53.0

Source: Center for Responsive Politics, *Congress Speaks: A Survey of the 100th Congress* (Washington, D.C., 1988), p. 89. Used with permission of Center for Responsive Politics.

TABLE 4-5 Survey Question: What Effect Have Political Action Committees Had on How Congress Works? (by Chamber)

	Members			Personal Staff			Committee Staff		
	House	Senate	Total	House	Senate	Total	House	Senate	Total
Positive effect	19.5%	15.4%	18.6%	10.9%	0.0%	8.2%	0.0%	0.0%	0.0%
No effect	20.7	11.5	18.6	17.4	20.0	18.0	17.9	16.0	17.0
Effect mixed	19.5	19.2	19.5	15.2	13.3	14.8	7.1	16.0	11.3
Somewhat negative effect	16.2	15.4	15.9	21.7	6.7	18.0	7.1	4.0	5.7
Negative effect	24.1	38.5	27.4	30.4	60.0	37.7	60.8	60.0	60.3
No opinion/Don't Know	0.0	0.0	0.0	4.4	0.0	3.3	7.1	4.0	5.7
n =	87.0	26.0	113.0	46.0	15.0	61.0	28.0	25.0	53.0

Source: Center for Responsive Politics, *Congress Speaks: A Survey of the 100th Congress* (Washington, D.C., 1988), p. 89. Used with permission of Center for Responsive Politics.

will see in succeeding chapters. Attempts to restrain PACs through legislation could produce unintended consequences for the entire political system. To repeat a point stressed throughout this book, more and more people are seeking political fulfillment through organizations. PACs do supplement our electoral process by informing, educating, and motivating voters. Restrictive legislation could depress voter turnout and further weaken public support for our national democratic institutions.

NOTES

[1]For some excellent sources on PACs, see Joseph E. Cantor, *Political Action Committees: Their Evolution and Growth and Their Implications for the Political System* (Washington, D.C.: Congressional Research Service, 1984); Larry Sabato, "Parties, PACs and Independent Groups," in *American Elections of 1982* Thomas E. Mann and Norman J. Ornstein (Washington, D.C.: American Enterprise Institute, 1983); Larry Sabato, *PAC Power* (New York: W. W. Norton & Co., Inc., 1984); and Michael J. Malbin, ed., *Money and Politics in the United States: Financing Elections in the 1980s* (Washington, D.C.: American Enterprise Institute, 1984).

[2]See Herbert E. Alexander, *Financing Politics: Money, Elections and Political Reform*, 3rd ed. (Washington, D.C.: CQ Press, 1984).

[3]96 S. Ct. 612.

[4]For more detail on independent PAC expenditures, see Joseph E. Cantor, *The Evolution of and Issues Surrounding Independent Expenditures in Election Campaigns* (Washington, D.C.: Congressional Research Service, 1982).

[5]Frank Sorauf, "Political Action Committees in American Politics: An Overview," in *What Price PACs?* (Washington, D.C.: Twentieth Century Fund, 1984), pp. 41–42.

[6]Frank Sorauf, "Who's in Charge? Accountability in Political Action Committees," *Political Science Quarterly*, 99 (1984), 591–614.

[7]See Sorauf, "Who's in Charge?"

[8]Quoted in the Congressional Quarterly *Weekly Report*, 38 (October 25, 1980), 3204.

[9]Michael J. Malbin and Thomas W. Skladony, "Campaign Finance 1984: A Preliminary Analysis of House and Senate Receipts," paper presented at American Enterprise Institute Public Policy Week, Washington, D.C., 1984, p. 1.

[10]Quoted in the *Washington Post*, August 10, 1980, p. F1.

[11]See Margaret Ann Latus, "Assessing Ideological PACs: From Outrage to Understanding," in *Money and Politics in the United States*, ed. Malbin, pp. 142–71.

[12]James B. Kau and Paul Rubin, *Congressman, Constituents and Contributors* (Boston: Marinus Nijhoff, 1982). Also see Henry W. Chappell, "Campaign Contributions and Congressional Voting," *Review of Economics and Statistics*, 64 (1982), 77–83; and W. P. Welch, "Campaign Contributions and Legislative Voting: Milk Money and Dairy Price Supports," *Western Political Quarterly*, 35 (1982), 478–95.

[13]Kirk R. Brown, "Campaign Contributions and Congressional Voting" (paper presented at the American Political Science Association, Chicago, 1983), p. 49.

[14]Quoted in Sabato, *PAC Power*, p. 136.

[15]This proved to be the case in the author's own research on the impact of PAC money and legislative voting. These findings were noted in Dennis W. Gleiber, James D. King, and H. R. Mahood, "PAC Contributions, Constituency Interest, and Legislative Voting: Gun Control Legislation in the U.S. Senate" (paper presented at the Midwest Political Science Association Meeting, Chicago, 1987).

[16]Elizabeth Drew, *Politics and Money: The New Road to Corruption* (New York: Macmillan, 1983), p. 156.

[17]Edward Roeder, "Pumping Oil Money in Congress," *Politics Today,* March/April 1980, p. 39. Also see Philip M. Stern, *The Best Congress Money Can Buy* (New York: Pantheon, 1988). Stern presents a number of brief cases studies where PAC money is perceived to wield a good deal of influence on the content of legislation.

[18]Michael J. Malbin, in *Money and Politics in the United States,* ed. Malbin, p. 252.

[19]Herbert E. Alexander, *The Case for PACS* (Washington, D.C.: Public Affairs Council, 1983), p. 29–32.

[20]See Sabato, *PAC Power,* p. 173.

CHAPTER FIVE
CONGRESS AND INTEREST GROUPS:
Legislating in a Changing Context

Traditionally, Congress has been a prime target of organized interests because its lawmaking authority has important consequences for all kinds of individuals and groups.[1] The interest-group focus on Congress has become much more intense in recent years, as the following example demonstrates.

In the final months of 1986, Congress passed the controversial Tax Reform Bill.[2] Like previous tax measures, this bill was of great concern to interest groups representing almost all segments of society. Members of the House and Senate tax-writing committees were under siege by dozens of lobbyists (Box 5-1). Among those interests vitally concerned with the pending legislation were savings and loan institutions, stockbrokers, oil and timber, banks, farmers, real estate brokers, and state and local government officials.

Lobbying strategies were, of course, varied because of the complexities and size of the tax reductions under consideration. The American Banking Association (ABA) concentrated on the House committee while mutual-fund advocates actively opposed any House and Senate attempt to change individual retirement account (IRA) provisions.

An alliance of 150 groups calling themselves the 15/27/33 Coalition pushed hard for passage of the bill. Their name stood for the new tax structure that would be established under the bill. The coalition comprised such elements as big corporations, advocates for the poor, banks, left-leaning and right-leaning women's organizations, and racial groups. Alphabetically, the groups ranged from the Aetna Life and Casualty Company to the Women's Equity Action League. Real estate associations, segments of the securities industry, and state and local government representatives lobbied most aggressively. State and

BOX 5-1   *A LAWMAKER'S VIEW OF WASHINGTON ARM-TWISTING*

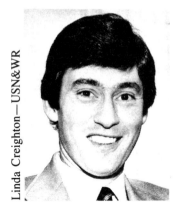

Linda Creighton—USN&WR

Downey: "Lobbying's golden age."

by KENNETH T. WALSH

Few legislators on Capitol Hill present a more inviting target for lobbyists than Representative Thomas Downey (D-N.Y.).

A member of both the House Ways and Means Committee and the Budget Committee, Downey, 36, is at the center of some of Washington's most intense battles, ranging from tax reform to Pentagon spending and domestic-budget cuts.

"It has gotten so bad that they wait for him in the halls," says Carolyn Blaydes, Downey's legislative assistant. "They know he takes certain doors, eats in certain places. They can find him if they want to."

Yet Downey says the best lobbyists know their limits. "They haven't lined up at the gymnasium yet," he says. "That would be a cardinal sin—just unforgivable."

Downey has appointments with an average of four lobbyists each day, usually to discuss tax issues. His staff handles many more lobbyists, both in person and on the phone.

"It has become unmanageable since tax reform started with the Treasury I proposal last November," says Blaydes. "I could see lobbyists 5 hours a day at 15-minute intervals. But you can't do meaningful interviews in that short a time. It's more like 20 to 30 minutes for each one, and sometimes a lot more."

Shower of favors. Representatives of interest groups often ply lawmakers with meals, tickets to social or sporting events and other treats. Downey's assessment: "A dinner or a ticket to a baseball game helps humanize a lobbyist—but I don't think it influences votes."

Adds the six-term congressman: "Good lobbyists never badger. If they do, members don't want to see them. A good lobbyist sees you only infrequently—and takes as little of your time as possible." Downey says skilled lobbyists not only present their own arguments but also summarize other views so a legislator is not caught unaware.

As with most members, Downey often finds lobbyists help him reach his own goals. For example, lobbyists are useful in his fight to save federal deductions of state and local taxes, which President Reagan seeks to abolish.

> Such a provision would hit especially hard in high-tax states such as New York, and Downey plans to work closely with home-state lobbyists and a variety of state and local officials to defeat the proposal.
>
> Like other lawmakers, he is bracing for an even bigger deluge of lobbyists later this year, as interest groups try to fine-tune the tax-reform proposals. Predicts Downey: "This period of time will be the golden age of lobbying. If you can walk and talk and type, you'll be employed by somebody."
>
> Source: *U.S. News & World Report,* June 17, 1985, p. 34. Copyright © 1985, U.S. News & World Report. Reprinted with permission.

local representatives were especially concerned because initial drafts of the bill abolished citizen deductions for property and sales taxes. The final version did retain a credit for property taxes paid.

Though the final bill was not heavily amended, 682 "transition" rules (easing the transition for taxpaying groups from the old rate to the new rate) were buried in it. Approximately fifty corporations with assets of $20 million or more were given large tax breaks, as Table 5-1 shows.

TABLE 5-1   A Sample of Corporate Tax Breaks Allowed by the 1986 Tax Reform Bill

Company	Tax Savings
United Telcom	$234,000,000
John Deere	212,000,000
Pacific-Texas Pipeline	187,000,000
Chrysler Corporation	78,000,000

Source: Congressional Quarterly *Weekly Report,* 44 (September 27, 1986), 2256–57.

These were one-time tax breaks and not permanent loopholes.

This brief example demonstrates the complexity of congressional decision making as well as the intensity of group involvement in it. To better understand the role of organized interests in the legislative process, we need to investigate various structural aspects of the legislative system. To this end we will note a number of recent changes within Congress itself that condition lobbying strategies and decision making. We will also analyze the committee/subcommittee system, note the broadening range of current lobbying strategies, examine "internal" legislative coalitions that also lobby, and conclude with a brief comment on congressional fragmentation. These analyses will contribute not only to a better understanding of interest group involvement in the legislative process, but also to a more accurate perception of Congress's policy-making processes.

SOME INSTITUTIONAL
CHARACTERISTICS

Before we proceed with these analyses, we need to note several aspects of the legislative system that help explain its policy outputs. First, the congressional system is complex, differentiated, and decentralized. All legislative systems have institutionalized subsystems—informal rules and procedures along with committees and subcommittees—that establish divisions of labor as well as distinct policy roles.

Second, Congress tends to go about its business in a highly fragmented manner. A host of actors and interests—party leaders, legislative coalitions, and groups—interact and affect the content of legislation. None of these entities, however, consistently dominates the system; rather there is a sharing of power and influence. Usually, though, congressional fragmentation helps status quo groups and inhibits groups seeking significant policy shifts.

Third, though not as numerous or compelling, some aspects of the system are integrative. Certainly the parties can provide centralized leadership in both chambers during policy making. Also, some members of Congress have strong policy commitments—agriculture, defense, the environment—and as the numbers of such legislators grow, opportunities for congressional consensus are enhanced, as is the success of broad-based interests.

Fourth, as a representative body, Congress is amenable to group penetration. This openness is an invitation accepted by more and more groups today. Two students of legislative politics characterize the situation this way:

> Although the number of bills whose origins stem from interest groups cannot be reckoned with precision, it is obviously great. Many ideas for new bills or for transformations of old ones are born in the offices of pressure groups and later drafted there for submission in the legislature.[3]

Finally, lawmaking is best perceived as a slow, deliberative process. A great deal of time and resources may be required in getting legislation passed. Each chamber has its own routine, rules, and procedures for handling legislation, and these are routinely followed. Thus, from introduction until enactment, days, months, or even years may pass. (For example, the initial Equal Rights Amendment for women was introduced in Congress in 1923.)

The legislative process also has a cumulative character. Bills pass through a series of stages before they become law. During each of these stages, organized or unorganized pressures are frequently brought to bear. Additionally, compromises or deals are struck along the way that influence the content of the legislation. Rarely does any bill get through the legislative labyrinth without some modification. Congressional decision making, then, reflects the efforts of a number of competing and cooperating forces interacting from time of proposal until enactment—legislative peers, interest groups, constituency, administrative personnel, and others. The relative importance of these forces will vary over time and from issue to issue.[4] But no one force will consistently dominate the legislative system.

We turn now to several changes within Congress that have import for pressure group involvement. These changes have taken place in congressional elections, congressional staffs, and the makeup of today's legislators.

THE NEW CONGRESS

The Congress of Sam Rayburn, Harry Byrd, or Richard Russell no longer exists.[5] Or to put it another way, Congress has changed greatly from what it was in the 1940s, 1950s, and early 1960s. In the old Congress, a small elite of committee chairmen, party leaders, and senior lawmakers made most of the policy decisions, negotiated with the president, and decided the general business of each chamber. Life "on the hill" was slow, collegial, and personal. There was always time for a good story over a glass of bourbon in the late afternoon.

But pressures for change began to build. A young president, Jack Kennedy, pressured Speaker of the House Sam Rayburn to expand the dinosaur-like House Rules Committee so that more liberal legislation could be passed. Some members even wrote books criticizing the old Congress—a "House Out of Order,"[6] and "The Sapless Branch."[7] Junior members demanded changes in the congressional establishment.

And then in the late 1960s and the 1970s, congressional elections produced a "new breed" of freshman not at all awed by the hallowed traditions of Capitol Hill or by the effete "gentlemen's club," the U.S. Senate. New members such as William Proxmire, Dale Bumpers, Richard Cheney, Tom Downey, and Richard Gephardt had gotten to Congress on their own and not because they had paid their dues to the local and state party apparatus.[8] Characteristically, these men were younger, self-starting, and policy-oriented. They came to Washington to legislate—to pass more environmental laws, more civil rights legislation, more regulatory reforms. The traditional niceties—being seen but not heard, not being too pushy in committee meetings, not challenging the leadership—held no attraction for them.

The case of the South deserves special attention. The Old South, as every schoolchild knows, was a virtual citadel controlled by rural, white Democrats after Reconstruction. Economically poor, the states of the old Confederacy stood at the bottom of the national ladder in per capita income, educational attainment, and opportunities for minority personal advancement. Nonetheless, Dixie's congressional contingent siphoned off millions of federal dollars for air and naval bases, dams and bridges, and farm subsidies. These grants were obtained through pork-barrel legislation and through the usual wheeling and dealing in the old Congress. But in the area of civil rights, the political status quo remained, year after year.

Nevertheless, sweeping changes were in the wind. An increasing number of liberal Democrats were elected to Congress. Lyndon Johnson won a landslide victory in 1964 and secured passage of the Civil Rights Act (1964) and the Voting Rights Act (1965). Gradually, a generation of southern moderates was elected to Congress—Sam Nunn, Wyche Fowler, Lawton Chiles, and Andrew Young. Simultaneously, a number of moderate governors were chosen by Southern voters—Jimmy Carter in Georgia, Ruben Askew in Florida, and William Winters in Mississippi. The election of these individuals demonstrated quite clearly that the old politics of racism were on the way out. Southern living standards, along with life-styles and politics, were coming to resemble those in other parts of the nation.

Finally, the new Congress features expanded congressional staffs that are taking on greater importance. They play a vital role in the legislative process and are therefore objects of heightened pressure group attention. Three types of staffs presently exist—personal staffs, committee and subcommittee staffs, and institutional staffs.[9]

Personal staffs serve individual members of Congress and work mainly on constituent and district problems. They operate offices within the districts and at the state level as well as in Washington. Committee and subcommittee staffs have grown rapidly since the end of World War II, and especially in the 1970s. This is not surprising, for subcommittees have also proliferated, as we will see later in this chapter. These staffers are intimately involved in drafting, assembling political support for, and amending legislation. Lobbyists and other group representatives spend a good deal of time cultivating relationships with these individuals. Finally, some of the newer congressional bureaucracies, such as the Office of Technology Assessment (OTA), the Congressional Budget Office (CBO), and the General Accounting Office (GAO), provide busy legislators with the important technical data they need in policy areas such as defense, the budget, and consumer products.

Whereas senators in the old Congress such as Alben Barkley, Robert Taft, and Harry Byrd functioned with half a dozen aides, today's lawmakers have several dozen. It should not be surprising that these busy legislators defer a good deal of their work and policy development to their staffs. Indeed, staffers have become indispensible. One former staffer who was elected to Congress quipped,

> People asked me how I felt about being elected to Congress and I told them I never thought I'd give up that much power voluntarily.[10]

These and other changes have contributed to a new, more politically oriented Congress. Its membership, both individually and collectively, is relatively more independent and less tradition-bound than the membership of one or two generations ago was.

TECHNIQUES OF INFLUENCE

In Chapter 3 we noted the wide array of techniques available to today's lobbyists and lobbies. These techniques have resulted from the growing preoccupation of interest groups with Congress as well as from the changing nature of that institution. Today's lobbies—agriculture, environmentalists, business, and so on—are increasingly adept at exploiting available techniques for their own needs and circumstances. A list of current lobbying techniques would probably look like Table 5-2.

These techniques show a good deal of similarity among the groups lobbying Congress. From Table 5-2 we can also discern the propensity for

TABLE 5-2   Percentage of Groups Using Various Lobbying Techniques (N = 174)

Testifying at hearings	99%
Contacting government officials directly to present your point of view	98
Engaging in informal contacts with officials—at conventions, over lunch, etc.	95
Presenting research results or technical information	92
Sending letters to members of your organization to inform them about your activities	92
Entering into coalitions with other organizations	90
Attempting to shape the implementation of policies	89
Talking with people from the press and the media	86
Consulting with government officials to plan legislative strategy	85
Helping to draft legislation	85
Inspiring letter-writing or telegram campaigns	84
Shaping the government's agenda by raising new issues and calling attention to previously ignored problems	84
Mounting grassroots lobbying efforts	80
Having influential constituents contact their congressman's office	80
Helping to draft regulations, rules, or guidelines	78
Serving on advisory commissions and boards	76
Alerting congressmen to the effects of a bill on their districts	75
Filing suit or otherwise engaging in litigation	72
Making financial contributions to electoral campaigns	58
Doing favors for officials who need assistance	56
Attempting to influence appointments to public office	53
Publicizing candidates' voting records	44
Engaging in direct-mail fund raising for your organization	44
Running advertisements in the media about your position on issues	31
Contributing work or personnel to electoral campaigns	24
Making public endorsements of candidates for office	22
Engaging in protests or demonstrations	20

Source: Kay L. Schlotzman and John T. Tierney, *Organized Interests and American Democracy.* Copyright © 1986 by Kay L. Schlotzman and John T. Tierney. Reprinted by permission of Harper & Row, Publishers, Inc.

multiple approaches. Today's lobbying not only is more intense but involves a number of interrelated activities.

But do all groups use the same general approaches, or do some groups specialize in certain techniques? The answer is found in Table 5-3.

TABLE 5-3   Percentage of Groups in Each Category Using Various Lobbying Techniques

	Sample	Corporations	Trade Associations	Unions	Public Interest Groups
Testifying at hearings	99%	98%	100%	100%	100%
Contacting officials directly	98	100	97	100	100
Informal contacts	95	98	97	95	96
Presenting research results	92	94	89	90	92
Sending letters to members	92	85	97	95	86
Entering into coalitions	90	96	91	100	92
Shaping implementation	89	90	91	85	92
Talking with press and media	86	67	89	95	96
Planning legislative strategy	74	81	85	85	83
Helping to draft legislation	85	86	94	85	74
Inspiring letter-writing campaigns	84	83	89	100	83
Shaping the government's agenda	84	79	77	85	100
Mounting grassroots lobbying	80	79	80	100	71
Having constituents contact	80	77	94	85	58
Drafting regulations	78	85	83	75	75
Serving on advisory commissions	76	74	74	95	67
Alerting congressmen to effects	75	92	74	85	57
Filing suit	72	72	83	95	79
Contributing to campaigns	58	86	66	90	29
Doing favors for officials	56	62	56	68	46
Influencing appointments	53	48	49	80	47
Publicizing voting records	44	28	37	90	75
Direct-mail fund raising	44	19	37	65	75
Running ads in the media	31	31	31	55	33
Contributing manpower to campaigns	24	14	23	70	33
Endorsing candidates	22	8	9	95	25
Engaging in protests	20	0	3	90	25
N =	(174)	(52)	(35)	(20)	(24)

Source: Kay L. Schlotzman and John T. Tierney, *Organized Interests and American Democracy.* Copyright © 1986 by Kay L. Schlotzman and John T. Tierney. Reprinted by permission of Harper & Row, Publishers, Inc.

The four types of groups represented in Table 5-3—labor unions, corporations, public interest organizations, and trade associations—show striking similarities in the techniques they employ. The techniques listed in the top half of Table 5-3 are used by 80 percent of all four types of organizations.

Some important differences, however, are also discernible in Table 5-3. Public interest groups are significantly less likely to make financial contributions (this would violate their tax-exempt status). Both public interest groups and labor unions are likely to engage in direct-mail fund raising and in publicizing candidate voting records. Furthermore, unions are quite likely to endorse candidates, donate manpower for campaigning, and engage in demonstrations.

Table 5-3 also shows 80 percent of the sample groups involved in grass-roots lobbying. The conventional wisdom used to be that public officials are skeptical of "inspired" mail as a barometer of their constituents' feelings. Nonetheless, today's lobbying organizations are not reluctant to exploit this technique. Rather than mass mailings of form letters, though, the emphasis now is on personal, handwritten letters. As one lobbyist notes,

> the member [of Congress] has to care that *somebody* out there in his district has enough power to get hundreds of people to sit down and write a postcard or letter—because if the guy can get them to do *that*, he might be able to influence them in other ways.[11]

Constituent mail is for legislators an important gauge of the mood and concerns of their constituents.

THE COMMITTEE AND SUBCOMMITTEE SYSTEM

At the core of congressional policy making are committees and subcommittees (Table 5-4). Legislation is screened and developed in each chamber by these subsystems. Given the growing complexity and variety of issues brought before Congress today, this division of labor and expertise is necessary for sustaining the strength of Congress as a national policy-making body.

The life of a bill is always tenuous, but it is more so at the committee or subcommittee stage. Victory here augurs well for passage; a major setback at this stage is rarely undone. Accordingly, interest groups and lobbyists concentrate most heavily on these subsystems. Two lobbyists elaborate:

> Once a bill clears committee the battle is usually four-fifths done, because they have a habit over there of backing up their committee actions in both houses. The main battle is to get appropriate legislation out of the committee. . . . Once that happens, you don't have any problem.[12]

> We watch the [House] Education and Labor Committee very carefully; but it's the

only one we're interested in. Otherwise you would spread yourself too thin. We have to control the labor committee. It's our life blood.[13]

Committee and subcommittee hearings afford groups an opportunity to present their positions on pending legislation and submit information and data either in opposition to or in support of the bill. Minor legislation may involve the organization's lobbyist, but in the case of major legislation organizational officers may testify in the belief that their views will carry greater weight among committee members. Most trade-offs and policy compromises occur at the committee level. A good deal of formal and informal interaction occurs

TABLE 5-4   House and Senate Standing Committees

House Committees	Senate Committees
Agriculture (8)[a]	Agriculture, Nutrition, and Forestry (6)
Appropriations (13)	Appropriations (13)
Armed Services (7)	Armed Services (6)
Banking, Financing and Urban Affairs (8)	Banking, Housing, and Urban Affairs (5)
Budget (0)[b]	Budget (0)
District of Columbia (3)	Commerce, Science, and Transportation (8)
Education and Labor (8)	
Energy and Commerce (6)	Energy and Natural Resources (5)
Foreign Affairs (8)	Environment and Public Works (6)
Government Operations (7)	Finance (8)
House Administration (8)	Foreign Relations (6)
Interior and Insular Affairs (6)	Governmental Affairs (6)
Judiciary (7)	Judiciary (8)
Merchant Marine and Fisheries (6)	Labor and Human Resources (6)
Post Office and Civil Service (7)	Rules and Administration (0)
Public Works and Transportation (6)	Small Business (7)
Rules (2)	Veterans Affairs (0)
Science and Technology (7)	Select Committee on Ethics (0)
Small Business (6)	Select Committee on Indian Affairs (0)
Standards of Official Conduct (0)	Select Committee on Intelligence (0)
Veterans Affairs (5)	
Ways and Means (6)	
Select Committee on Aging (4)	
Select Committee on Children, Youth, Families (0)[c]	
Select Committee on Hunger (0)[c]	
Permanent Select Committee on Intelligence (3)	
Select Committee on Narcotics Abuse and Control (0)	

[a]Number of subcommittees in parentheses.
[b]The House Budget Committee divides itself into eight "task forces" rather than appointing subcommittees.
[c]These committees divide into "task forces" rather than appointing subcommittees.

among the petitioning groups, the committee members, and the staff responsible for the final legislative details. The committee room is the focus of this interaction "simply because [it] is the only place where it is possible to arrange a compromise acceptable to all major interests affected."[14]

An important procedural change occurred in 1973. House Democrats approved a "Subcommittee Bill of Rights" that has made subcommittees powers in their own right. These subsystems in effect were made permanent and became less subject to the control or whim of committee chairs. Each subcommittee has its own budget, staff, and jurisdiction, and the assurance that legislation falling under its jurisdiction will be referred to it. Subcommittee chairs are elected, rather than designated by the full committee. In 1977 the Senate adopted similar rules decentralizing its committee system. Two students of legislative affairs comment on this change:

> Cutting a committee's jurisdiction into small pieces and placing real responsibility for decisions in the discrete subcommittees *encourages* particularized single-interest groups to disengage from umbrella lobby groups (that is, lobby groups that aggregate numerous interests in a policy domain into one lobby effort) and expend concentrated effort on the particular subcommittee determining the fate of their particularized interest. Concerned with only a few policy interests, these subcommittees are apt to become the captives of these clientele groups. The move to subcommittee government has fueled the rise of single-interest groups, increasing the probability of clientele dominance of congressional policy making.[15]

Much of the real work of Congress today is done by the numerous subcommittees—hearings, bill drafting, amending, and so on. This decentralization of legislative authority means that lobbyists spend a good deal more time and effort in today's Congress than they did in the old Congress.

COMMITTEE MEMBERSHIP
AND COMMITTEE CHAIRS

Interest group preoccupation with congressional committees and subcommittees goes beyond the mechanics of policy influence. Groups are also intensely interested in committee and subcommittee makeup. A number of factors are considered when assignments are made—professional qualifications, ideology, constituency makeup, party affiliation, region, and so on. Naturally, certain interests have special concerns with certain committees and subcommittees—farm associations with agricultural committees, veterans' organizations with veterans' affairs committees, and taxpayers' organizations with taxing and spending committees.

Legislators, therefore, do not sit back and wait for their assignments. They choose them with great care and actively work for their choice. According to Richard F. Fenno, members have three basic goals in mind when considering their committee assignments—reelection, institutional power, and policy making.[15] A member primarily concerned with reelection is likely to seek an assignment on a committee that serves this objective. For example, the House Post Office and Civil Service Committee and Public Works and Transportation Committee dispense benefits that enhance reelection. The House Foreign Affairs Committee and Education and Labor Committee tend to attract members with strong policy orientations. Those members seeking to enhance their status or influence within the House are drawn to the Ways and Means Committee or the Appropriations Committee, as very few congressional decisions carry greater weight than those involving taxing and spending policies.

This self-selection process tends to tilt committees and their subcommittees in favor of certain interests and policy directions. House and Senate agriculture committees are made up of a disproportionate number of legislators from farm states. Similarly, the House Education and Labor Committee along with its Senate counterpart disproportionately represent heavily unionized constituencies. Self-selection also leads to important differences among committees and subcommittees in terms of prestige and member attractiveness. Newly elected legislators often end up on less prestigious committees—District of Columbia, or Post Office and Civil Service—whereas the more senior members are found on the more attractive ones—Ways and Means, Appropriations, and Rules. Members move from one committee assignment to another, usually from the less prestigious to the more attractive ones.

Committee chairs are generally the ranking members of the majority party in each chamber. Though the "rule of seniority" is not formally written into the rules of Congress, its philosophy has been firmly embedded in legislative procedures throughout this century. Heading a committee increases a member's chamber status as well as placing him or her in a key position to influence legislation. This fact is not lost on lobbying organizations.

Today, though, elevation to a chair is not automatic. In the early 1970s, both parties in the House of Representatives agreed that seniority would not be the *only* factor considered in caucus or conference voting on committee and subcommittee chairs. A few years later, the Senate also adopted this change. Modification of the seniority rule has led to the replacement of a few committee heads by less senior members. But too many legislators are satisfied with the seniority system to allow it to be scrapped. Nevertheless, a new relationship now prevails between committee chairs and their committee members. (See Box 5-2 and Box 5-3 for profiles of a Senate and a House chair.)

INTERNAL LEGISLATIVE CAUCUSES AND COALITIONS

Thus far we have focused on strategies utilized by external forces seeking to influence congressional policy making. But the legislative system is also subject to pressures from within as legislators seek benefits or pursue political

BOX 5-2   *PROFILE OF A SENATE CHAIR*

Sam Nunn, a longtime Washington insider, is now a political figure—Chairman of the Senate Armed Services Committee. He thus continues the tradition of southern congressmen heading either the House or Senate Armed Services Committee—Carl Vinson, Ga.; Mendell Rivers, S.C.; Edward Hebert, La.; and John Stennis, Miss.

Nunn came to the Senate when that body was in general revolt against the administration's Vietnam War policies. He quickly gained a reputation for hard work on the Armed Services Committee—studying long Pentagon reports, intensively questioning military witnesses before the committee, and offering provocative alternative policies.

In the 1980s he worked with others, including Les Aspin, his counterpart in the House, to develop alternative military policies that would strengthen, not weaken the nation's military posture in the world. As a result, he differed with both presidents Carter and Reagan on various military policy initiatives. Nunn criticized Carter for cutting defense spending to dangerously low levels. Although he supported Reagan's Strategic Defense Initiative (SDI), Nunn was quick to point out that it could never be an effective shield for an entire population, as Reagan claimed.

Nunn's senatorial influence goes beyond his position as committee chair. He has the respect of both parties on military issues. On nonmilitary questions, Nunn's instincts are conservative. Though his voting record may look like that of a modern Dixiecrat—against gun controls, for more aid to the Nicaraguan Contras, and for more research funds for SDI—he is no knee-jerk conservative. He maintains an open mind on socioeconomic issues before the Senate. He is something of a loner. He does not actively campaign on behalf of his Senate peers, but he does freely endorse them. This defuses any charges by Republican opponents that some Democratic senators are soft on defense.

BOX 5-3 *PROFILE OF A HOUSE CHAIR*

Like Senate Armed Services Committee Chairman Sam Nunn, D-Ga., Les Aspin deals easily with defense experts as a peer rather than a patron. Both . . . attacked President Reagan's defense program in detail for lacking coherence.

And each is trying to move the Democratic Party to the right on defense—though not necessarily to the same degree—because he thinks a more hard-line policy would be correct on its merits and advantageous to the party at the polls.

But while Nunn seems to hold much of the Democratic Party and the national press in thrall, Aspin, 48, is straining to hold his committee chairmanship.

Part of the difference is that some critics accuse the Wisconsin Democrat of deception. They allege he solicited their votes for the chair in 1985 by promising to oppose the MX missile and then reneged. Aspin denies any such promises were made.

For most of his first decade on the Armed Services Committee, as a liberal isolated from the panel's mainstream, Aspin's chief means of influence was a cascade of pungent and well-timed press releases, some of them detailed critiques of Pentagon policy, others lighthearted zingers.

Their cumulative impact was to type Aspin by the mid-1970s as a "liberal Pentagon critic." In fact, he often took a harder line than many of his fellow liberals. As early as 1979, for instance, he argued that the Carter administration—and liberals in general—were underestimating the danger of Soviet meddling in developing countries.

By 1983, Aspin was an Armed Services subcommittee chairman, a fixture in the Washington defense community and a proponent of building the MX missile. He defended the missile as a bargaining lever against Moscow, a political payoff to Reagan for moderating his arms control policy, and a chance for Democrats to prove they were not soft on defense.

But critics charged that Aspin had been co-opted by the White House and had walked away from his earlier stand against the missile.

Aspin also arouses some suspicion by his plain zest for political wheeling and dealing. On the other hand, some leading liberal activists credit Aspin's energy and political skill for the interlocking web of amendments, timetables and rules that turned . . . debate on the [1986] defense authorization bill into a political rout for Reagan. . . .

But critics complain that he plays his own hand too close to the vest while trying to broker political deals.

Source: Congressional Quarterly *Weekly Report,* Vol. 45, No. 3 (January 17, 1987), 106.

objectives for their constituencies. Approximately one hundred coalitions and caucuses exist within Congress today. Let us look briefly at the role these voluntary associations play in congressional policy making.

Obviously, these internal associations differ from traditional pressure groups in their makeup and in their immediate access to members of Congress, but their approaches are quite similar. They consist of incumbent chamber members with the usual organizational attributes—a title, some staff, a membership list, and a leadership structure. The legislative network allows instant access to chamber members and leadership along with significant opportunities for lobbying, dissemination of information, and involvement in lawmaking. The degree of access to legislators and opportunities for policy influence exceed those of most private interests. However, private interests do complement internal associations by activating their memberships in common lobbying activities.

Of course, these coalitions and caucuses vary in length of tenure, organizational sophistication, size, and policy influence. Like traditional interest groups, they demonstrate a wide range of issue concerns and exist for a variety of purposes, as Table 5–5 demonstrates.

In addition to pursuing their policy concerns, internal associations perform several other important functions: representation, informational exchanges, policy development, and coalition building. Like special interest groups, these voluntary associations may have broad or narrow policy concerns and they seek to establish relationships with certain sectors of the national bureaucracy.

The Congressional Black Caucus

An excellent example of a legislative caucus is the Congressional Black Caucus (CBC). As a national constituency caucus, the CBC seeks to influence the congressional agenda and mobilize support for its policy objectives. The CBC came into being in 1971, largely through the efforts of its first chairman, former congressman Charles Diggs (D–Mich.).[17] The political climate was ripe for the appearance of such an organization. The reapportionment revolution of the 1960s established a number of predominantly black congressional districts in many major cities—Chicago, Detroit, Los Angeles, Baltimore, and so on.

TABLE 5-5   A Sample of Congressional Caucuses

Type of Caucus	House	Senate	Bicameral
Party	Budget Study Group Democratic Research Organization Republican Study Committee Wednesday Group	Moderate/Conservative Democrats Wednesday Group Steering Committee	
Personal Interest	Human Rights Arts Space	Caucus on the Family Senators for the Arts Drug Enforcement	Arms Control and Foreign Policy Coalition for Peace Through Strength Environmental and Energy Study Conference Renewable Energy Clearinghouse on the Future
Constituency Concerns: National	Black Caucus Hispanic Caucus Local Government Caucus		Caucus for Women's Issues Viet Nam Veterans in Congress
Regional	Border Caucus Conference of Great Lakes Congressmen Sunbelt Council Tennesee Valley Authority Caucus	Border Caucus Western States Coalition Midwest Conference of Democratic Senators	Pacific Northwest Trade Task Force San Diego Congressional Delegation
State/District	Rural Caucus Federal Government Task Force House Caucus on North American Trade Export Task Force	Senate Caucus on North American Trade Senate Export Caucus	Crime Caucus Friends of Ireland Committee on the Baltic States and Ukraine
State/District Commercial	Coal Group Port Caucus Steel Caucus Footwear Caucus Textile Caucus Automotive Caucus	Coal Caucus Copper Caucus Rail Caucus Wine Caucus Footwear Caucus Tourism Caucus	Alcohol Fuels Caucus Jewelry Manufacturing Coalition Wood Energy Caucus

Source: S. W. Hammond, D. P. Mulholland, and A. G. Stevens, "Informal Congressional Caucuses and Agenda Setting," Western Political Quarterly, 38 (1985), 584–604. Used with permission.

Additionally, passage of the 1965 Voting Rights Act stimulated registration by black voters throughout the country. Further, the political climate early in the Nixon administration was one of extended confrontation between the White House and black members of Congress. These tensions generated a sense of common purpose among the congressmen as well as a growing sense of ethnic identity, fostering a push for caucus formation.

MEMBERS OF THE CONGRESSIONAL BLACK CAUCUS (100th CONGRESS)

William Clay, Mo.	Augustus F. Hawkins, Calif.
Cardiss Collins, Ill.	Charles A. Hayes, Ill.
John C. Conyers, Mich.	Mickey Leland, Texas
George W. Crockett, Jr., Mich.	John Lewis, Ga.
Ronald V. Dellums, Calif.	Kweisi Mfume, Md.
Julian Dixon, Calif.	Major R. Owens, N.Y.
Mervyn M. Dymally, Calif.	Charles B. Rangel, N.Y.
Mike Espy, Miss.	Gus Savage, Ill.
Walter E. Fauntroy, D.C.	Louis Strokes, Ohio
Floyd Flake, N.Y.	Edolphus Towns, N.Y.
Harold E. Ford, Tenn.	William H. Gray III, Pa.
Alan Wheat, Mo.	

Today, the CBC is firmly established and politically active. Its agenda for the 1990's includes such issues as greater minority employment throughout the private sector, continuance of voting rights legislation, more public housing for low-income black families, and more public support for minority entrepreneurs. The caucus also offers it own federal budget for congressional consideration.

The CBC is one of the most visible and institutionalized caucuses in Congress. While other caucuses and coalitions operate with relatively modest resources, the CBC maintains a permanent staff that performs a multitude of tasks. The staff publishes a magazine through a foundation, issues periodic legislative alerts, produces studies, briefs caucus members on pending legislation, and suggests various legislative strategies. These activities, coupled with significant public and private linkages, make the Black Caucus unique among legislative groups. The CBC regularly solicits opinions from a network of advisers throughout the country who help formulate policy positions and generate political support within black communities. The network includes many black lawyers, businesspeople, bankers, economists, and other professionals.

Legislative caucuses and coalitions offer a range of benefits to their members.[18] They raise relevant issues to a level of public debate and policy formulation. Caucuses have contributed to congressional procedural and policy reforms—democratizing the selection of committee and subcommittee chairs, further decentralizing decision making, and moderating party policies on issues of concern. Additionally, legislative coalitions offer more points of access to the chamber membership, they often operate as precommittee mechanisms for issue formation, and they frequently help integrate opinion on divisive issues. These are important constituent services at a time when party services in some of these areas are weakening.

Given the proliferation of groups in the private sector over the 1980s, there is reason to believe that public-sector groups such as these coalitions will continue to increase. The movement of Congress and other national institutions into new policy frontiers will provide the impetus for additional group formation. Of equal significance is the way these public-sector interest groups now conduct their political activities. Legislative coalitions and caucuses demonstrate the adaptability and sophistication inherent in many of today's lobbying organizations.

THE FRAGMENTATION OF CONGRESSIONAL POWER: A NEW CHALLENGE FOR INTEREST GROUPS

A persistent theme in this chapter is the decentralization of power within Congress today. The proliferation of subcommittees has contributed to this decentralization. Another decentralizing aspect of subcommittees is their participation in "issue networks" (discussed more fully in the next chapter). These networks are displaying "iron triangles" of policy making consisting of committee or subcommittee personnel, agency personnel, and concerned interest groups. Issue networks are more complex and contain more participants than do traditional iron triangles. These new networks, incidentally, are largely invisible outside Washington, but they are quite influential in policy choices within their domain. One writer describes the attraction that these new relationships hold for legislators:

> Policy-conscious members of the House now find it preferable to be big fish in the small ponds constituted by "their" issue networks than give their proxies to congressional leaders. Even if the influence of Congress is less than it was in the old system, members of low-to-medium seniority find that their own influence is now much more substantial.[19]

Faced with an increasingly decentralized, individualistic legislative system, interest groups and their representatives must now interact with legislators on a broader front and expend more resources. As one observer explains,

> the many changes on Capitol Hill over the past decade—the proliferation of subcommittees, the greater importance of Congressional staff . . . the greater importance of policy entrepreneurs both among elected representatives and staff . . . all of these things have altered the environment of legislative lobbying and left pressure groups bent on influencing officials with little choice but to escalate the range and volume of their activities.[20]

SUMMARY

Interest groups and Congress need each other. Interest groups contribute to the definition of policy alternatives, illuminate issues, marshal evidence, and promote bargaining. By serving as a source of voting cues on a variety of bills, these functions help overworked legislators fulfill their mandates. But it is unrealistic to contend that certain groups steadily dominate legislative voting. Legislative successes by one set of interests can spur counteractivity by other interests. Also, legislators are not mere ciphers waiting to be manipulated by this or that organization. Not all legislators share the same orientation toward environmentalists, or religious fundamentalists, or labor unions, or gun control organizations.

Congressional responses to today's petitioners are shaped to a great degree by that institution's own internal processes. No legislation goes through the legislative labyrinth without some modification. Pressure groups and lobbies are displaying more sophistication and a broader range of tactics today than they did in the 1950s and 1960s. This is only natural, given the ongoing changes within Congress itself. Further refinements of and changes in group tactics will undoubtedly continue.

But regardless of the changes in Congress and a new generation of interests emerging on the political horizon, traditional lobbying practices will not be completely abandoned in favor of the new. As two students of interest group politics point out,

> the explosion of group activity is not confined to those methods particularly appropriate to an age either of electronic media and data processing or of stronger links between legislators and constituents. Rather, the increase has taken place across *all* categories of interest group techniques, the old-fashioned as well as the modern.[21]

NOTES

[1]Some excellent sources on Congress and its policies are Charles O. Jones, *The United States Congress: People, Place, and Policy* (Homewood, Ill.: Dorsey, 1982); W. J. Keefe and M. S. Ogul, *The American Legislative Process: Congress and the States,* 7th ed. (Englewood Cliffs, N.J.: Prentice-Hall, 1988); R. B. Ripley, *Congress: Process and Policy,* 3rd ed. (New York: W. W. Norton & Co., Inc., 1983); and Christopher J. Deering, ed., *Congresstional Politics,* (Chicago: Dorsey, 1989).

[2]For more on congressional action on the 1986 Tax Reform Bill, see the Congressional Quarterly *Weekly Report* (44) for the months of September and October 1986.

[3]Keefe and Ogul, *The American Legislative Process,* p. 280.

[4]On this point, see John W. Kingdon, *Congressmen's Voting Decisions,* 2nd. ed. (New York: Harper & Row, Pub., 1981).

[5]For an excellent in-depth study of the "older" Congress, especially the U.S. Senate, see William S. White, *Citadel: The Story of the U.S. Senate* (New York: Harper & Row, 1956).

[6]Richard Bolling, *House Out of Order* (New York: Harper & Row, 1965); Joseph Clark, *The Sapless Branch* (New York: Harper & Row, 1964).

[7]Joseph Clark, *The Sapless Branch,* (New York: Harper & Row, 1964).

[8]See W. M. Lunch, *The Nationalization of American Politics* (Berkeley: University of California Press, 1987).

[9]Keefe and Ogul, *The American Legislative Process,* pp. 169-73.

[10]Quoted in Lunch, *The Nationalization of American Politics,* p. 123.

[11]Quoted in K. L. Schlotzman and J. T. Tierney, "More of the Same: Washington Pressure Group Activity in a Decade of Change," *Journal of Politics,* 45 (1983), 371.

[12]Quoted in Richard F. Fenno, *Congressmen in Committees* (Boston: Little, Brown, 1973), p. 31.

[13]An AFL-CIO official quoted in John M. Bacheller, "Lobbyists and the Legislative Process: The Impact of Environmental Constraints," *American Political Science Review,* 71 (1977), 257.

[14]Keefe and Ogul, *The American Legislative Process,* p. 162.

[15]L. C. Dodd and B. J. Oppenheimer, *Congress Reconsidered,* 2nd ed. (Washington, D.C.: Congressional Quarterly Press, 1981), pp. 45-46.

[16]Fenno, *Congressmen in Committees,* p. 1.

[17]For a discussion of the events leading up to the formation of the Black Caucus, see Margerite Ross Barnett, "The Congressional Black Caucus," *Proceedings, American Academy of Political Science,* 32 (1975), 34-50. For a more recent evaluation of the Black Caucus, see the Congressional Quarterly *Weekly Report,* 43 (April 13, 1985), 675-81.

[18]William Hammond et al., "Informal Congressional Caucuses," *Western Political Quarterly,* 38 (1985), 584-605.

[19]Lunch, *The Nationalization of American Politics,* p. 127.

[20]Testimony of John Tierney before the Senate Committee on Governmental Affairs, quoted in *The Transformation in American Politics* (Washington , D.C.: Advisory Commission on Intergovernmental Relations, 1986), pp. 234-35.

[21]Schlotzman and Tierney, "More of the Same," p. 370.

CHAPTER SIX
ADMINISTRATIVE POLICY MAKING:
New Relationships and Actors

Our national bureaucracy has become an increasingly independent and powerful political force over the past quarter century. Bureaucratic personnel (or bureaucrats) have more to do and more individuals and groups to interact with—lobbyists, members of Congress, congressional staffers, citizens' organizations, state and local officials, interest groups, and so on—than in any previous period in our history. By tradition, most citizens have been far less interested in bureaucratic politics than in congressional politics. But because Congress has seen fit to add new agencies and responsibilities to the bureaucracy, more individuals and interest groups are giving greater attention to it.

THE GROWTH OF BUREAUCRATIC POWER AND INDEPENDENCE

The size and scope of today's bureaucracy result from a number of factors. Briefly, our bureaucracy expanded in influence as the result of three phases of political innovation—the Progressive era, the New Deal era, and the Great Society era and its immediate aftermath.[1]

The turn-of-the-century Progressive period led to the establishment not only of a more professional public service but to new responsibilities as well. The passage, for example, of the Pure Food and Drug Act (1907) initiated public surveillance of the manufacturing, distribution, and sale of drugs and food. The Federal Reserve Act (1913) established a Federal Reserve Board that initiated public–private cooperation in banking. This action was taken to prevent future bank closings and the recurrence of the "panics" (or recessions) so common in the country during the 1880s and 1890s.

The stock market crash in 1929 stimulated additional bureaucratic growth and responsibilities during Franklin Roosevelt's New Deal programs. Government involvement in the economy led to the establishment of a number of agencies, including the Securities and Exchange Commission (SEC). This agency was given authority to regulate stock exchanges along with the sales of stocks in interstate commerce. The National Labor Relations Board (NLRB) was created to monitor labor–management practices in the workplace. In 1938, the Civil Aeronautics Board (CAB) came into being with responsibility to regulate fares and freight rates in the growing airline industry. These and other New Deal agencies were generally responsible for managing their clientele in such a fashion that the stability of the marketplace was not disturbed and the nation's economy remained stable.

The 1960s and 1970s saw another spurt in the size and scope of the federal bureaucracy. Broad legislation in the fields of civil rights, affirmative action, consumerism, and environmentalism produced a new generation of administrative agencies—the Consumer Product Safety Commission (CPSC), the Environmental Protection Agency (EPA), the National Highway Traffic Safety Commission, the Occupational Safety and Health Administration (OSHA), and the departments of Energy and Education, to name only a few.

Bureaucrats received broad grants of authority in these three periods. The environmental and civil rights legislation are obvious examples. Congressional phraseology and the power to implement such legislation have had the effect of greatly expanding bureaucratic power:

> Ambiguity in the law gives bureaucrats power because someone must interpret the words and phrases that are left undefined. For example, what are "reasonable efforts"? How much compliance is "substantial"? To provide a seemingly easier example, what is a "federal program or activity"? If students at a college accept federal loans to go to school, has the college become a federal "program or activity" as a result?[2]

Bureaucrats, then, have the unenviable task of deciding "legislative intent." Most of the time this is quite difficult, and interpretation of new legislation can spark new controversy.

In this chapter we will note the basis for increased interest group–bureaucracy interaction and then examine the new set of relationships characterizing that interaction. We will then review administrative lobbying and conclude the chapter with a discussion of White House–interest group relationships.

INTEREST GROUPS AND
THE BUREAUCRACY

Interest groups and administrative agencies have a natural affinity for each other because both are *policy specialists.* They interact for a variety of purposes—policy formation and/or modification, regulatory pursuits, lobbying, and information exchange—across a broad range of issues—sex discrimination in public employment, environmental pollution, nuclear energy production, veterans' benefits, and so on. These relationships can range from the very formal and adversarial to informal lobbying contacts.[3]

Generally, though, interest groups and public agencies maintain close relationships for their mutual benefit—veterans' organizations with the Department of Veterans Affairs (formerly the Veterans Administration), business associations with the Small Business Administration or the Department of Commerce, and farm organizations with the Department of Agriculture. The rewards emanating from these contacts include service on intraagency advisory boards and committees, informal contacts with influential bureaucrats, opportunities to present testimony before administrative tribunals, or merely the reinforcement of working relationships.

IRON TRIANGLES

The working relationships between interest groups and agencies quite frequently evolve into what the prevailing literature characterizes as *subgovernments* or *iron triangles.*[4] These relationships are characteristically exclusionary, involving a few interest groups and agency personnel along with selected members of Congress. Consumer or housing policies, say, will be monopolized by virtually independent communities of like-minded officials, as illustrated in Figure 6-1.

In recent years, iron triangles have sprouted across Washington. One consists of farm groups, congressional agricultural committees, and the Department of Agriculture. Another is made up of labor unions, congressional labor committees, and the Department of Labor. From a political standpoint, these alliances have helped reduce the level of conflict in our highly diverse and fragmented society and have encouraged cooperation (though some might call it collusion).

The participating interest groups, members of Congress, and agency personnel each stand to gain by making policy quietly and cooperatively. Committee personnel frequently have constituents with a narrow (or economic) perspective, interest groups are deeply concerned with even the minutest policy details, and bureaucrats want broad powers and adequate budgets. All three sides, therefore, benefit from their triangular relationship: the interest groups gain favorable policies from the agency, the agency maintains goodwill with

FIGURE 6-1   An Iron Triangle

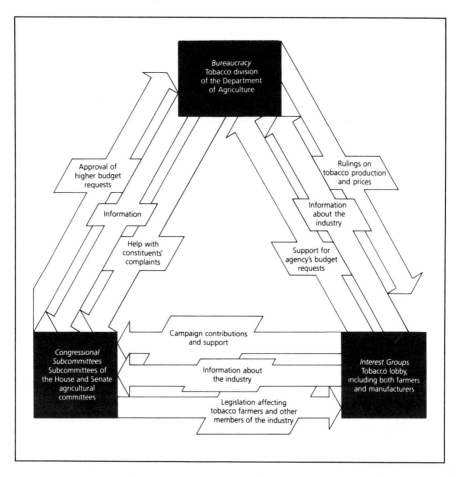

Adapted from "Iron Triangle: One Example" by Robert L. Lineberry, *Government in America: People, Politics, and Policy* 3rd ed. (Boston: Little, Brown, 1980) p. 419. Copyright © 1986 by Robert L. Lineberry. Reprinted by permission of Scott, Foresman and Company.

grateful members of Congress and may receive greater congressional funding as a result, and the legislators gain constituent favors that will be helpful come election time.

THE EMERGENCE OF ISSUE NETWORKS

A new set of relationships among administrative agencies, interest groups, and Congress is emerging in the nation's capital. Not that the triangular relationships have disappeared from the scene; rather they have been significantly modified. According to Hugh Heclo, new, fluid "issue networks" are emerging that are more elaborate and diverse as well as more conflictory than triangular relationships.[5] Heclo theorizes that issue networks are not only changing the processes of administrative policy making but are also serving as seedbeds for organizations advocating new legislation. Consequently, policy making is no longer limited to a mere handful of public officials but also includes journalists, academicians, public interest groups, policy experts, and state and local participants from time to time.

Traditionally, farm policy consisted mainly of maintaining stable prices for commodities (corn, wheat, oats, rice) and stable interest rates on the money farmers had to borrow between planting time and harvest. Involved with these concerns were certain Department of Agriculture personnel, congressional agricultural committees and subcommittees, and a few farm lobbyists.

Today, the situation is more complex. Farm surpluses are occasionally used as leverage in foreign policy (a grain embargo was placed on the Soviet Union after it invaded Afghanistan). Agricultural policies have also become tied to oil consumption because of the Arab boycotts against those Western nations that aided Israel during the 1973–74 Arab–Israeli war. Oil powers American farm machinery as well as being a component in fertilizers and pesticides. Domestically, farm policies involve a multi-billion-dollar food-stamp and welfare program in addition to a number of human-service programs. It used to be that mainly agricultural politicians were concerned with these matters, but now other kinds of experts are involved—energy experts, foreign-policy and international-trade experts, social-service and human-nutrition experts.

Today's bureaucrats must cope with increasingly difficult issues—energy consumption, international trade, the environment, and so on. Even the most cerebral of politicians do not have all the answers. Issue networks, then, offer opportunities for broader discussion than the older subgovernments do. Network participants generally have stronger academic credentials and more issue expertise, and policy discussions are conducted on a more sophisticated level. The resulting policy choices tend to be based not so much on political expediency as on rigorous examination of the facts at hand. Although this new system may professionalize decision making, there is concern that the resulting policies may be less popular than those under the old system. Mandarin-like bureaucrats, far removed from public pressure, may not serve the long-term interests of the bureaucracy.

LOBBYING THE AGENCIES

Let us now look more closely at administrative lobbying by interest groups. Once Congress passes legislation relating to farm subsidies, veterans' benefits, or excise taxes on small business, opportunities exist for concerned groups to help decide what the law really means.* In our relatively decentralized political system, administrative boards, commissions, departments, bureaus, and other agencies are given a good deal of discretion in interpreting and implementing new legislation.

John E. Chubb's study of energy-related interest groups' interaction with regulatory agencies notes a variety of lobbying approaches.[6] In the case of oil, Chubb found varying degrees of contact between the regulatory agencies and their clientele (Table 6-1). The large, affluent oil companies and the small associations of oil producers continually utilized a broad range of formal and informal contacts. The more diffuse and less affluent citizens' organizations lobbied more sporadically and with less intensity. It is not surprising, then, that the industry-related organizations were more successful with the regulators than the latter groups were.

TABLE 6-1   Frequency of Group Interaction with Two Petroleum Regulatory Agencies, 1974-78 (N = 76)

Interest Groups	Constant	Frequent	Sporadic	Infrequent	None
Environmental Groups			11%	22%	67%
Consumer and Public-Interest Groups			11	22	67
Petroleum and Gas Industry	69%	12%	6		12
Electric Power Industry				22	78
Conservation and Renewable- Energy Groups					100
Labor Unions				12	88
Commercial Users		8	31	38	23

The two regulatory agencies were the Federal Energy Agency (a precursor of the Department of Energy) and the Economic Regulatory Administration (now within the Department of Energy).

Source: John E. Chubb, *Interest Groups and the Bureaucracy: The Politics of Energy* (Stanford, Calif.: Stanford University Press, 1983), p. 134. Used with permission of the publishers, Stanford University Press. Copyright © 1983 by the Board of Trustees of the Leland Stanford Junior University.

Like legislative relationships, agency–clientele relationships are reciprocal. Agencies need the technical assistance and political intelligence their constituents provide. Clientele groups want favorable policy outputs and opportunities for future influence in agency decision making.

Indirect lobbying frequently involves interest group participation in the selection of agency personnel. Environmentalists, consumer organizations, and

---

*Most federal agencies contain advisory committees (about 900 exist today). These committees consist of representatives of the various interests regulated by the agency—Defense, Interior, Agriculture, Justice, and so on—and subject to its jurisdiction. These committees, in effect, institutionalize group representation in agency policy making.

conservative interests, for example, want supportive appointees throughout the bureaucratic structure. From high-level presidential appointments to lower management and administrative positions, coalitions of organizations lobby for the selection of one of their own.*

But qualifications for appointment are changing. Bureaucratic nominees are less partisan and less parochial. Professional competency and loyalty to the president carry more weight now. In the Washington of the 1940s, 1950s, and early 1960s, many of the assistant secretaries, special assistants, and other high-level appointees—those actually participating in policy formation—were politicians with mandates from party officials and/or concerned interest groups. Today, technocrats and strong policy advocates of the left and right are frequent appointees.[7] Among the technocrats, some typical appointments by the Reagan administration are listed in Table 6-2.

TABLE 6-2   Technocrats in the Bureaucracy

Name	Occupation	Government Position and Background
James Barnes	lawyer	deputy administrator of the EPA: special assistant to the EPA administrator, 1970–73; lawyer in the Justice and Agriculture departments; reappointed to the EPA as general counsel in 1983; and deputy administrator of that agency in 1985
John Pendergrass	industrial hygenist	assistant secretary of labor for safety and health: biologist with the Tennessee Valley Authority, 1948–1951; industrial hygenist with 3M Company, St. Paul, Minnesota
Rosemary Collyer	lawyer	general counsel, National Labor Relations Board: appointed chair, Federal Mine Safety and Health Commission, in 1981; appointed to the NLRB in 1985

These and similar appointees, according to Hugh Heclo, represent a departure from the past:

> these "political" appointees as a group have been distinguished by nothing so much as their common lack of experience in party politics, their unfamiliarity with agency programs, and their general protectiveness of their own organizational jurisdictions. All have been managerial or subject matter experts.[8]

The strong policy advocates, or ideologues, among the appointees are members of policy-oriented interest groups or think tanks representing the

---

*During the formation of George Bush's administration, such organizations as the Heritage Foundation, the Chamber of Commerce of the U.S., a coalition of approximately eighty women's organizations, conservative religious orders, and environmental organizations submitted thousands of resumes of individuals for appointment throughout the executive branch.

political right or left. During the Carter administration, many of Ralph Nader's lieutenants were appointed throughout the bureaucracy. For example, Carole Tucker Foreman of the Consumer Federation of America served as Assistant Secretary of Agriculture for Food and Consumer Services during this period, and Brent H. Rushford, founder of the Center for Law in the Public Interest (Los Angeles), was appointed Assistant General Counsel, Department of Defense.

The Reagan administration appointed administrators representing the political right. James Watt, from the conservative Mountain States Legal Foundation, was Reagan's initial Secretary of the Interior. Edwin Meese, cofounder of the Pacific Legal Foundation, a conservative public law firm, was a White House adviser during the first Reagan administration and then served briefly as Attorney General in the second administration. William J. Bennett of the right-wing Heritage Foundation was appointed by President Reagan to chair the National Endowment for the Humanities.

This gradual substitution of technocrats and ideologues for politicians throughout the bureaucracy represents a new dimension in public policy making. Where earlier policy making was conducted in terms of interests and involved a mere handful of consensual officials, ideas are now becoming increasingly important. Public policy making, as a result, is more routinized and deliberate than accidental. Issues are increasingly decided on merit and careful examination of the facts rather than through political compromise.

Another type of interest group lobbying occurs when clientele groups perceive potential interference with or threats to their agency relationships. Farm organizations may rally behind the Farm Credit Administration or the Department of Agriculture; civil rights groups will coalesce behind the Equal Employment Opportunity Commission or the Civil Rights Commission; environmental groups will support the Council on Environmental Quality or the Environmental Protection Agency.

During the later 1970s and early 1980s, various business interests—used-car dealers, insurance companies, cereal manufacturers, undertakers, and others—sought to weaken the Federal Trade Commission's regulatory authority over their jurisdictions. This action, however, activated a combination of groups—labor unions, consumer associations, and senior citizens—who wanted the commission's authority left alone. These organizations feared increased costs for the services offered by these businesses if the FTC's authority was weakened. They perceived themselves as a consumer–labor coalition that would "Save the FTC" from destruction.[9]

Forbidden by law to indulge in direct lobbying,* FTC personnel nonetheless played a key role in generating and maintaining opposition to congressional legislation that would have stripped the commission of its authority. Staff personnel coordinated communications, provided relevant materials, and

---

*Although no one has been prosecuted under this 1913 statute, it does attempt to restrain the more aggressive agency efforts to generate public support.

participated in periodic strategy sessions with FTC supporters. A former FTC commissioner characterizes staff involvement in the lobbying as follows:

> Through our press office, we made certain that factual background documents reached the hands of any reporter, columnist, or editorial writer who might wish to be informed of the commission's plight.[10]

Bureaucracy–interest group relationships have become much more atomized and difficult. During the 1940s and 1950s these relationships were cozier and decision making was simpler. But now there are many more adversarial interest groups on the scene, each with its own network of influence. Administrative policy making, as a result, is more chaotic, less predictable, and frequently more confrontational.

INTEREST GROUPS AND THE WHITE HOUSE: FROM TRANSIENTS TO PERMANENT GUESTS

Since the beginning of the republic, an endless chain of petitioners—farmers, veterans, proabortionists, business people, conservatives, state and local representatives—have sought presidential support of their pet projects. All presidents, from George Washington on, have had to deal with these entreaties. Many of the petitioners' concerns were handled routinely by staff aides, but others came to involve the president personally.

Presidential access for interest groups should be viewed as a product not only of interest group demands but of presidential initiatives. Presidents Franklin Roosevelt, Harry Truman, and Richard Nixon were lobbied by black civil rights organizations for more federal appointments as well as for their backing for civil rights legislation.[11] Jewish organizations lobbied Lyndon Johnson and Richard Nixon for political support and military aid to Israel during the Arab–Israeli wars of the 1960s and 1970s. During his final years in office, President Reagan was heavily lobbied by oil interests for a continuation of their tax breaks in the face of congressional calls for tax reform.

Presidents receive a number of advantages from their group relationships. First, petitioning groups can provide the votes essential to electoral victory for an incumbent administration. Second, interest groups can provide a sitting president with increased leverage over Congress. Interest groups can help compensate for the weakening of political parties and the election to Congress of people who are less amenable to presidential control. Working with like-minded organizations allows an administration to utilize its network of contacts and put additional heat on legislators or committees opposing presidential legislation. To this end, the White House cultivates its lobbying base. Finally, groups can help presidents through "intelligence gathering." They can alert presidents to potential "fire storms" of opposition or to impending actions that might be detrimental to administration goals.[12]

As recently as Lyndon Johnson's administration, White House-interest group relationships existed mainly on an ad hoc basis; many groups found representation through cabinet secretaries. (Johnson did, however, utilize a number of party officials as well as members of his staff as intermediaries with group representatives.) But this type of representation became increasingly unsatisfactory as time went by. As a result, the Office of Public Liaison (OPL) was established in 1974 to formalize relationships between the two sides. Additionally, Presidents Ford, Carter, and Reagan developed full-time, formal relationships with a growing number of group petitioners. In the Reagan administration, for example, OPL staffers held "portfolio management responsibilities" with a range of interest groups—Jews, farmers, Catholics, consumers, the elderly, labor unions, and so on.[13]

During President Carter's tenure, conscientious efforts were made by the OPL staff to organize broad ad hoc coalitions in support of the president's programs. Various interest group representatives were brought to the White House for briefings and consultation on the budget, foreign policy, health care, and other matters high on the president's agenda. The feedback from these representatives helped the president ascertain the extent of group support in these and related policy areas.

The OPL also coordinated meetings between the president and leaders from organized labor, business, black and Hispanic organizations, and environmental, women's, and consumers' organizations. Discussions focused mainly on issues of concern to the groups, but also covered more general topics of importance to the president. The White House also sought to have several meetings annually with a broad spectrum of interest group representatives in order to ascertain what their main concerns were. Under Carter, some groups—feminists organizations, environmentalists, and consumers—were favored more than others and as a result had more White House access. The Reagan White House was oriented more toward conservative business and religious fundamentalist organizations.

A set of *constituency representatives* were added to the Carter White House staff—special assistant for consumer affairs, special assistant for ethnic affairs, counselor for the aging, and so on. These representatives, incidentally, had a history of political activism and leadership experience, which gave them a ready-made network of political contacts.* These individuals supplemented existing OPL contacts, as a former OPL head notes:

> The people who represented blacks, Hispanics, consumers, Jews, seniors and women . . . all had the title of Special Assistant to the President and we worked

*Constituency representatives in recent administrations include Esther Peterson, long active in labor and women's affairs; Louis Martin, a long-time activist in organized labor and the Democratic party; and Nelson Kruikshank, with long service in the American Federation of Labor.

with them when we wanted to use those groups as part of the coalitions we would build or as part of consultation on policy issues.[14]

White House–interest group relationships are much more structured and formalized now. The incorporation of "portfolios" has helped diversify both the staff composition and the policy objectives of the White House. It has also helped apprise presidents of the concerns of the elderly, certain racial groups, and business organizations. White House responses to group petitions will, of course, depend on the president's perspective of the organizations and their political objectives.

Today, more and more groups are appealing to the White House for presidential intercession. Incumbent presidents have in effect become *conflict managers*. The growing number of competing interest group demands has resulted in what Thomas E. Cronin calls "the swelling of the Presidency."[15] Many presidential aides, as well as personnel in the Office of Management and Budget, the Office of Policy Development, and the Council of Economic Advisors, are involved in sorting out and responding to these demands. Added to this burden is the continuing atrophy of the political parties, which virtually eliminates them as group mediators or policy makers.

Interest group–White House relationships raise questions about future presidential leadership. Will the routinizing of these relationships ultimately lead groups to appeal directly to the president, bypassing other channels of negotiation and reconciliation? The grievances of veterans, victims of AIDS, and the elderly can often be handled more expeditiously at the local level than by the Washington bureaucracy. Certainly, presidents must be adept at group cultivation and consultation which allows some access. But in order to have the political flexibility and freedom to respond to other demands of his office, a president must be selective in handling group demands. For the present, at least, the White House appears to have a significant range of discretion in both the structuring of group relationships and the utilization of them when needed.[16]

SUMMARY

Administrative policy making is significantly different today from what it was a generation ago. The increased preoccupation of interest groups with an expanded national bureaucracy has forced Washington officialdom to alter its traditional policy-making processes. The older system of a few private interests interacting with a small number of bureaucrats and members of Congress on policy formation or modification is fast disappearing. Issue networks are replacing the older, triangular relationships and thereby allowing for broader interest group participation.

The size and scope of the federal bureaucracy will undoubtedly continue to expand. That the national government has undertaken significant responsibilities in the areas of civil rights, the environment, and occupational safety has set the stage for future undertakings. This will inevitably lead to the formation of more interest groups and their involvement in the political process. These potential groups, however, will probably be less tied to traditional economic and geographical divisions within the country; more likely they will be based in national movements emanating from emerging issues.

Finally, the White House, as a key center of national policy making, will remain the focus of a large number of adversarial interest groups. The Office of Public Liaison is an official acknowledgment of both the maturity and the increasing political clout of groups. In the opinion of Thomas Cronin, a miniaturization of politically important interest groups and professions is appended to today's White House establishment.[17] Interest groups have upgraded their status from temporary guests to permanent residents.

NOTES

[1] A good source on the Progressive era is Richard Hofstadter's *The Age of Reform* (New York: Random House, 1955). For a concise analysis of Franklin Roosevelt's New Deal, see W. E. Leuchtenberg, *Franklin D. Roosevelt and the New Deal* (New York: Harper & Row, Pub., 1963). Doris Kearns's *Lyndon Johnson and the American Dream* (New York: Harper & Row, Pub., 1976) offers a good analysis of the Great Society.

[2] William M. Lunch, *The Nationalization of American Politics* (Berkeley: University of California Press, 1987), pp. 171-72.

[3] An excellent study of interest group–agency interaction is found in John E. Chubb, *Interest Groups and the Bureaucracy: The Politics of Energy* (Stanford, Calif.: Stanford University Press, 1983). Also see James Q. Wilson, ed., *The Politics of Regulation* (New York: Basic Books, 1980); and Francis E. Rourke, *Bureaucracy, Politics, and Public Policy*, 3rd ed. (Boston: Little, Brown, 1984).

[4] See Theodore J. Lowi, *The End of Liberalism*, 2nd ed. (New York: W. W. Norton & Co., Inc., 1979); and Dorothy B. James, *The Contemporary Presidency* (New York: Pegasus, 1969).

[5] Hugh Heclo, "Issue Networks and the Executive Establishment," in *The New American Political System*, ed. Anthony King (Washington, D.C.: American Enterprise Institute, 1978), pp. 118-24.

[6] Chubb, *Interest Groups and the Bureaucracy.*

[7] Lunch, *The Nationalization of American Politics*, pp. 180-82.

[8] Hugh Heclo, *A Government of Strangers* (Washington, D.C.: Brookings Institution, 1977), p. 79.

[9] See Micheal Pertschuk, *Revolt against Regulation: The Rise and Pause of the Consumer Movement* (Berkeley: University of California Press, 1982).

[10] Ibid., p. 107.

[11] See Joseph A. Pika, "Interest Groups and the White House: Comparing Administrations" (paper presented to the American Political Science Association, Chicago, 1985).

[12] See John Kessel, *Presidential Parties* (Homewood, Ill.: Dorsey, 1984).

[13] Pika, "Interest Groups and the White House," p. 6.

[14] Ann Wexler, cited in ibid., p. 21.

[15] Thomas E. Cronin, *The State of the Presidency*, 2nd ed. (Boston: Little, Brown, 1980), pp. 243-47.

[16] The cooperation that business and trade associations extended to President Reagan was crucial in congressional passage of the 1982 budget. A steering committee consisting of the Amer-

ican Business Conference, the National Association of Home Builders, the National Association of Manufacturers, and other organizations kept the White House briefed on where opposition to this piece of legislation might occur. See Martha Joynt Kumar and Michael B. Grossman, "Political Communications from the White House: The Interest Group Connection," *Presidential Studies Quarterly,* 16 (1986), 92–101.

[17]Cronin, *The State of the Presidency,* p. 245.

CHAPTER SEVEN
JUDICIAL POLITICS:
Groups Turn to the Courts

American courts have always been political institutions, more powerful in this country than their counterparts in other Western democracies are. But over the past twenty-five years, they have moved closer to becoming *explicitly* political.[1] This change has great significance for both individuals and interest groups. Especially after the arrival of Earl Warren as chief justice of the Supreme Court, that body embarked on a period of change and reform virtually unprecedented in its history. The Warren Court inaugurated changes in such sensitive areas as race relations, representation in state and national legislatures, and criminal procedures for police. Reflecting on these changes, one commentator writes,

> The courts have changed their role in American life. American courts, the most powerful in the world—they were that when Tocqueville wrote and when Bryce wrote—and now far more powerful than ever before. . . , through interpretation of the Constitution and the laws, now reach into the lives of the people, against the will of the people, deeper than they ever have in American history.[2]

This chapter is devoted to an examination of the relationships between the federal courts and interest groups. We will look at various group strategies before the federal bench, interest group responses to Supreme Court decisions, the role of interest groups in the selection of judicial personnel, and off-the-bench activities of federal judges. Our goal will be a more accurate and complete understanding of the role of courts in national policy making and of the success or failure some organizations experience in their attempts to influence judicial policy making.

UNIQUE ASPECTS OF THE
FEDERAL COURTS

We first need to stress several elements of the federal judiciary that affect judicial policy making. These factors help condition group lobbying as well as the decision-making process. They also help legitimize judicial decisions and broaden their public acceptability. The first element is judicial *style*. Courts cannot initiate policy, as does Congress or the bureaucracy; only through litigation (the bringing of cases to court) can judicial policy be made. Most cases handled by the courts, incidentally, do *not* involve major policy decisions. The second element is judicial *access*. A group or an individual seeking access to the courts is required to engage a lawyer and meet the special requirements of court "jurisdiction." The parties involved must also have legal standing* in the eyes of the court and be affected by the decision. Third, judicial *procedures* are quite different from the procedures of the other two branches of government. The use of propaganda or public relations techniques, for example, have no place in court. Formal communications are filed according to prescribed procedures and usually pertain to legal arguments and points of law. Fourth, generally speaking, courts limit their decisions to *specific cases*. Whereas the president or Congress may announce or legislate broad policy changes on, say, pollution, economic regulation, or foreign trade, courts address their findings to the case at hand. Finally, judicial process presents the *appearance of objectivity*. Individuals and groups fully expect a member of Congress to think and act in partisan terms, but the black-robed judge must preserve decorum in the court and be a paragon of impartiality. Generally, too, judicial decisions are made not through the kind of bargaining and compromise inherent in lawmaking, but mainly through intensive investigation of the facts and of points of law. This does not preclude, of course, interaction and case discussion among judges themselves.

Therefore, despite liberalization of access to the courts in recent years, interest groups lobby the judiciary in significantly different ways than they do the other branches of government. The kind of direct access to legislators or bureaucrats that is available to groups does not exist in interest group–judiciary relations. Rather, the avenues of influence are more indirect. As David Truman notes, "circuitous lines of access are found in the other branches of government also, but the circuitry is accentuated in the judiciary."[3] Two key factors—the nature of the judicial function and its relative detachment from the usual political pressures—determine the types of strategies available to interest groups seeking to influence judicial policy making. Let us turn now to a number of those strategies.

---

*Rules on legal standing have been liberalized. Between 1968 and 1982, Congress passed a body of legislation allowing individuals and groups greater freedoms in bringing suits.

JUDICIAL STRATEGIES

Litigation

Litigation is a direct approach to influencing the federal judiciary. It involves bringing a series of suits before the courts to gain a policy determination favoring the litigating group. Quite often, litigation is a device for groups lacking access to the legislative or executive branch. These are the groups

> that are highly dependent upon the judiciary process as a means of pursuing their policy interests, usually because they are temporarily, or even permanently, disadvantaged in terms of their abilities to attain successfully their goals in the electoral process, within the elected political institutions or in the bureaucracy. If they are to succeed at all in the pursuit of their goals they are almost compelled to resort to litigation.[4]

The success of litigation as a group strategy is conditioned by a number of resources.[5] First, the amount of money an organization allots to litigation affects its strategy, the kinds of issues it will pursue, and its chances of success. The NAACP Legal Defense Fund's financial resources were crucial to the success of the landmark *Brown* v. *Board of Education of Topeka* case in 1954. Second, if interest groups can cultivate the support of the federal government through litigation or by filing an *amicus curiae* brief (to be discussed shortly), their chances for success are greatly improved. Third, by continually increasing its use of litigation—in other words, through longevity—an organization utilizing test-case strategies enhances its chances for victory. One writer, noting the NAACP's Legal Defense Fund and similar funds of other organizations, argues that "repeat players" accrue certain benefits, such as "advance intelligence" and credibility before the courts. A fourth crucial resource is expert legal staff. A talented staff dedicated to organizational goals allows the organization to keep abreast of potential test cases, to monitor ongoing cases, and to prepare litigation if the organization desires. Finally, establishing liaison or coalitions with like-minded organizations—other environmentalists, labor unions, antiabortionists, or religious fundamentalists, for example—improves a group's chances for court influence.

Today, groups of all political stripes are litigating. It is not unusual, therefore, to find the American Civil Liberties Union (ACLU), the AFL–CIO, the Business Roundtable, and the National Right-to-Life Committee in court. Motives consist of a variety of social and economic concerns—unionization, employment discrimination, pornography, the rights of criminals, and many more.

Litigation is also driven by other forces. Take Congress, for example. A good deal of the legislation of the 1960s and 1970s—voting rights, affirmative action, and environmental laws in particular—required clarification. No law, no matter how detailed, can cover every eventuality during implementation by a public agency. Courts, therefore, become involved in resolving the ambiguities, in deciding what the law "really" means. As we have noted, liberalization of the concept of legal standing encouraged more groups to pursue litigation. Congress has also "passed the buck" to judicial bodies by establishing the Legal Services Corporation. This agency, which primarily serves poor clients, has initiated hundreds of suits in behalf of illegal aliens, to safeguard poor people's right of access to federally funded hospitals, and to clarify residency requirements for welfare payments.

The courts themselves, through their collective decision making, have added to the amount of interest group legislation as well as to the establishment of new groups. Court decisions, remember, are "disturbances" in the classic Truman sense of the term (see Chapter 1). The 1973 case of *Roe* v. *Wade* is a case in point.

In *Roe* v. *Wade* the Supreme Court decided that an abortion is a woman's constitutional right. This decision energized a broad array of pro- and antiabortion organizations, some of which persist to this day. The antiabortion forces consist mainly of such organizations as the Moral Majority, the Christian Voice, the Catholic Church, the National Right-to-Life Committee, and a number of ad hoc Christian fundamentalist organizations at the national, state, and local levels. The prochoice coalition includes such organizations as the American Civil Liberties Union, the National Abortion Rights Action League (NARAL), the National Organization for Women (NOW), and numerous ad hocs at various government levels.

Because of the traditionally conservative attitudes within state governments with respect to abortion and family matters in general, the anti-*Roe* decision, antiabortion forces were able to wage a relatively successful lobbying campaign at the state level. This strong grass-roots campaign resulted in approximately two dozen states passing legislation narrowing the applicability of *Roe* v. *Wade.*

On the other side, prochoice organizations gained encouragement from the *Roe* decision and continued to litigate before the Supreme Court. The Court responded affirmatively and struck down most of the restrictive state laws through a series of rulings in *Connecticut* v. *Menillo* (1975); *Planned Parenthood of Central Mo.* v. *Danforth* (1976); *Belloti* v. *Baird* (1976); *Beal* v. *Doe* (1977); *Colautti* v. *Franklin* (1979); *Belloti* v. *Baird* (1979); *Harris* v. *McRae* (1980); *H. L.* v. *Matheson* (1981); and the *City of Akron* v. *Akron Center for Reproductive Health* (1983). In all of these cases, the Supreme Court consistently upheld the right of a woman to terminate a pregnancy if that was her desire.*

That *Roe* v. *Wade* was brought before the Supreme Court in the first place, along with the landmark cases dealing with reapportionment and school desegregation, led one observer to note that

---

*During its 1988–89 session, the Supreme Court modified this position in *Webster* v. *Reproductive Health Services* allowing some state restrictions.

the Warren and Burger Courts, with prodigious help from the lower courts, have regularly reinterpreted the Constitution and statutes to expand judicial power, but the most significant single change of the past two decades may be that the rules governing access to the court system have been greatly relaxed. More litigants can now bring more cases of all types, including those that have the most profound political implications.[6]

Amicus Curiae Briefs

Amicus curiae (friend of the court) briefs represent a more indirect route to judicial influence. *Amicus* briefs are interest group inputs to court personnel of additional data and arguments relevant to an impending judicial decision. Samuel Krislov notes that

> where the stakes are highest for groups, and where needs on the part of judges for information and for sharing of responsibility through consultation are at their peak, access [for amicus briefs] has appropriately, and almost inevitably, been [at] its greatest . . .[7]

Amicus briefs allow a number of groups to be heard for the record, not just those that are party to the suit. Additionally, these briefs inform the courts on the possible or probable consequences of their decisions for the contending groups. An AFL-CIO brief, a Common Cause brief, or a Jewish Defense League brief, while demonstrating support of or opposition to an impending decision, also argues why the court should decide a certain way. Though less costly and less time-consuming than litigation, the submission of a brief has its limitations. By merely submitting a brief, an interest group has little control over strategy and policy input. Depending, of course, on the circumstances, litigation may be more fruitful in the long run.

Despite such limitations, *amicus* submission, especially before the Supreme Court, has been increasing for some time now. Relatively low before World War II, it has risen consistently since then (Tables 7-1, 7-2, and 7-3).

TABLE 7-1   *Amicus Curiae* Participation in Supreme Court Cases

Years	Percentage with *Amicus* Briefs N = 2016	Total Number of Cases
1928–1940	1.6% (03)	181
1941–1952	18.2 (67)	368
1953–1966	23.8 (149)	626
1970–1980	53.4 (449)	841

Source: Karen O'Conner and Lee Epstein, "Amicus Curiae Participation in U.S. Supreme Court Litigation: An Appraisal of Hakman's 'Folklore,'" *Law and Society Review,* 16:2 (1981–82), pp. 316–17. Tables 7-1 through 7-3 reprinted by permission of the Law and Society Association.

TABLE 7-2   *Amicus Curiae* Participation in Supreme Court Cases, 1970-1980

Case Type	Percentage with *Amicus* Briefs		Percentage without *Amicus* Briefs		Total Number of Cases per Category
	N =		N =		
Unions	87.2%	(75)	12.8%	(11)	86
Sex Discrimination	77.5	(31)	22.5	(9)	40
Race Discrimination	67.7	(42)	32.3	(20)	62
Free Press	66.7	(16)	33.3	(8)	24
Information Act	63.6	(7)	36.4	(4)	11
Church–State	62.9	(22)	37.1	(13)	35
State–Federal Employees	55.0	(11)	45.0	(9)	20
Military	52.9	(9)	47.1	(8)	17
Indigents	52.5	(32)	47.5	(29)	61
Obscenity	51.6	(16)	48.4	(15)	31
Conscientious Objectors	50.0	(5)	50.0	(5)	10
Elections	48.9	(23)	51.1	(24)	47
Free Speech	44.8	(13)	55.2	(16)	29
Criminal	36.8	(120)	63.2	(206)	326
Others	64.0	(27)	36.0	(15)	42
Totals	53.4	(449)	46.6	(392)	841

Source: O'Conner and Epstein, "Amicus Curiae Participation," p. 316.

The high-water mark in *amicus* briefs submitted to the Supreme Court occurred in the *Bakke* case (1978).[8] Allen Bakke, a thirty-four-year-old engineer, was rejected for admission to the University of California at Davis Medical School. Each year, the medical school at Davis had one hundred vacancies available for incoming freshmen. Of the total, sixteen were set aside for minority students—blacks and Hispanics. Bakke, who obtained a higher entrance

TABLE 7-3   *Amicus Curiae* Participation in Supreme Court Cases, 1928-1966 and 1970-1980 (Selected Categories)

Case Type	Percentage of Cases with *Amicus* Briefs, 1928–1966		Percentage of Cases with *Amicus* Briefs, 1970–1980	
	N =		N =	
Unions	51.2%	(41)	87.2%	(86)
Free Press	46.8	(32)	66.7	(24)
Race Discrimination	27.3	(157)	67.7	(62)
Church–State	26.8	(67)	62.9	(35)

Source: O'Conner and Epstein, "Amicus Curiae Participation," p. 317.

score than most of the minority applicants, was denied admission. Charging "reverse discrimination," Bakke appealed to the Supreme Court. That court ruled in Bakke's favor, stating that a quota was "no less offensive when it serves to exclude a racial majority."

Some fifty-seven *amicus* briefs were submitted when Bakke appealed to the United States Supreme Court. Approximately three-fourths of the briefs supported the right of the state of California and the State Board of Regents to establish and maintain a selective admission program for minorities. The following is a sample of the organizations submitting *amicus* briefs:

PRO-BAKKE	PRO-STATE BOARD OF REGENTS
American Federation of Teachers	American Bar Assocation
American Jewish Congress	American Federation of State, County and Municipal Employees
Anti-Defamation League	American Medical Colleges
Chamber of Commerce of the U.S.	Americans for Democratic Action
Fraternal Order of Police	Carnegie Commission on Higher Education
National Medical and Dental Association	NAACP Legel Defense and Education Fund
Polish-American Congress	National Association of Affirmative Action Officers
Sons of Italy	Society of American Law Teachers
Young Americans for Freedom	YMCA

Why would the American Jewish Congress and the Anti-Defamation League have supported Bakke? The answer lies at least in part in the Jewish politics of that time. The reason for the position of these two organizations was the rising disenchantment among American Jews with the application of affirmative action during the 1970s. In the recent past, Jews themselves faced discrimination and quota restrictions in American colleges and universities, especially those in the East. They were also subject to discrimination in areas such as employment and housing. Originally, Jewish organizations supported affirmative action programs as a way of bringing about equal opportunities for disadvantaged minorities. But by the late 1970s, many Jewish organizations viewed affirmative action programs in terms of quotas and racial preferences—policies they have traditionally opposed.

In summary, the Supreme Court has adopted a more liberal position on the submission of *amicus* briefs, and disadvantaged groups have been quick to exploit this opportunity. *Amicus* briefs grant the Supreme Court a broader constituency, and this allows greater "elbow room" for decision making. Further, *amicus* briefs are relatively modest in terms of resource demands when compared with an actual suit or legislative lobbying. But although the submission of a brief reduces group costs, it may also reduce group influence.

By filing a brief, the contesting group enters the process relatively late, when strategies and other policy considerations have already been established by other organizations. Nonetheless, *amicus* briefs are still frequently submitted by today's interest groups.

Judicial Selection

Another indirect route for group influence is judicial selection. Given the importance of the Supreme Court in such areas as voting rights, government regulation, and abortion rights, it is little wonder that interest group activity in the judiciary is most intense in the selection process.

Although there are no constitutional or statutory provisions governing membership on the nation's highest court, a number of factors have traditionally been important:

1. the nominee's legal qualifications
2. partisan identification
3. personal relationships with relevant public officials
4. public policy views
5. various religious, sexual, and geographical considerations

The weight of these has varied over time as well as with the political circumstances at the time of nomination. More recently, ideology has come to replace political relationships and experience as a criterion.

The exercise of affirmative action during the Carter administration led to the appointment of more women and minorities to the lower federal courts. President Carter urged U.S. senators, who usually controlled the appointments, to establish judicial selection panels in their respective states to screen potential candidates. This had the result of depoliticizing the selection process and weakening the role of the party. Nevertheless, most of the appointees were Democrats.

The Reagan administration deemphasized the state selection panels, preferring to rely almost exclusively on ideological criteria for appointment. Potential appointees had to have "correct" positions on issues such as abortion, prayers in public schools, and busing schoolchildren to achieve racial balance. Not surprisingly, the overwhelming majority of Reagan judicial appointees were white, conservative Republicans. A leading authority on judicial appointments proclaimed that "there has been more consistent ideological screening under Reagan"[9] than at any other time in the history of the federal court system.

The controversy over the nomination of former federal judge Robert H. Bork to the Supreme Court illustrates the role of ideology and the involvement of interest groups in the selection process. In the fall of 1987, the Senate Judiciary Committee considered Bork for a vacancy on the high court. A federal judge with strong academic and conservative credentials, Bork has written extensively on the Supreme Court and its role in interpreting the Constitution.[10]

Generally speaking, Bork has been quite critical of the Court's activist role and its decision making, specifically in such areas as personal privacy, voting rights, legislative reapportionment, abortion, and civil rights. He believes that there is virtually no constitutional basis for the majority of the Court's rulings in these areas. The appropriate role for the Court, according to Bork, is that of interpreting the laws, not making them. Judicial self-restraint should be the prevailing philosophy of the Court.

Bork's nomination activated broad coalitions both in support and in opposition:

ORGANIZATIONS SUPPORTING JUDGE BORK

American Conservative Union
American Farm Bureau Federation
Black Americans for Life
Christian Action Council
Coalitions for America
Concerned Women of America
Eagle Forum
Federal Criminal Investigators Association
Focus on the Family
Fraternal Order of Police
International Association of Chiefs of Police
Knights of Columbus

National Association for Evangelicals
National District Attorneys Association
National Family Institute
National Law Enforcement Council
National Right to Life Committee
National Right to Work Committee
National Sheriffs Association
National Troopers Coalition
Society of Former Special Agents of the FBI
Southern Baptist Convention (Public Affairs Committee)

ORGANIZATIONS OPPOSING JUDGE BORK

AFL-CIO
American Civil Liberties Union
Common Cause
Leadership Conference on Civil Rights
NAACP (National Association for the Advancement of Colored People)
National Abortion Rights Action League
National Coalition of Black Lesbians and Gays

National Coalition to Abolish the Death Penalty
National Council of Churches
National Education Association
National Gay and Lesbian Task Force
National Organization for Women
National Women's Political Caucus
People for the American Way
Planned Parenthood Federation of America
Sierra Club

In a number of ways, the controversy over the Bork nomination was unprecedented—the number of pro and con witnesses testifying before the Senate Judiciary Committee (122), the length of Bork's testimony before the committee (four and a half days), supporting testimony by a former president and former chief justice of the Court (Gerald Ford and Warren Burger), and the high level of personal involvement by President Reagan during the confirmation hearings.

Generally, the anti-Bork forces argued that the nominee's conservative philosophy would tip the Court's balance, allowing a rollback in recent gains in the areas of civil rights, abortion-on-demand, and voting rights. Conservative interests wanted Bork confirmed for exactly those reasons—to reverse the perceived moderate-to-liberal drift in Court decisions. Bork was ultimately rejected by the Senate fifty-eight to forty-two, along party lines. Senate Democrats voted virtually en masse against the nomination while the bulk of Senate Republicans voted to confirm.*

As expected, the organizations just listed and their allies lobbied intensely during the Senate hearings. Most senatorial offices experienced substantial increases in letters, phone calls, telegrams, and constituent visits. See pages 150-156 for some examples of conflicting group positions on the Bork nomination.

JUDICIAL DECISIONS AND GROUP RESPONSES

Given the federal court's expanded role in national policy making, what are the prospects for decisional compliance or noncompliance? The Supreme Court, one must remember, has *no* enforcement mechanism of its own. It must rely on others—state and local officials and court personnel, public commissions, federal officials and agencies—to carry out its mandate.

Compliance depends in part on how those affected by a court decision accept that decision. Some federal court decisions have affected a broad range of individuals and groups—admissions officers of public schools, colleges, and universities; labor union officials; local school boards; religious orders and hospitals. A whole range of procedures, informal practices, and behavioral patterns are altered or disturbed in the wake of a court decision.

Our federal system with its inherent decentralization of power contributes to a broad array of responses to judicial decisions. Some individuals may seek to evade the responsibilities assigned to them by the decision. There may be conflicting interpretations of the decision. Or the decision may be seen as ambiguous. Responses in Southern states by state officials, local school boards, and conservative interests to the Supreme Court's 1954 school desegregation decision, though generally hostile, displayed a good deal of variation. The Virginia legislature, for instance, initiated a new body of laws aimed at frustrating compliance. Louisiana invoked its "police power" as a shield against further federal intrusion. The Carolinas perpetuated segregation by adopting a

---

*Only two Democratic senators broke ranks and voted for Bork—David Boren and Ernest Hollings. Both cited his excellent qualifications for the Court vacancy. A number of moderate Republicans—Arlen Spector, Lowell Weicker, John Chafee, and Robert Packwood—resisted intense White House and organized conservative pressures and voted against confirmation.

pupil-placement plan that assigned students to their existing schools. Finally, some states allowed the leasing of public school facilities to private organizations, which then operated the schools on a segregated basis. Most of these activities, however, were eventually overturned by federal circuit courts having responsibility for enforcing the 1954 decision.

Group compliance to the Court's decisions on legislative reapportionment came more quickly. The ruling in *Baker* v. *Carr* (1962) ordered a more

---

October 8, 1987

The Honorable XXXXX XXXXXXXX, XX.
U. S. Senate
Washington, D. C. 20510-xxxx

Dear Senator:

On behalf of the tens of thousands of Right to Work supporters in your state, I urge you to take a stand in favor of freedom of choice by voting to confirm Judge Robert Bork to the United States Supreme Court.

Throughout his career, Judge Bork has proven himself to be an independent thinker with a deep sensitivity to individual rights.

Unfortunately, the union bosses of the AFL-CIO and NEA are demanding a rubber stamp on the High Court for their compulsory unionism agenda. Using forced dues taken from workers as a condition of employment, Big Labor has launched a vicious smear campaign against Judge Bork.

Senator, I want to make it clear to you that a vote against Judge Bork is a vote in favor of compulsory unionism. Right to Work supporters in your state will hold you accountable.

Once again, Senator, I urge you to put the freedom of individual workers above the greedy, narrow self-interests of union bosses by voting to confirm Judge Bork to the United States Supreme Court.

Sincerely,

Reed Larson

RL/wp

WASHINGTON D.C. HEADQUARTERS: 8001 BRADDOCK ROAD, SUITE 500 ●
SPRINGFIELD, VIRGINIA 22160 ● TEL. (703) 321-9820
"Americans must have the right but not be compelled to join labor unions"

Used with permission of the National Right to Work Committee. This letter was sent to all members of the Senate.

EDITORIALS

Advise and Consent

The AFL-CIO opposes the nomination of Judge Robert H. Bork to be an associate justice of the Supreme Court.

The President is intent on perpetuating the "Reagan revolution's" social and political program beyond his term of office by putting the courts in the hands of judges whose first fealty is to that program.

It is the Senate's right and responsibility to stand up to this ideological court packing.

Our review of Judge Bork's academic work and his public career make it plain that he is a man moved not by deference to the democratic process, nor by allegiance to any recognized theory of jurisprudence, but by an overriding commitment to the interests of the wealthy and powerful in our society.

His agenda is the agenda of the right wing.

So far as we have been able to ascertain, he has never shown the least concern for working people, minorities, the poor or for individuals seeking the protection of the law to vindicate their political and civil rights. The causes that have engaged him are those of businessmen, of property owners and of the executive branch of government.

He condemns "liberal judges" who allegedly decide cases out of "partisanship." The decisions he derides include many of the landmarks guaranteeing civil liberties, racial justice and equal treatment under law.

In contrast, we have not found in Judge Bork's writings even a whisper of disapproval of any Supreme Court decision in the last 50 years taking a limited view of individual rights or a broad view of government power, or any suggestion that right-wing judges have ever improperly relied on their personal values in construing statutes or in fashioning constitutional principles.

Aside from seeking to drain the Bill of Rights of most of its force, Judge Bork has concentrated his energies on attempting to liberate big business from most of the limits on corporate power stated in the antitrust laws. In pursuit of this goal, he is an extreme judicial activist, ready and willing to jump all the hurdles put in his way by legislative enactments and dozens of longstanding judicial precedents.

Judge Bork has demonstrated no capacity for statecraft. His place is on the lawyer's side of the bar, openly arguing for the privileged who have been the beneficiaries of his endeavors all along.

For these reasons, the AFL-CIO opposes his nomination to the Supreme Court and urges the Senate to refuse its "advice and consent."

—From an Executive Council statement, Aug. 17, 1987.

Source: *AFL-CIO News,* April 29, 1987, used with permission.

PRIORITY MESSAGE   PRIORITY MESSAGE

TELL YOUR SENATOR TO OPPOSE BORK

As you read this issue of FORUM, the Senate Judiciary Committee is conducting hearings on the nomination of Robert H. Bork to the Supreme Court. A full Senate vote is expected in October.

Robert Bork's record, both in and out of public life, is the record of an ideological extremist. On the bench and in his public statements, he has consistently opposed civil rights. He has said, for example, that the Supreme Court was wrong to uphold the provisions of the 1965 Voting Rights Act that banned literacy tests.

He has attacked the constitutional right to privacy, calling the lead Supreme Court decision enunciating the right "unconstitutional."

He has an extraordinarily narrow view of the First Amendment's protection of freedom of speech. By Bork's standard, the right to advocate civil disobedience is unprotected by the Constitution and censorship of artistic expression is permissible.

His interpretation of the Constitution and the Bill of Rights invites an intolerable mixing of church and state.

The White House is promoting Bork as an advocate of "judicial restraint," but in fact Bork is a judicial activist. He shows deference to legislative intent and judicial precedent only when it suits his ideological predispositions.

Bork's own writings and speeches indicate that he would vote to turn back the clock of progress, retrenching on civil rights gains made in the past four decades, undermining the constitutional right to privacy, and restricting free speech clearly protected from such restrictions in the First Amendment of the Bill of Rights. Bork's nomination poses an intolerable threat to individual liberties promised in the Constitution, won through decades of struggle and defended by landmark Supreme Court decisions. He must be rejected.

Please write your senators and urge them to vote against Bork's nomination. Write to:
Your Senator
U.S. Senate
Washington, DC 20510

Source: *Forum*, Fall 1987, ("The Newspaper of People for the American Way Action Fund").

EAGLE FORUM

August 1987

PHYLLIS SCHLAFLY
PRESIDENT

LEADING THE PRO-FAMILY MOVEMENT SINCE 1972

316 Pennsylvania Ave., S.E., Suite 203, Washington, D.C. 20003 (202) 544-0353

Hqrs. Office: Box 618, Alton, IL 62002 (618) 462-5415

The Bork Nomination

Let me explain why it is so important that you let both your U.S. Senators know at once that you want them to confirm President Reagan's nomination of Judge Robert Bork to the U.S. Supreme Court.

Most of the major issues that the American people are concerned about were caused by Supreme Court decisions: (1) tying the hands of the police while vicious criminals are coddled and turned loose to commit more crimes; (2) requiring forced busing of little children across town, in arrogant disregard of the wishes of their parents (both black and white); (3) inventing a new "right" of any woman to kill her unborn baby for any reason of her choice, resulting in some 20 million such killings since 1973; (4) overturning the convictions of dozens of pornography peddlers, so that porn has grown to an $8 billion business making money out of degrading women and family life; (5) forbidding the mention in public schools of God, the Bible, and the Ten Commandments, while allowing schools to impose on minor children curricula that are anti-religious, anti-moral, anti-family, or anti-patriotic.

All these problems are caused by activist Federal judges. Yet, they enjoy life tenure and are responsible to no one. They can't be fired or defeated for reelection. Fortunately, President Reagan has nominated a man who is qualified, experienced, and NOT a judicial activist. He believes that judges should NOT engage in judicial legislation or policy-making, but should stick to the Constitution. That man is Robert Bork.

Liberal Democrats and some Republicans, with the cooperation of big media, are waging a political attack on Bork. Senator Joseph Biden and Paul Simon should excuse themselves from service on the Judiciary Committee because they have a conflict of interest with their own Presidential campaigns. They are using Bork to posture for media attention to assist their Presidential campaigns.

Write both your Senators at the Senate Office Bldg., Washington, DC 20510, and say "PLEASE CONFIRM ROBERT BORK FOR THE COURT."

American Civil Liberties Union ● 132 West 43rd Street ●
New York, New York 10036
Norman Dorsen, President ● Eleanor Holmes Norton, Chair, National Advisory Council ●
Ira Glasser, Executive Director
Public Information Department: 212/944-9800 (day) ● 212/944-9846 (night line)

PR 23-87

For Release, Monday, August 31, 1987 at 1:30 p.m.
ACLU ANNOUNCES OPPOSITION TO BORK;
URGES SENATE TO REJECT NOMINATION

Washington, D.C.

The American Civil Liberties Union today announced that it would oppose United States Senate confirmation of Supreme Court nominee Robert Bork and would mount a major national campaign to block his appointment.

The decision was made this past weekend at a special meeting in New York of the ACLU's National Board of Directors.

ACLU President Norman Dorsen, who is Stokes Professor of Law at New York University Law School and former law clerk to the late Justice John Marshall Harlan, said at a news conference in Washington today that "it is a mistake to think of Robert Bork as a conservative jurist within the tradition of Justice Harlan, Justice Frankfurter or the recently resigned Justice Lewis Powell."

"Judge Bork is, in fact, more radical than conservative," Dorsen said. "He is certainly well outside of the mainstream of conservative judicial philosophy that governed decisions of justices like Harlan, Frankfurter or Powell. If Robert Bork's views were to prevail, the most critical function of the Supreme Court—the protection of individual rights—would atrophy, and the system of checks and balances that protects such rights would be upset. America would become a different place and many freedoms that ordinary Americans now take for granted would be threatened. It is impossible to examine Judge Bork's record as a whole and conclude otherwise."

Source: Used with permission of American Civil Liberties Union.

EDITORIALS

Have You Contacted Your U.S. Senators About the Confirmation of Judge Bork?

By the time you have finished the next sentence, I trust you will have already written/called/sent a telegram to your two United States Senators supporting the confirmation of Supreme Court nominee Judge Robert Bork.

Let me take just one second to restate an obvious but fundamentally important fact of political life: there is no way you could exaggerate the weight politicians place on personal contacts from their constituencies. After all, it is you and I who will determine whether they change addresses. But in the case of Judge Bork's nomination the importance of your message is even greater. Our federally-endowed—amply so, by the way—pro-abortion opposition is in the process of spending millions of dollars in advertising with just one goal in mind: make Judge Bork out to be some kind of monster. To an extent that campaign of distortion has unquestionably succeeded. How many people were able to watch four and one-half days of Judge Bork's testimony? How many will see a full-page ad in their local paper painting Bork in extremist hues? The results are opinion polls demonstrating that many people who did not hear Judge Bork (or anyone else for that matter, defending him) are skeptical. It is our job as citizens who have followed this nomination carefully to contact our Senators to make two points. First, that Bork is extraordinarily competent, with a richly varied background in the law, and a razor-sharp mind. Second, that they oughtn't to knuckle under to such extremist special interests as NOW, NARAL, and Planned Parenthood. Please, take time now.

As someone who has closely followed the Bork hearings, I can honestly say I thought I had seen it all. Maybe I had, but I never saw it all put together in one place. Senator Alan Simpson of Wyoming, no friend of the right to life movement but a staunch supporter of Judge Bork, observed early on in the confirmation hearings that the way you defeat nominees (and ideas) in Washington is to pin the label extremist on them: you're really in luck if you can successfully intimate that the person is unsympathetic to women and minorities. The fact that there may be no basis for such charges is beside the point. The objective is to cast doubt, at a minimum, assassinate the individual's character, preferably. That is why the attacks on Bork sound so much alike. The anti-Bork forces are trying to drum into people's minds a very simple— and very distorted—message: Bork is "outside the mainstream."

The coalition opposing Bork has played the game well, if dishonorably. They held off opening the hearings for the same reason they delayed the committee vote once testimony had concluded. To rally every organization in America that might conceivably oppose Bork publicly. Again, this is very shrewd. The more they smear Bork, the more skeptical the public grows, the less courage it takes those organizations ambivalent about going public to oppose Bork. Ditto for the petty harassments and manipulation that went on at the hearings. For example, letting the most vituperative critics go on and on until by the time proponents testify, it is too late to get their support for Bork included in the nightly network news.

Some people had predicted that Bork would endure some tough sledding but that he would nevertheless be fairly easily confirmed. They forgot several facts of life. First, from city hall to the halls of Congress, Democrats play hard ball. They really play for keeps. Also, as we have repeatedly demonstrated, Bork is Armageddon for the Abortion Establishment. They will do anything necessary to defeat him. Moreover, as we have seen in prior battles over abortion during the Reagan years, the pro-abortion coalition knows how to delay, distort, and divide. Skilled technicians, they learned their lessons well.

Make no mistake about it, the Bork nomination is going down to the wire. You can rest assured Bork's opponents will leave nothing to chance. As rich as they are, they have so many more cards to play than those who support Bork. We have only one card to play—the willingness of people like you to take the time and effort to demonstrate to your elected officials that those who understand Judge Bork, realize he is an extraordinary jurist. But one card is enough if each and every one of you not only personally contacts his or her senators, but prods friends, family, and social organizations into making their voices heard. Won't you please help?

Source: *National Right to Life News,* October 15, 1987. Used with permission.

democratic division of seats in the Tennessee House, and *Wesberry* v. *Sanders* (1964) applied the same principle to congressional districts. In these and subsequent cases, a Court majority accepted the arguments of urban interests across the nation that urban underrepresentation in state legislatures violated the Constitution.

As the Warren Court handed down cases of this type with increasing frequency, criticism of the courts and the Supreme Court in particular increased among such organizations as the John Birch Society and Americans for Constitutional Action and among intellectuals from the political center to the right. Even so, the Warren Court continued on its assertive, interventionist way. Thus, within the short span of six years, general compliance to the principle of equal representation—"one person, one vote"—was attained.

Through a series of decisions over the past twenty-five years, the Supreme Court has almost unanimously rejected religious exercises in public schools—bible reading, recitation of prayers, or moments of "silence." But many school districts, particularly in the South, have continued religious activities in the classroom. In 1983, as the result of extensive lobbying by religious fundamentalists and political conservatives, the Tennessee legislature passed a bill requiring public schools to begin each day with a moment of "silence." The object of the lobbying coalition was to bring religious "meditation" or "reflection" into the classroom. Presently, a national coalition of the Moral Majority, the Eagle Forum, and other politically conservative organizations are lobbying for a constitutional amendment that would overturn earlier Court decisions banning school prayer. The Reagan White House supported the activities of this coalition, and the president himself declared it is

nonsense [that] we are told our children have no right to pray in school. . . . Sometimes I can't help but feel the First Amendment is being turned on its head.[11]

In March 1984, the Senate voted to reject a proposed constitutional amendment to permit organized, recited prayers in public schools.

These examples of compliance and noncompliance reveal a spectrum of interest group responses to judicial decisions. Organization behavior, it appears, depends upon the perceived effect or threat a decision has for this or that interest group. Our decentralized political system allows groups a good deal of latitude in deciding what course of action is in their best interests.

JUDICIAL LOBBYING: OFF-THE-BENCH ACTIVISM

Certainly a rational argument can be made that people who receive a judicial appointment should remove themselves from the "political thicket." "Politics as usual" does not square with judicial impartiality and rules of procedure. Operating as they do in a political environment, though, many federal judges continue to practice the art of politics, but in a more discreet manner.

Off-the-bench politics persist throughout the federal judiciary, as we will see shortly. Former chief justice Warren Burger maintained an active political profile through frequent speeches before bar associations in addition to articles in national magazines. Justice Burger also lobbied Congress for legislation establishing a new court of appeals and a tenth justice to the high court to handle administrative matters, and for help to reduce the Court's case load. Other justices have spoken out on such issues as crime, civil rights, governmental reform, and the Court's role in society.

As a whole, today's federal justices are more politically involved than ever before and more organized. Shedding traditional inhibitions, federal justices are establishing trade associations, hiring legislative representatives, conducting grass-roots campaigns, and even initiating lawsuits on questions and disputes that arise between themselves and the other branches of government.

The motivations behind these typical pressure group activities are economic as well as social and legal, as one writer notes:

> Often the judges' off-the-bench activities are devoted to ordinary pocket book issues. They regularly press for higher salaries for themselves and better life insurance and annuities for their survivors. They have also begun to seek exemptions for Social Security taxes and more favorable treatment on federal income taxes.[12]

A *Los Angeles Times* study noted instances in which the judiciary has attempted to influence social- and criminal-law policies:

> —On several occasions over the last five years, the judges have registered their opposition in Congress to bills requiring that the proceedings of the federal courts of Puerto Rico be conducted in Spanish. (The bills have never passed, and as a result, federal law still requires that the court proceedings generally be conducted in English.) The judges complained that this legislation would have "an adverse effect upon the administration of justice" and noted that it would make it more difficult for judges from the U.S. mainland to help reduce the court backlog in Puerto Rico.

> —The federal judiciary has also worked quietly for the defeat of proposals, supported both by civil libertarians and by the American Bar Assn., to permit individuals to bring lawyers with them when they are called to testify before a grand jury. The judges told Congress these proposals would "turn a grand jury proceeding into an adversary one."

—The judges have formally asked Congress to amend the federal bail laws to make it clear that judges may consider "the safety of any other person or the community" in deciding whether or under what conditions to release a defendant on bail. They have also sought revisions of federal law to make it clear that persons found not guilty by reason of insanity may afterward be confined to mental hospitals in civil proceedings.

—In 1978, a group of federal judges objected to the new Ethics in Government Act, the federal law that requires members of the judiciary and all other high-ranking federal officials to file financial disclosure statements listing their assets, liabilities and outside income.

—The judges went to court, arguing that the law violated their constitutional rights to privacy. Their lawsuit delayed the release of the judges' disclosure statements for nearly two years. During that time, the public had access to the financial statements of members of Congress, Cabinet members and all other high-ranking officials except federal judges. Finally, in 1981, the lawsuit was thrown out and the judges' disclosure forms were released.[13]

In 1981, a group of federal judges established the Federal Judges Association (FJA) with the aim of lobbying Congress for better salaries, retirement benefits, and other economic amenities. The FJA currently has approximately 300 members (out of a total of almost 700 federal judges), who contribute $200 annually in dues. U.S. District Judge Spencer M. Williams (San Francisco district) heads the organization and regards it as both a lobbying and a grass-roots organization.

We know which judges are friendly with which congressmen. When there's a problem, the judges can contact the congressmen in their district and talk to them. . . . The judges are merely exercising their rights. Every other group in this country has an organization to talk to Congress.[14]

The association maintains a "federal coordinator" for national legislation relating to the courts.

The FJA is modeled after the California Judges Association, a group of state judges that has had considerable success with the state legislature over the past decade. Supplementing the association more informally are a number of private organizations of judges, operating within their own state or region. Association members are convinced that their organization serves its constituency better than did the older Judicial Conference. Critics of the conference point out that it has not won much sympathy or support from either Congress or the executive branch. U.S. District Judge Laughlin E. Waters (Los Angeles district) emphasizes the need for a change:

The Chief Justice [of the Supreme Court] is our nominal spokesman, but his time is too fragmented. There's no way he can cover 500 members of Congress. I don't think the official structure representing the courts "the Judicial Conference" is at all adequate. It just can't move fast enough on these things.[15]

This heightened judicial activism has touched off a debate among lawyers and scholars. Some believe judicial activism harms the judicial image of impartiality and jeopardizes the judiciary's special status within society. Geoffrey C. Hazard of the Yale Law School offers the following opinion:

> The position of being an authority figure and being a supplicant are inconsistent. I think judges are compromising their role.[16]

Monroe H. Freedman of Hofstra University's law school concurs, characterizing off-the-bench activism as "unseemly and inappropriate." Numerous public interest lawyers agree. Nonetheless, there is strong support within the FJA for continued activism, at least until a number of relevant economic and legal issues are resolved.

SUMMARY

Americans have always been litigious. Alexis de Tocqueville observed more than 150 years ago that every political question in the young nation was ultimately a judicial one. They are important agents for challenging established policies and reinforcing new ones. As a result, today's judiciary is determining what kinds of apprenticeship programs private industry may offer its minority workers, what level of living conditions states must maintain in their prison systems, when an abortion may be performed, or what constitutes a "religious exercise" in public schools.

It should not be surprising, then, that interest groups are developing and refining strategies for influencing judicial decisions. Lobbying the judiciary, though, requires strategies somewhat different from those employed before the other two branches of government.

Once they hand down a decision, the courts must look to others for its implementation. This may mean relatively quick compliance or a series of organizational strategies designed to limit the effects of the decision.

Finally, just because federal judges and justices don the "black robe of impartiality," they do not necessarily become political eunuchs. Like members of the other two branches of government, judges will organize and lobby for those benefits they deem important to their careers.

NOTES

[1]On the federal judiciary and its political role, see Lawrence Baum, *The Supreme Court,* 2nd ed. (Washington, D.C.: Congressional Quarterly Press, 1985); Thomas P. Jahnige and Sheldon Goldman, *The Federal Courts as a Political System,* 3rd ed. (New York: Harper & Row, Pub., 1985); C. A. Johnson and B. C. Canon, *Judicial Policies: Implementation and Impact* (Washington, D.C.: Congressional Quarterly Press, 1984); and Bob Woodward and Scott Armstrong, *The Brethren: Inside the Supreme Court* (New York: Simon & Schuster, 1979).

[2]Nathan Glazer, "The Imperial Judiciary," PUBLIC INTEREST, Fall 1985, p. 106.

[3]David Truman, *The Governmental Process* (New York: Knopf, 1971), p. 489.

[4]Richard C. Cortner, "Strategies and Tactics of Litigants in Constitutional Cases," *Journal of Public Law,* 17 (1968), p. 287.

[5]See Lee Epstein, *Conservatives in Court* (Knoxville: University of Tennessee Press, 1985). Court victories by liberal organizations during the 1960s and 1970s generated a surge of litigation by conservative associations in response.

[6]William M. Lunch, *The Nationalization of American Politics* (Berkeley: University of California Press, 1987), p. 140.

[7]Samuel Krislov, "The Amicus Curiae Brief: From Friendship to Advocacy," *Yale Law Review,* 72 (1963), 703-4.

[8]For a detailed analysis of the *Bakke* case, see Allan P. Sindler, *Bakke, DeFunis and Minority Admissions: The Quest for Equal Opportunity* (New York: Longman, 1978).

[9]Sheldon Goldman, quoted in Ronald Brownstein, "Labor Wants Respect," *National Journal,* November 2, 1985, p. 2340.

[10]See Judge Bork's address to the American Enterprise Institute, *Tradition and Morality in Constitutional Law* (Washington, D.C.: American Enterprise Institute, 1984).

[11]Quoted in the *Wall Street Journal,* March 5, 1984, p. 1.

[12]*Los Angeles Times,* November 4-5, 1983, "U.S. Judges Now Court Legislators," by Jim Mann, p. 1. Copyright © 1983 *Los Angeles Times.* Reprinted by permission.

[13]Ibid.

[14]Ibid.

[15]Ibid.

[16]*Los Angeles Times,* November 7, 1983, "Fraud: Deciding When to Prosecute," by Leslie W. Werner, p. 18. Copyright © 1983 *Los Angeles Times.* Reprinted by permission.

CHAPTER EIGHT
PUBLIC INTEREST GROUPS:
Peoples' Lobbies

The 1960s and 1970s may well be remembered because of a number of significant political developments—the proliferation and strengthening of congressional subcommittees, the modification of the congressional seniority system, the establishment and intrusion into the electoral process of PACs, and the continued erosion of political party influence. One other important occurrence was the emergence of a new kind of political interest group, the "public" interest group. This organization is unique from its predecessors because of its involvement in "causes," or the pursuit of ideas.

Given their twenty-five years of existence, their recognized political influence, and the continuing controversy surrounding their activities, public interest groups deserve our close examination. In this chapter we will analyze these organizations first by noting some of their common characteristics and then by considering several public interest groups individually.

ORGANIZATIONS FOR
THE MASSES

In Chapter 2 we briefly noted the key role Ralph Nader played in the rise of the public interest movement. His example activated thousands of individuals across the nation to challenge large corporations, corrupt politicians, and various special interest representatives. He was the first political entrepreneur to fully appreciate the institutional lessons of the civil rights movement: Washington's officialdom could be effectively lobbied by activist organizations through effective use of the mass media, especially television. Nader, incidentally, became a television celebrity in his own right and a much sought after public speaker.[1] His message basically is that the American people are being short-changed by big business because public regulatory policies are generally ineffective. Nader calls for numerous citizen organizations that can effectively counter the extensive political influence of large, private firms.

Today, over two thousand public interest groups are championing various causes or ideas "in the public interest." Some of their recent successes include nonsmoking restrictions on domestic airline flights, automobile recalls due to defective parts or operation, nutrition labels on cereal boxes and soup cans, and flame-resistant sleepware for infants.

The composition of public interest groups distinguishes them from the more traditional interest groups. Many have small staffs (six to twenty) with no regular memberships per se. These groups are usually pitted against organizations with more money and manpower. Consequently, most public interest organizations rely not only on their powers of persuasion but also on their savvy for creating sympathetic constituencies and mobilizing public opinion. Demonstrations, sit-ins, and other media events allow these organizations to reach broader audiences as well as tapping new sources of money. Whereas in the Washington of the 1940s and 1950s demonstrations were a sure sign of weakness, now they indicate public support and political clout.* Publicity enhances an organization's respectability and its access to influential policy makers.

One other distinguishing characteristic of public interest groups is their emphasis on subject-matter expertise as opposed to propaganda. Public interest organizations develop their public positions or ideas through extensive investigation and research. They rely heavily on statistics and computer-generated data compiled by expert staffs. A good deal of the data is aimed at increasingly knowledgeable public officials, but the general public is targeted, too. Its support can be crucial in political battles.

With this in mind, let us look more closely at several public interest groups—Common Cause, the Natural Resources Defense Council, the CATO Institute, and Citizens for Tax Justice. These organizations are quite representative of the public interest groups currently active in national politics. We will discuss these four groups in the context of their political orientations and their involvement in the political process.

COMMON CAUSE:
A CITIZENS' LOBBY

One of the best-known and most visible public interest organizations today is Common Cause. Established in 1970, it represents a unique departure from

---

*For example, by organizing "Earth Day" on April 20, 1970, and holding thousands of rallies and demonstrations nationwide in behalf of cleaning up the nation's environment, environmental groups contributed significantly to enactment of legislation in this area over the next couple of years.

traditional interest group establishment and activism. The organization is the brain child of its founder, political entrepreneur John Gardner. As a former high official in Lyndon Johnson's administration, Gardner became increasingly concerned with the perceived privileged access of narrow, private interests to many public institutions, and with the apparent lack of significant countervailing centers of power. He became increasingly convinced of the need for a "citizens' lobby" to speak for a set of "public goods" that were inadequately represented by the existing lobby system.

Gardner's perceptions and the solutions he offers are a throwback to muckraking Progressives. He believes, as did those earlier reformers, that the political system, though somewhat flawed, is basically sound. But it is constantly being undermined by narrow, selfish interests. Common Cause is a vehicle for revitalizing the political role of the individual citizen and for increasing public participation in the political process. Gardner writes,

> Our nation's founders did not leave us a completed task . . . they left us a beginning. It is our obligation to define and dislodge the modern obstacles to the fulfillment of our founding principles. Because, as visionary as they were, our founders could not have foreseen *how dominant special interests would become* through the accumulation of wealth and power, and through skillful secret dealings with government officials.

> In the face of this, people like you and me—people who reject apathy and cynicism—must join forces to fight for open and accountable government. How? By joining Common Cause and supporting our efforts to create direct and immediate changes in the political system.[2]

Common Cause was established as a Washington-based lobbying organization (Figure 8-1). Emerging at the end of the black civil rights movement and in the early phases of the environmental movement, Common Cause profited from the examples and experiences of both. It combines traditional American idealism with pragmatic and scientific skill. Wishing to avoid the mistakes of the earlier Progressives, Common Cause indulges in bargaining and political compromise with former opponents, establishes and works for attainable political goals, and avoids pushing for complex or "scientific" political solutions in the name of "economy and efficiency."

A number of factors contributed to the founding of Common Cause. There was, for example, growing public discontent with public institutions and their policies. Public officials came to be generally perceived as inefficient, self-serving, and basically indifferent to the needs of the broader elements of society. The political influence of private corporations and labor unions was also viewed cynically by large segments of the public. It was not surprising, therefore, that many people responded positively to initial mail solicitations from Common Cause (see Box 8-1 and Figure 8-2).

Additionally, growing public anger with a long and bloody Asian war, the revelations of Watergate, and the perceived inability of state and local authorities to deal adequately with urban violence produced a political backlash. The

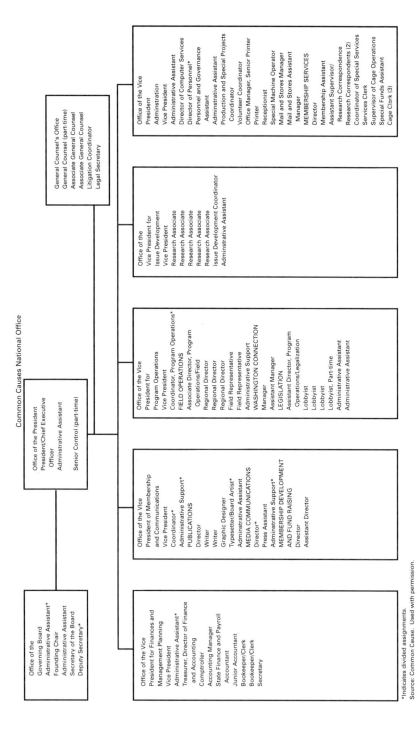

FIGURE 8-1 Common Cause National Office

Source: Common Cause. Used with permission.

BOX 8-1   *THE FIRST AD FOR COMMON CAUSE*

"Everybody's organized but the people."

John Gardner asks you to join him in forming a mighty "Citizen's Lobby," concerned not with the advancement of special interests but with the well-being of the nation.

I know that many of you share my concern over what is happening to our country.

That is why I am coming to you; to ask you to join me in forming a new, independent, non-partisan organization that could be an effective force in rebuilding America.

It will be known as Common Cause.

It will not be a third party, but a third force in American life, deriving its strength from a common desire to solve the nation's problems and revitalize its institutions of government.

Wherever you touch the public process in this country today, almost without exception, you will find a failure of performance.

The air we breathe is foul. The water we drink is impure. Our public schools are in crisis. Our courts cry out for reform. Race conflict is deepening. Unemployment is rising. The housing shortage has driven rents through the roof.

The things that government is supposed to do, it is not doing. The things it is not supposed to do—interfering with the lives and liberties of its citizens—it is doing.

How we can work together in Common Cause.

The first thing Common Cause will do is to assist you to speak and act in behalf of legislation designed to solve the nation's problems. We will keep you up to date on crucial issues before Congress. We will suggest when and where to bring pressure to bear.

Common Cause is an outgrowth of the Urban Coalition Action Council. Operating under a governing board of extraordinary diversity (mayors, leaders from business, labor, minority and religious groups), the Action Council proved to be astonishingly effective in influencing major legislation. So we know from first hand experience that citizen action can get results.

I shall not attempt to list here all the issues with which Common Cause will be concerned.

We believe there is great urgency in ending the Vietnam war now. We believe there must be a major reordering of national priorities, and that the Government cannot go on spending $200,000,000 a day for "national defense". We believe the problems of poverty and race must be among our first concerns. We will call for new solutions in housing, employment, education, health, consumer protection, environment, family planning, law enforcement and the administration of justice.

We intend to take the phrase "Common Cause" seriously. The things that unite us as a people are more important than the things that divide us. No particular interest group can prosper for long if the nation is disintegrating. Every group must have an overriding interest in the well being of the whole society.

One of our aims will be to revitalize politics and

government. The need is great. State governments are mostly feeble. City government is archaic. The Congress of the United States is in grave need of overhaul. The parties are virtually useless as instruments of the popular will. We can no longer accept such obsolescence.

Most parts of the system have grown so rigid that they cannot respond to impending disaster. They are so ill-designed for contemporary purposes that they waste taxpayers' money, mangle good programs and frustrate every good man who enters the system.

The solutions are not mysterious. Any capable city councilman, state legislator, party official, or Member of Congress could tell you highly practical steps that might be taken tomorrow to make the system more responsive. But there has been no active, powerful, hard hitting constituency to fight for such steps. We can provide that kind of constituency.

Skeptics say "But you can't really change such things." Nonsense. The Congress of the United

After spending the last 5 years in Washington as Secretary of Health, Education & Welfare and as Chairman of the Urban Coalition, John Gardner is convinced that only an aroused and organized citizenry can revitalize "The System" and change the nation's disastrous course.

States has changed in dramatic ways since its founding. Why should we assume it has lost the capacity to change further?

The political parties have changed even more dramatically since the birth of the Republic. They can change again.

Many of you share my anger at institutions and individuals that have behaved irresponsibly. But, if we're going to focus our anger, a good place to begin is with ourselves.

We have not behaved like a great people.

We are not being the people we set out to be. We have not lived by the values we profess to honor. And we will never get back on course until we take some tough, realistic steps to revitalize our institutions. We had better get on with it.

In recent years we have seen too much complacency, narrow self-interest, meanness of mind and spirit, irrational hatred and fear. But as I travel around the country, I see something else. I see great remaining strength in this nation. I see deeper reserves of devotion and community concern than are being tapped by present leadership. I see many, many Americans who would like to help rebuild this nation but don't know where to begin.

I invite you to be among the first to join us in Common Cause.

We cannot and should not depend on big contributors. The money to support our work must come from the members themselves.

We therefore ask you to enclose a check for $15 with your membership application.

If you can afford more, send an additional contribution.

With a large and active membership, we can begin to remake America.

—*John W. Gardner*

Common Cause

Source: Common Cause. Used with permission.

August 1970. The first ad for Common Cause. Six months later, the new organization had 100,000 members.

FIGURE 8-2   Membership of Common Cause

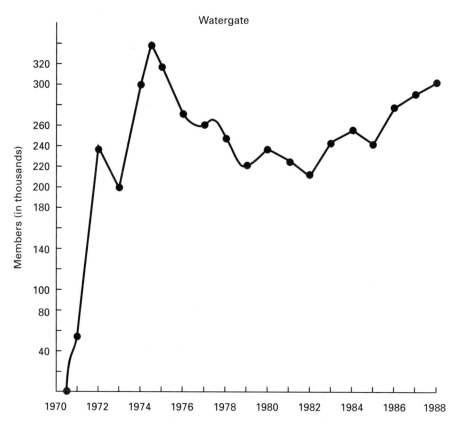

Membership characteristics: college-educated; median income of $40,000; middle-aged (early fifties); professional background; moderately liberal; predominantly Protestant.

early 1970s was the optimum time for the establishment of a national citizens' lobby.

Finally, modern technology also facilitated the establishment of Common Cause. Computer-based direct mailings have made membership solicitation and fund raising relatively easy. Computers can break down membership lists by state and congressional district for speedy and direct activation of members. Supplementing the mails are cheaper long-distance telephone networks. Wide Area Telephone Systems (WATS) lines give organizations the means for quick communication with local branches. Periodic telephone "alerts" on pending legislation, issue development, or executive appointments can bring pressure on members of Congress. Regular mailings are frequently too slow to deal with the political exigencies of the moment.

Common Cause utilizes traditional lobbying activities—testimony before congressional and administrative committees, research and publication, and grass-roots pressures—but with unique emphases. Lobbying is frequently directed toward legislators' *district* (or local) offices, not at Washington. Rather than becoming bogged down with or dismissed by Washington staffers as "just another lobby," Common Cause concentrates on the district level—the idea being that the local office is more of a service agency. The novelty of lobbying at this level is that pressure on the member of Congress is accomplished through the close and continuing contacts maintained between the district and Washington offices.

Another unique aspect of Common Cause lobbying is its congressional testimony. The organization seeks out experts in various fields who are *not* members, but who are concerned about a particular issue and are favorably disposed to Common Cause and its views. Securing such people eliminates the need for time-consuming staff briefings and research. In the opinion of its officers, in both its testimony and its public image Common Cause does not seek to substitute conviction or dogma for background research and public knowledge. It seeks to counter opposition objections on merit, and on the facts involved, rather than through rhetoric or abstract theories.

During the floor stage of legislation, Common Cause works with sympathetic members of Congress to persuade the "undecided."[3] It is better strategy to allow these intermediaries to persuade wavering legislators than becoming directly involved. Depending on the circumstances, Common Cause seeks to generate a moderate amount of constituent pressure on a vacillating representative or senator. Too much pressure can be counterproductive. While the legislation is on the floor, local units of Common Cause will write the legislator urging him or her to support the organization's position.

Common Cause frequently participates in lobbying coalitions. In the area of environmental policy, for example, Common Cause consistently follows the lead of the Sierra Club, the Wilderness Society, or Friends of the Earth on issues such as strip mining, nuclear plant construction, or offshore drilling. However, in the area of governmental reforms, Common Cause is the acknowledged leader. It will direct coalitional efforts when Congress is considering, say, redistricting legislation, public financing of congressional races, or internal, procedural reforms. The League of Women Voters periodically becomes involved in these issues, but strategies will be mainly in the hands of Common Cause.

An important aspect of a coalitional lobbying is respecting the "turf" of other coalitional members. An organization will be the acknowledged leader on a certain issue before Congress because it has experience, expertise, and access. For example, the Sierra Club will take the lead when legislation is pending before Congress on the establishment of new park lands or wilderness areas. A distinct division of labor prevails. Common Cause would *not* lobby independently in the area of environmental policy.

The advent of the Reagan administration in 1980 marked some shifts in the political strategies of Common Cause. One obvious change was the appearance of a new publication, *Common Cause Magazine.* It is a glossy trade magazine published in bright colors and featuring article-length investigative reporting on such topics as PACs, lobbyists and lobbying, state politics, bureaucratic inefficiencies, and proposals for governmental reforms. The magazine's purpose is to inform and periodically alert members on relevant issues.

In 1981 and 1982, Common Cause sought to enhance its lobbying capabilities by establishing a number of "action teams" in those congressional districts where legislators were uncommitted on issues of organizational concern.[4] An action team involves a dozen or so Common Cause members who lobby their representative in a personal, continual, and informed manner. The national staff provides background, update memos, and other pertinent briefing materials necessary for lobbying the representative and briefing the local media on the issues at hand. The main objective is to let the member of Congress know action team members personally, not just abstractly. A second goal is to inform the public official that his or her activities are being closely monitored by Common Cause.

Some of the initial Reagan administration policies offered a series of challenges to Common Cause and its allies. Campaigning on the theme of "getting government off the back of the American people," Reagan had called for the elimination of the Legal Services Commission (which provides legal services to the poor), changes in voting rights legislation, modifications in the powers of the Federal Election Commission, the eventual abolishment of the recently established departments of Energy and Education, and opposition to public financing of congressional campaigns.

For Common Cause and its allies, most of these policy positions represented a challenge to the hard-won victories gained through interest group activism in the 1960s and 1970s. Philosophically, the Reagan administration's positions were anathema to the majority of the public interest constituency. As a result, Common Cause launched a broad lobbying effort to blunt administration policy initiatives. Membership was expanded significantly through mass-mail solicitations stressing that the country was being moved in the wrong direction.

Campaign finance reform, for example, remains one of the prime political objectives of Common Cause. Its lobbying efforts on this issue are both direct and indirect—congressional committee testimony, staff briefings by Common Cause personnel, information exchanges with other public interest groups, and information dissemination to local media in selected congressional districts. This last tactic is quite important, according to one student of Common Cause:

> The great majority of Senate and House members employ a full-time press aide, who follows the local press. . . . Thus, favorable mentions of Common Cause-sponsored reforms in the local press are likely to be known to members . . . and be regarded as significant. If a congressman votes against a reform that some local newspapers like, the member of Congress may be criticized in the local press, which is something to be avoided. A congressman who is undecided on a bill often can assume that he will be criticized by the local Common Cause

unit if he does not vote for the measure. Adding the criticism to criticism by hometown newspapers may be enough to sway his vote.[5]

Common Cause is fighting the battle of campaign reform virtually alone. Given the prevailing deregulatory climate in Washington, additional public regulations do not appear to be attractive to other reform-minded groups. In fact, Common Cause's consistently hard line generates periodic congressional backlash, as represented by the following remarks from Senator Steven Symms of Idaho:

> Common Cause supports many liberal causes and is noted for its self-righteous complaints about the amount of money business and political action [groups] spend trying to influence legislation.[6]

Having failed to generate congressional action on campaign reform, Common Cause resorted to increased litigation. For example, it brought suit against the Committee to Re-Elect the President to force it to disclose donations it solicited in order to reelect Richard Nixon. This suit played a role in discrediting a system of financing presidential elections in which a person or organization could give unlimited amounts of money to a presidential candidate. The suit also led to enactment of the 1974 Federal Election Campaign Act. Common Cause was also a party to a suit brought by James Buckley, Eugene McCarthy, and the Civil Liberties Union in the mid-1970s testing the constitutionality of this act. More recently, Common Cause turned its guns on political action committees (recall the organization's "Declaration of War on PACs" in Chapter 4). In March 1985 the U.S. Supreme Court rejected the position of Common Cause that existing legislation limited PAC contributions in presidential campaigns to $1000.

Finally, Common Cause is seeking through its publications to alert the public to the ever-increasing amounts of private interest money in congressional campaigns. *Common Cause Magazine* constantly updates the amount of PAC money made available to members of Congress and who the big contributors are. To gain a wider audience, the organization also disseminates these data to like-minded organizations—the League of Women Voters, Public Citizen, and the AFL-CIO's Committee on Political Education. By publicizing these increasing donations, Common Cause wants to trigger public demands that Congress pass legislation limiting the amounts of money in congressional races. The Common Cause position on this issue is expressed by John Gardner:

> Our system is being corrupted and compromised by the power of money to dictate political outcomes. The capacity or willingness of government to find solutions to any of the problems that plague us—inflation, inequitable taxes, unemployment, housing, urban chaos, dirty air and water—is complicated by the commanding power of monied interests to define the problem and set limits to public action.[7]

Today Common Cause is one of the most established and successful public interest groups on the national political scene. It has activated thousands of middle-class liberals and professionals interested in governmental reform. Numerous congressional and executive branch meetings that were closed to the public twenty-five years ago are open now. The privileged groups of the 1950s and 1960s compete for influence on a more equal basis with a new generation of lobbies.

THE NATURAL RESOURCES DEFENSE COUNCIL

The Natural Resources Defense Council (NRDC) represents another dimension in the universe of public interest groups. The NRDC was established in 1970 as the result of a series of meetings between Yale Law School students and a group of experienced lawyers participating in the Scenic Hudson Preservation Conference. (At this time, the environmental movement was in full bloom.) The conference was called to rally public opposition to and develop strategy against further electrical generation projects on the Hudson River. A grant from the Ford Foundation helped to bring these two groups together.

Today, these are the Wall Street lawyers of the environmental movement. Whenever an environmental cause needs first-class representation or policy analysis, those involved usually turn to the NRDC. The organization's scientific and legal expertise has put it at the center of the major environmental debates of the 1970s and 1980s.

An organization with seventy thousand members and an expert staff of 125 lawyers, resource experts, consultants, and others, the NRDC has pioneered the lawsuit as a strategy for protecting the nation's environment (Box 8-2). Initially, the council began to institute lawsuits against public agencies not in compliance with newly adopted environmental laws. It quickly gained the reputation of a highly professional, aggressive advocate for implementation of clean air and clean water legislation as well as for the basic provisions of the National Environmental Policy Act.

Council operations expanded considerably in the 1980s to include more environmental research and greater emphasis on citizen education (Figure 8-3). In 1986, the NRDC entered into an unprecedented agreement with the Soviet Academy of Science to establish monitoring stations near nuclear weapons test sites in both countries. The council is also responsible for congressional approval of legislation calling upon both the United States and the Soviet Union to jointly assess the environmental consequences of a nuclear war.

Like its political strategies, the council's issues concerns have expanded in recent years (Figure 8-4). Initially concerned with energy consumption and land conservation, the organization is now deeply committed to issues such as

BOX 8-2   *NRDC LAWSUITS*

"Citizen Suits" Become a Popular Weapon In the Fight Against Industrial Polluters

BY BARRY MEIER
Staff Reporter of The Wall Street Journal

A new mobile laboratory tests for chemical pollutants in Connecticut soil, courtesy of General Electric Co. Olin Corp. is underwriting environmental-law enforcement in Louisiana. Bethlehem Steel Corp. is helping to clean up Chesapeake Bay.

This corporate largess wasn't volunteered. The contributions stem from "citizen suits," an increasingly common type of environmental lawsuit in which activists sue polluters on their own behalf and then help to decide how any settlement funds will be spent. Over the past four years, an estimated 600 citizen suits have been filed against scores of companies by individuals and such environmentalist groups as the Natural Resources Defense Council and the Sierra Club.

Not surprisingly, the suits have ignited controversy. Some corporate officials argue that many of the actions are frivolous. Others charge that the suits are being used to coerce contributions for pet projects.

Despite such contentions, the number of citizen suits is expected to continue rising, along with the stakes involved. Congress recently approved amendments to the Clean Water Act—the federal statute under which most of the suits are filed—that increase daily fines for each violation to $25,000 from $10,000. And a new round of citizen actions is anticipated. "Three years from now I expect to have a couple hundred of these cases going," says James Thornton, a lawyer with the New York-based NRDC, which has brought more than 100 citizen suits.

Targeting the Companies

Citizen suits began in the 1970s as a result of provisions in federal environmental legislation. Typically, they were directed against the federal and state governments, with the aim of compelling them to enforce the laws. In the early 1980s, the focus of the suits started to shift toward the polluters themselves.

Nearly all U.S. environmental laws empower citizens to sue companies for pollution and recover legal fees in addition to damage or settlement awards if successful. But most citizen suits are brought under the Clean Water Act because it requires companies to file public reports listing pollutant discharges into public sewerage systems, says Katharine H. Robinson, a lawyer with the New Haven-based Connecticut Fund for the Environment.

Records showing discharges above permitted limits serve as a legal admission of guilt, lawyers say. If the government hasn't moved to penalize the offender, private action can be taken. "It's like shooting fish in a barrel, and we've shot a lot of fish," says Mr. Thornton, who contends the suits are a way for citizens to plug a gap in federal and state enforcement.

Moreover, lawyers note that because of the size of the fines involved, nearly all citizen suits are quickly settled. "These are no-risk lawsuits," says John Proctor, a

Washington-based attorney who has defended companies in citizen actions. "It's like going to the bank."

Some of the settlements have been substantial. For example, Bethlehem Steel's participation in the Chesapeake Bay cleanup arose from a recent $1.5 million settlement of a citizen suit brought against it by the NRDC and the Chesapeake Bay Foundation, another activist group. As part of the plan, the company also agreed to pay an additional $500,000 to cover the groups' legal expenses.

While companies can pay settlement awards to the federal or state governments, most agree to give the money to an environmental group or specific project. "If you make a contribution, it's tax-deductible," says John Frawley, a top environmental official with Hercules Inc., a Wilmington, Del.-based chemical producer that is currently negotiating settlement of a citizen suit brought against it by the New Jersey Public Interest Research Group.

A 'Fitting Resolution'

Activists such as Mr. Thornton contend that environmental donations are a fitting way to resolve citizen actions. They also note that companies are free to donate settlement proceeds to government agencies, but don't because they would lose tax benefits.

Not all citizen suits end in acrimony. Two years ago, in the face of a citizen suit brought by the NRDC, officials at a Texas Instruments Inc. metal-finishing plant in Attleboro, Mass., convinced the activists that the facility's violations weren't serious. The NRDC dropped the action, and plant officials in turn funded a one-day seminar on pollution controls for several hundred local metal-finishing companies, says Gilbert Perkins, a group vice president for materials and controls.

Some groups are also opting for conditional settlements. Furman Foods Inc., a Northumberland, Pa.-based food company, recently agreed to pay $25,000 to settle a citizen suit brought by the Atlantic States Legal Foundation, says Mr. Proctor, who represented the company. But under the plan, no money changes hands if Furman doesn't violate its permit in the future.

"Management likes it because they've gotten the message," Mr. Proctor says, "and they tell employees they'd better comply or it's going to cost them money."

Source: "'Citizen Suits' Become a Popular Weapon in the Fight Against Industrial Polluters" by Barry Meier *The Wall Street Journal,* April 17, 1987, p. 17. Reprinted by permission of *The Wall Street Journal.* Copyright © 1987 Dow Jones & Company, Inc. All rights reserved worldwide.

public health and international pollution. In the former area, council litigation has attained important policy changes:

1983   NRDC lawsuit forces the National Steel Company to comply with air pollution control laws and pay $2.5 million in back penalties.

1984   NRDC lawsuit compels oil refineries to tighten pollution-control standards and reduce toxic discharges by 400,000 pounds per year.

1985   NRDC wins "citizen suit" that finds Bethlehem Steel Corporation liable for 350 pollution violations at Chesapeake Bay plant.

1986   NRDC stops Norfolk Southern Corporation from building a coal transfer operation in Delaware Bay.

FIGURE 8-3   NRDC Stratagies

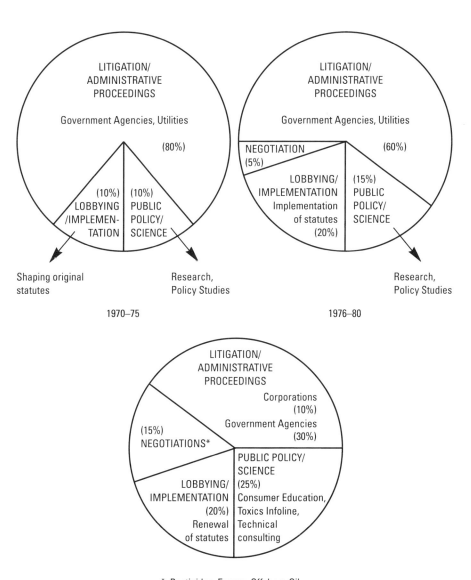

1970–75

1976–80

* Pesticides, Energy, Offshore Oil,
   Nuclear Verification

1981–87

Source: Natural Resources Defense Council. Used with permission.

FIGURE 8-4   Issues of Concern to the NRDC

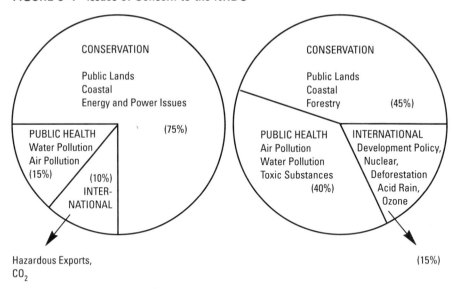

CONSERVATION

Public Lands
Coastal
Energy and Power Issues

(75%)

PUBLIC HEALTH
Water Pollution
Air Pollution
(15%)

(10%)
INTER-
NATIONAL

Hazardous Exports,
CO₂

1970–75

CONSERVATION

Public Lands
Coastal
Forestry   (45%)

PUBLIC HEALTH
Air Pollution
Water Pollution
Toxic Substances
(40%)

INTERNATIONAL
Development Policy,
Nuclear,
Deforestation
Acid Rain,
Ozone

(15%)

1976–80

(25%)
CONSERVATION
Public Lands
Coastal
Northwest Energy
Forestry/Agriculture

(25%)
INTERNATIONAL
Development Policy
Global Warming
Acid Rain, Arms Control
Tropical Deforestation

PUBLIC HEALTH
(50%)
Air Pollution
Water Pollution
Toxic Substances
Pesticides
Antibiotics

1981–87

Source: Natural Resources Defense Council. Used with permission.

The council's lobbying activities are an important supplement to its litigation. Staff personnel are actively involved in the formation and progress of nearly every environmental bill coming before Congress today. This involvement usually takes the form of technical and legal analysis of specific proposals, expert testimony before various House and Senate committees and subcommittees, and informal consultations with key legislators. Frequently, lobbying is coordinated with other public interest groups as well as interests of the more traditional type.*

Various executive agencies, especially the Environmental Protection Agency (EPA), have been objects of council pressure. The NRDC is concerned with the implementation as well as the enforcement of the Clean Air Act, the Clean Water Act, and the Toxic Substances Control Act. It closely monitors and occasionally challenges EPA decisions under these laws that might allow major polluters to expand or modernize plants in localities already experiencing high levels of water and air contamination. It has even conducted private enforcement, detecting violations the EPA has failed to tackle and suing dozens of companies to "clean up their act." In the process, it has gained greater public credibility.

The council combines scientific research with public education as a way of stimulating greater public awareness of and participation in environmental matters. A flood of articles, technical reports, pamphlets, books, press releases, and studies on the nation's environment emanate from the council. These publications cover a multitude of environmental problems, such as air and water pollution, management of public lands and national forests, nuclear proliferation, energy conservation, and international pesticide use. Additionally, the council sponsors periodic educational workshops for citizens and groups desiring a more active role in protecting the environment. Each year, staff attorneys conduct the New York University Law School Clinic, instructing law students in the intricacies of environmental law. The NRDC also offers a limited number of internships to graduate and postgraduate students annually. These positions offer the appointee unique training and experience in environmental law and public policy making.

The council also publishes the *Amicus Journal.* Its primary purpose in doing so is to provide the general public with thought and opinion on environmental affairs, especially those having national and international significance. To this end, the *Journal* publishes a diverse range of articles and opinions.**

The council's annual budget is about $12 million and is increasing yearly (Figure 8-5). About 45 percent of the budget comes from membership dues, 40 percent comes in the form of grants from private foundations such as the

*In 1980 and again in 1981, the NRDC joined 146 other organizations to lobby against budget cuts sought by the Reagan administration in social services and environmental programs.

**In 1983, the editorial staff of the *Journal* received the George Polk Award for Special Interest Publications, for excellence in environmental reporting.

FIGURE 8-5   NRDC Budget (in millions of dollars)

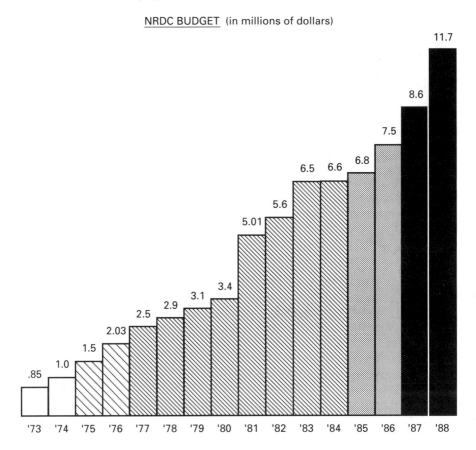

NRDC BUDGET (in millions of dollars)

Source: Natural Resources Defense Council. Used with permission.

Rockefeller, Columbia, New York Community, and Public Welfare foundations. The remainder is from contracts and fees accruing from the council's
educational activities.

What is the general perception of the NRDC as a public interest group? A
1985 poll of EPA and congressional staffers by the *Environmental Forum,*
a magazine of environmental issues, rated the NRDC the most positively in
a survey of some twenty environmental groups (Table 8-1). On the criterion
of ability to articulate policy preferences and effectively lobby for them, the
ratings of these organizations are virtually the same. A former EPA official
characterizes the political role of the NRDC this way:

> It's the most effective of the environmental groups. They are able to file good
> lawsuits, they're effective on Capitol Hill, they can use the media, and they're
> good at reacting with the agency (EPA).[8]

TABLE 8-1   Organizations

Organization	Average Score
Natural Resources Defense Council	4.21
National Wildlife Federation	3.67
Conservation Foundation	3.46
Environmental Defense Fund	3.41
National Audubon Society	3.32
League of Women Voters	3.23
Sierra Club	3.06
National Clean Air Coalition	2.81
Environmental Policy Institute/Center	2.66
Friends of the Earth	2.55
The Nature Conservancy	2.48
League of Conservation Voters	2.38
Clean Water Action Project	2.28
Izaak Walton League	2.19
Duck Unlimited	2.14
Resources for the Future	2.14
Defenders of Wildlife	1.95
Environmental Action	1.94
World Wildlife Fund	1.71
Solar Lobby	1.35
	(Median 2.65)

Key: 5 = most positive rating
      1 = least positive rating

Source: *Environmental Forum Magazine, Washington's Lobbying Groups: How They Rate* (Washington, D.C.: Environmental Law Institute, April 1985), p. 13. This report is based on survey data from approximately 100 questionnaires sent to Washington's perceived environmental policy makers. Used with permission.

THE CATO INSTITUTE

An important component of today's public interest movement are the "think tanks," cause- or idea-based groups that are technologically sophisticated and independent of (sometimes even hostile to) the political system. These organizations initially emerged on the political left because of the organizing capabilities of Ralph Nader, but numerous think tanks representing conservative interests have since appeared.

Typical of conservative think tanks is the CATO Institute, a Washington-based research foundation established in 1977. It is named for the *Cato Letters,* libertarian pamphlets disseminated in the American colonies prior to the Revolutionary War. Institute founders claim the *Letters* played an important role in laying the philosophical foundation for the American Revolution.

Because of its conservative orientation, the institute deplores and opposes the "bewildering array of governmental programs aimed at combatting hunger, poverty, unemployment and other social problems." Not only do these programs fail to alleviate problems, according to the Institute, they waste billions of taxpayers' dollars. In addition, the national government has become so pervasive that it is stifling individual liberties and interfering with the proper functioning of a free economy. What is badly needed is a renaissance of our "original" ideas on personal freedom, peace, and humanity. If this rebirth could be accomplished, the nation would be better able to deal with the critical issues it faces daily.

Most of the institute's activities are in public policy research. It has over twelve hundred sponsors and between five and six thousand subscribers to its publications. These publications are designed to stimulate public policy debate and assist the layman in choosing the best alternatives. Approximately thirty books a year are published on a broad range of subjects—agriculture, energy use, judicial philosophy, privatization of the oil and gas industry, U.S. involvement in NATO, and so on. Numerous monographs and several journals are also available to subscribers and interested public officials. Most of these publications come from various staff members (twenty-five) and from approximately sixty college and university professors throughout the country holding adjunct positions with the institute.

Every year CATO sponsors four or five conferences on major public policy issues—taxation, the environment, property rights, etc. The institute also sponsors a monthly "Policy Forum" on Capitol Hill. Participating in these seminars are thirty to forty government policy analysts, congressional staffers, and White House personnel. The purposes of the Capitol Hill conferences, of course, are to publicize CATO's positions on important issues and to maintain its linkages to important policy makers. The institute does very little lobbying, preferring instead to present testimony to Congress, but only when it is asked to do so.

CATO's annual budget is about $2.5 million. Its primary sources are as follows: foundation grants (70 percent), individual grants (10 percent), sales of publications (15 percent), and sponsors (5 percent).[9] In a relatively short period, the CATO Institute has established itself as one of the country's authoritative centers for conservative political thought and has become well known by the general public.

CITIZENS FOR TAX JUSTICE

When a public interest group of modest means takes on a rich and powerful adversary, it must compensate by attracting new constituencies and finding ways of promoting its cause. Citizens for Tax Justice (CTJ) did just that in helping to reform the federal income tax code in 1986.

CTJ was founded in reaction to California's passage of Proposition 13 (1978), which drastically cut that state's property taxes and with them a number of public services. A prime purpose of the organization is to give ordinary citizens a greater voice in the formulation of tax laws at all levels of government. It is especially concerned with the level of taxation borne by low- and middle-income families across the nation. CTJ takes the position that there must be some correlation between one's income and the amount of taxes one pays.

The group's role in tax reform began in 1984 when its director, Robert McIntyre, a Nader-trained lawyer, and his staff of seven began compiling the annual reports of the nation's largest corporations over the period 1981–85. These reports were obtained from the files of the Securities and Exchange Commission. For several months, the staff extracted tax data from these reports as well as the amount of annual corporate profits.

During the summer of 1986, CTJ published its findings in a report entitled *130 Reason Why We Need Tax Reform.* The report states that

> out of 250 corporations surveyed in this report, 130—or more than half of the total—were able to pay absolutely nothing in federal income taxes, or receive outright tax rebates, in at least one of the five years from 1981 to 1985. . . . These 130 companies, ranging from Aetna Life & Casualty to Xerox, earned $72.9 billion in pre-tax domestic profits in the years they did not pay federal income taxes. But instead of paying $33.5 billion in income taxes, as the 46 per cent statutory rate purports to require, they received $6.1 billion in tax *rebates.*[10]

To maximize the effect of its findings, CTJ made them available to the mass media. Almost overnight, newspapers across the country began running features about "corporate freeloaders" such as AT&T, Boeing, General Mills, Texaco, and du Pont.* The thoroughness and accuracy of the report left little room for the listed companies to charge bias or claim harassment. They had only themselves to blame, since the report was based on *their* figures, not those of CTJ. These news stories produced citizen outrage that cut across ideological lines, along with demands for tax reforms.

The timing of the report was also strategic. Its release came at the same time the House and Senate tax-writing committees were in conference considering changes in the federal income tax code. Numerous copies of the CTJ report found their way into committee hands. Some of the labor unions that helped fund the report began grass-roots campaigns for tax reform. Members of the American Federation of State, County and Municipal Employees deluged members of the conference committee with pennies to help defray the federal deficit. Their message was that the pennies weren't much, but they were more than 130 big corporations were paying! The Communication Workers

---

*Editors at the *New York Times* liked the information about defense contractors so much they ran it twice, by two different reporters.

of America targeted the conferees in a letter-writing campaign that strongly denounced the 130 businesses for not paying their fair share of income taxes. Helping to garner conservative support for tax reform were a number of firms that were paying high taxes, such as Whirlpool, Ralston-Purina, Raytheon, McGraw-Hill, and Bristol-Myers. They too complained about their competitors' "freeloading."

Though not completely satisfied with the tax reform bill that Congress passed in 1986, a subsequent CTJ publication noted that

> tax reform is working. It isn't working perfectly. There are some hitches. There are some problems. . . . But tax reform represents a giant step in the direction of fairness: the number of corporate tax avoiders has been greatly reduced, most of the worst offenders of the past decade have begun to pay their fair share.[11]

CTJ is now scrutinizing corporate loopholes in state tax codes. Next on the list are billionaires who use real estate deals to duck or reduce their taxes.

Though CTJ cannot be given sole credit for recent tax reforms, it did play an important role in garnering additional support for the eventual reforms that were made. As just noted, both liberal and conservative organizations based their demands for tax reform on CTJ data. Because of this and other accomplishments, the *Washington Monthly* in 1988 rated CTJ as one of the best public interest groups in the country.[12]

SUMMARY

Probably the most important political development of the 1970s and 1980s (and for the immediate future as well) was the emergence and political involvement of public interest groups. Established and led by skillful entrepreneurs such as Ralph Nader and John Gardner, these groups have influenced the nature and performance of our national government. Their major weapons of influence are expertise, a crucial element when a group is testifying before legislative and bureaucratic institutions; publicity, which provides linkages to both public officials and new constituencies in addition to establishing organizational credibility; and litigation, an alternative channel of access when the other two branches of government are not responsive.

Today there are hundreds of public interest groups, or people's lobbies, from the far right to the far left. This new generation of political groups is less interested in the "bread and butter" issues of earlier pluralist battles. Public interest groups, in contrast, mobilize in behalf of social movements, such as the women's movement and the antiwar movement, or in support of certain causes, such as "prochoice," a "nuclear freeze," or a "balanced budget." Just what degree of influence these latter-day interest groups will have on policy making is hard to predict. But they are now an established part of the Washington scene and undoubtedly will remain so well into the 1990s.

NOTES

¹See David Broder, *Changing of the Guard* (New York: Simon & Schuster, 1980).

²From an early Common Cause mailing, "Common Cause: Modern Americans Fighting for Principles as Old as the Republic"; cited in Andrew McFarland, *Common Cause: Lobbying in the Public Interest* (Chatham, N.J.: Chatham House, 1984), p. 40.

³McFarland, *Common Cause,* p. 130.

⁴Ibid., pp. 136–37.

⁵Ibid., p. 127. Common Cause is also making a major effort to bring about badly needed state reforms—eliminating incestuous relationships between state regulatory agencies and interests under their jurisdiction, conflict-of-interest relationships among public figures, and more citizen participation on various state boards and commissions.

⁶Quoted in the Congressional Quarterly *Weekly Report,* August 27, 1983, p. 1732.

⁷John Gardner, *In Common Cause* (New York: W. W. Norton & Co., Inc., 1972), p. 56.

⁸Quoted in *The Wall Street Journal,* January 13, 1986, p. 50.

⁹Foundation for Public Affairs, *Public Interest Profiles* (Washington, D.C., 1987), p. K19.

¹⁰Robert S. McIntyre and Jeff Spinner, *130 Reasons Why We Need Tax Reform* (Washington, D.C.: Citizens for Tax Justice, 1986), p. 2.

¹¹Robert S. McIntyre, J. M. Crystal, and David C. Wilhelm, *The Corporate Tax Comeback: Corporate Income Taxes after Tax Reform* (Washington, D.C.: Citizens for Tax Justice, 1988), p. 2.

¹²"The Best and Worst of Public Interest Groups," Rita McWilliams, *Washington Monthly,* March 1988, pp. 19–27.

CHAPTER NINE
WHERE ARE WE HEADED?

A major theme of this book is that our national politics are predominantly group-based; as a result, political power and influence are fragmented. The older concept of power, according to which iron triangles, consisting of a few national party officials, senior congressmen, and high-level bureaucrats and a handful of interest groups called most of the shots, is less relevant now. Generational changes such as rising income, higher educational attainment, and the mass media have contributed to changes in the political status quo. A range of newcomers are now active participants, and their activities are changing forever our political processes and institutions. In order for us to chart our political future, we need to know where we are. Therefore, in this chapter we will examine our changing political system in the context of group interaction and then turn to political systems and changes that will likely determine the nature and direction of interest group politics in the years immediately ahead.

GREATER INSTITUTIONAL OPENNESS AND ACCESSIBILITY

Members of Congress, legislative staffs, agency bureaucrats, judges, and other public officials are targets of conflicting interest group pressures. An ever-widening array of associations of state and local officials, middle-class reformers, tax-cutting associations, and other groups are now part of the Washington scene. In addition, latter-day entrepreneurs in the mold of a Nader, a

Gardner, or a Schlafly have greater opportunities through current technologies to press their claims than interest group representatives had a generation ago.

Recent changes in Congress, for example, make that body more amenable to interest group appeals. For the most part, today's congressional elections are much more candidate-centered: the individual runs his or her own campaign with little party involvement. As a result, House and Senate incumbents are relatively free to campaign on and stress those issues that will enhance their careers.

In addition, there is the continuing decentralization of power within Congress. Large increases in staff size, the modification of the seniority system, and the proliferation of subcommittees are the chief factors in this trend. Subcommittees especially have contributed to the establishment of issue networks, in which affected interests interact not only with legislative and administrative personnel but also with various policy analysts, public interest lawyers, and journalists. As a result, legislative policy making is more chaotic now, but more opportunities exist for group inputs. The older, more controlled legislative process of norms and folkways has been significantly modified.[1]

The recent increases in the size and scope of the national bureaucracy have stimulated interest groups to maintain their preoccupation with its various components, particularly in terms of appointments and policy influence. With respect to the latter, newer agencies such as the EPA, the Occupational Safety and Health Administration (OSHA), and the Consumer Product Safety Commission (CPSC), are objects of intense pressures. These and similar agencies are often called upon to interpret and administer broadly written laws due to a lack of congressional consensus on agency jurisdiction or administrative responsibilities. Decisions made and actions taken by these agencies are frequently challenged by clientele groups and their allies. Litigation is a common response by these groups because of precedents set during the implementation of environmental, public health, and civil rights laws.

The federal courts are yet another channel of broadening group access. Recent years have witnessed an easing of restrictions on one's legal standing to sue. The concept of what a lawsuit is has also expanded, and the courts are quite willing to entertain more cases of a political nature.

Naturally, these developments have contributed to the expansion of judicial power and influence. Congress occasionally passes ambiguous or vague legislation, and federal jurists then have opportunities to decide what the new legislation means. Initially, public interest groups turned to the courts for policy clarification more than their predecessors did. But now interest groups of every political persuasion and makeup are litigating today. The Supreme Court has been an important catalyst. Since the Warren Court, judicial activism has been the dominant theme. Though the Rehnquist Court may choose to apply judicial power differently from its predecessors, no significant shift is perceptible at this writing. In any case, both liberal and conservative interests will continue to litigate before the high court given its willingness to entertain political cases.

IS THE PARTY OVER?

Though this book has diagnosed political parties as suffering from atrophy, it is much too soon to write their epitaph.[2] Granted, fewer voters today identify with a major party and still fewer vote a straight party ticket. Generational changes such as increasing educational levels, greater affluence, and increased exposure to television have helped make voting more volatile and less partisan.

Another important factor in the weakening of parties is the political resourcefulness of so many interest groups. Since the 1970s, many interest groups have been adopting techniques of influence traditionally used by political parties. A number of labor unions and business associations, for instance, began involving themselves in voter education and mobilization. Later on, such activities as voter registration, get-out-the-vote drives, and dissemination of incumbent voting records were added. As a result, there has been a gradual blurring of the distinctions between party politics and those involving interest groups.

The skill of interest groups in employing "party" strategies is an indication of their growing strength and public acceptability at a time when public support for the major parties continues to decline. The intermingling of party and interest group functions will continue, however. Many Washington-based interest groups have expanded their electoral activities in addition to establishing political action committees. There is little evidence to show that this trend will be reversed in the near future.

Political parties, though, may be going through a transitional phase, organizationally and functionally. The last decade of the twentieth century may very well see the emergence of a "new" national party system. We may, in fact, see evidence of this already in both major parties.

The insurgency and infighting among Democrats at the 1968 and 1972 national conventions are a case in point. While the 1968 convention nominated Vice-President Hubert Humphrey less than enthusiastically, it also established the McGovern-Fraser Commission on delegate selection and the O'Hara Commission on rules and procedures. In 1972, a challenge to the rules established by these commissions led to the unseating of a number of the "old guard" and the seating of more women, minorities, and young delegates. A series of court challenges to these changes were ultimately rejected by the Supreme Court. As a result, each Democratic convention is free to determine its own rules on delegate selection.

Suffering the ignominy of Watergate and the resulting loss of additional seats in Congress, the Republican National Committee (RNC) is leading the push for organizational changes. A good number of changes, both technological and procedural, are already in place. For example, the RNC has a computerized donor list that is constantly updated. It can therefore almost instantaneously tap contributors across the country that are most likely to contribute when asked. The RNC also offers a range of technical advice to both incumbents and first-time challengers to incumbent Democrats—polling, political advertising, and campaign strategies. From time to time, too, the committee conducts seminars and conferences on issue development, public-speaking techniques, and relationships with the press. A media division within the national committee makes available tapes, news programs for targeted districts, and ads that emphasize the accomplishments of the Republican party. Last, the RNC serves as a go-between for Republican candidates and the PACs that are most likely to contribute to them.

On the basis of these party developments, a "new" national party system oriented toward issues rather than traditional interests may be in the offing. Certainly the recent influx into the party system of more independent-minded candidates along with middle-class campaign workers and volunteers augurs change. Rejecting the usual party rewards of jobs or government contracts, the latter individuals are more issue- or idea-oriented—"prochoice," "proenvironment," "cut taxes," and the like. Issues or ideas are increasingly important in the minds of many of today's voters.

If these party changes continue in the direction they are taking, what are the consequences? First, besides becoming more issue-oriented, the major parties will be less partisan in their appeals. Many of the "old guard" of both parties will undoubtedly be replaced by middle-class activists on both the political left and right. And, even though some state and local party organizations will continue in their traditional ways, the "new" national party leadership, through the use of inducements like those just noted—money, campaign advice, information exchange, and so on—could gradually assume greater authority. But at this stage, this is highly speculative.

What would be the consequences of a centralized, idea-based party for interest groups? One source perceives the following scenario:

> Journalists, academics, publicists and intellectuals of all types gain when politics is thought to be largely about slogans and symbols. When politics revolves around the well-chosen phrase, sparkling rejoinder, and the airtight argument, those with a great deal at stake will hire lawyers, researchers and thinkers to defend themselves.[3]

Additionally, "good government" organizations, public interest groups, and publicity-wise entrepreneurs of liberal and conservative persuasion stand to improve their political leverage. Interest group testimony before various public bodies will be more academic and professional in both content and presentation. Public decision making in this type of system will be driven more by expertise than by partisan considerations.

Political parties, like our other political institutions, are in transition. One cannot accurately predict what the results will be. But, given what has already been noted, there is a good deal of evidence that both parties are adapting to the new political environment. Predictions of their imminent demise or displacement must therefore be viewed with a good deal of skepticism.

DEREGULATION: A REORDERING OF PUBLIC AND INTEREST GROUP RELATIONSHIPS

A new trend in national policy making with consequences for interest group relationships over the next decade is governmental *deregulation.* Presently, national economic regulatory authority is undergoing a transformation that is freeing a number of existing economic systems—airlines, railroads, trucking, savings and loan institutions, and cable television—from government regulation.[4] Governmental regulatory policies initiated in the early 1930s and 1940s, conferred numerous economic benefits and favors on certain industries. The airline and trucking industries, for instance, gained certain competitive advantages over time that resulted in increased profits. These industries adjusted their planning and operations in ways that allowed them to benefit from public regulatory policies. These policies (to be discussed shortly) sheltered these and other industries from the usual competitive groups and forces of a free and open market system.

Generally speaking, there are two kinds of public regulations, economic and social. *Economic regulation* (more traditional) refers to those laws and regulations under which private businesses may operate with respect to prices, rate or return, and entry or exit. *Social regulation* (relatively new) refers to those laws and regulations concerned with the welfare of workers, consumers, and the public. In the discussion that follows, emphasis will be on the former rather than on the latter, since deregulation is occurring more extensively in the former. What has deregulation meant, for instance, for affected interests in the airline industry?

Airline Deregulation

We will briefly note the nature of early governmental regulation of the airlines and then consider how some relationships within the airline industry have been altered by deregulation.

In 1938, Congress established the Civil Aeronautics Board (CAB), ostensibly to regulate the fledgling airline industry with respect to air carrier routes, passenger fares, and freight rates. But, as time went by CAB policies led to the cartelization of the industry rather than to an intended free-market economy. CAB policies consistently and systematically limited the processing of applications of new companies seeking to enter the market. At the same time, the board remained relatively indifferent to increasing consumer complaints about ticket prices and quality of service. In effect, the CAB had become a "captured" agency. The regulator and the regulated developed an almost incestuous relationship to the virtual exclusion of airline passenger interests.*

The movement for airline deregulation caught fire in early 1975 when President Gerald Ford received a report detailing the problems of government regulation and those of the airlines in particular. As a result of the report, President Ford placed deregulation high on his political agenda. Over the following months, a series of newspaper and magazine articles appeared generally critical of CAB policies. These in turn led to studies, conferences, and public discussion of the airline industry. But because of strong industry pressure, deregulation legislation made little headway in Congress.[5]

The succeeding Carter administration was committed to airline deregulation as part of its plan to reduce governmental intervention in the private sector. With both the president and key congressional leaders on the same side, deregulation had solid governmental backing. Supporters of deregulation were quite diverse when compared with its opponents:

FOR DEREGULATION	AGAINST DEREGULATION
American Conservative Union	Airline Pilots Association
Americans for Democratic Action	Most major air carriers: American
Common Cause	Braniff, Continental, Delta, Pan
National Taxpayers Union	American, TWA
United Airlines	Unions representing flight attendants and baggage handlers

Congress passed the Air Transportation Deregulation Act in October 1978, and President Carter immediately appointed Alfred Kahn as CAB chairman to initiate deregulation procedures as specified in the law. Chairman Kahn articulated the need for this kind of legislation:

> Whenever the government intervenes in the economy in one way or another . . . it typically confers benefits on some groups of people and, directly or indirectly, burdens on others. In doing so, it necessarily creates vested private interests in a continuation of [a] particular activity.[6]

How has deregulation altered interest group relationships within the airline industry over the past decade? In answering this question, we will frame our discussion in the context of the nature of airline competition today, management–labor relationships, and governmental supervision.

---

*The major beneficiaries of CAB regulatory policies were the bulk of the *major carriers,* such as American, Braniff, Delta, Eastern, Northwest, and TWA; *airline employees,* who attained relatively high salaries and fringe benefits for themselves through their unions; *small cities* such as Tulsa, Little Rock, and Joplin, which were receiving subsidized air service; and *airport operators* holding long-term leases with the major air carriers.

Airline deregulation is transforming the industry from a highly structured, government-controlled business to a more market-oriented, highly competitive one. New airlines have emerged and prospered while others, such as Braniff* and Frontier, have largely disappeared. At the same time, Texas Air has acquired Western Airlines, US Air has taken over PSA, American Airlines now owns Air Cal, and Northwest Airlines has absorbed Republic. A large number of small commuter airlines have emerged to serve people in those cities where major air carriers have significantly cut back or abandoned their routes. Deregulation is thus producing greater entrepreneurial volatility within the industry.

Deregulation is also significantly altering labor–management relationships within the industry. Under regulation, salaries were quite high, with mechanics averaging about $30,000 per year and pilots slightly over $100,000 per year. The major unionized airlines were paying between 33 and 37 percent of their operating budgets in salaries.[7] The CAB allowed the airlines to pass on these high labor costs to consumers, which is not the case today. (The CAB was phased out in December 1984.) With deregulation, newer and nonunion airlines hired pilots, flight attendants, baggage handlers, and other personnel at much lower salaries. As a result, salaries were only 19 to 27 percent of the operating budgets of newer airlines.

With economic survival on the line, a series of mergers and consolidations took place in the 1980s. The surviving airlines developed a much tougher stance in bargaining with its employees. As a result, hundreds of airline employees lost their jobs or were forced to take significant pay cuts and reductions in fringe benefits in order keep their jobs. Additionally, alterations were made in work rules that required longer hours and the size of flight crews were reduced on certain aircraft. In early 1989, the owner of Eastern Airlines threatened to declare bankruptcy if further employee concessions were not granted. Thus, the relationship between the two sides is more confrontational now than what is was a decade ago.

Finally, deregulation has produced a significantly different relationship between the airline industry and government authorities. The Federal Aviation Agency (FAA) is now a major voice in airline supervision. In this position, the FAA is much more consumer-oriented and regulatory in its policies than the old CAB was. For the first time, air carrier management is responsible for flight scheduling, air congestion at major airports, and meeting maintenance agreements for all fleet aircraft. The FAA is more aggressive in monitoring airline compliance in these and related areas.

Due to the recent increase in air crashes and other operational problems, the FAA is implementing more stringent requirements that include more frequent and thorough aircraft inspections and additional flight crew training.[8] The agency has also temporarily grounded aging aircraft showing undue fuselage

*Braniff has reemerged but is operating on a limited scale.

stress or minor deterioration. It is also pressuring airlines to install additional safety equipment, especially that warning of possible midair collisions.

The older, cozier relationships airlines had with the CAB no longer exist.[9] A number of airlines have disappeared, and others have merged in order to survive. This volatility certainly was not a characteristic of the earlier regulatory period. Labor–management relationships are more confrontational now, given the increased competition within the industry and the reluctance of Congress to intercede in behalf of this or that airline. Finally, the Reagan administration came into office opposed to any new regulations in general and to any provisions favoring labor in the marketplace. Thus, transition from a regulated system to a deregulated one has been turbulent and will continue to be. As of now, there appears to be some sentiment in the Congress for a return to a limited amount of regulation.

Just what deregulation will mean in other sectors of the economy is not clear. Lack of cooperation and understanding between the White House and Congress as to how far deregulation is to proceed has slowed the movement. The Reagan administration left office with a more flexible structure that seeks to balance governmental protection with market efficiency. But true deregulation will require further examination of laws that built the federal regulatory agencies. Whether dismantling these agencies and canceling their statutory authority is the way to go is debatable.

POLITICAL INTEREST GROUPS: MORE OF THE SAME

We have already noted that interest group politics are different both qualitatively and quantitatively from what they were twenty-five years ago. Interest group politics have changed in at least three different ways. First, during the late 1960s and early 1970s, interests on the left organized and became influential—environmentalists, consumers, feminists. In a way, these were the politics of equality. These groups and their allies simply were not a part of the pressure group system of 1950s and early 1960s. But, by profiting from both the successes and failures of earlier interest-related organizations, they and various entrepreneurs showed themselves to be quite adept at exploiting the available technologies of television, mass mailings, and computer-oriented fund raising. As a result of the political activities of these and allied organizations, a good deal of legislation exists today in fields of environmental, consumer, and affirmative action law.

As a result of these victories by these liberal organizations, the political right organized. Conservative think tanks, political interest groups, and public law firms sprang up to challenge many of these newly passed laws in federal courts. And, through their use of technology, conservative organizations have successfully linked up and activated "true believers" across the nation on behalf of causes that generate a good deal of passion and emotion—abortion, gun control, prayers in public schools, a balanced budget amendment, and so on. Though not always successful in their pursuits, conservatives have nevertheless succeeded in having programs such as welfare and revenue sharing reduced or phased out altogether. Ideologically oriented interest groups will continue to play an important role in our national politics in the years ahead.

Second, the emergence of public interest groups has permanently changed the character of group politics. Individuals like Ralph Nader and Richard Viguerie (a political conservative) burst on the scene about a quarter century ago to run circles around older and larger interest groups. These two entrepreneurs have amply demonstrated that blending expertise with effective use of modern technology generates publicity, which in turn attracts supporters and money. The speed and memory of computers make fund raising relatively easy and economical. Computer lists can also be cross-tabulated and culled for appeals to a certain type of donor or to a large audience of millions. Utilization of this technique has allowed these and other entrepreneurs to activate millions of middle-class Americans in support of their cause or ideas. The emergence of public interest groups has led to the politization of a large segment of Americans who were nonparticipants in the older post–World War II interest group system.

Finally, traditional interest groups took a political beating during the late 1960s and early 1970s. The temporary decline of business, organized labor, and various professionals, despite relatively greater resources, was indeed painful. As a result, many private firms, business associations, taxpayers organizations, and local organizations either began expanding their existing Washington facilities or hired an established lobbying firm. Not only were these older organizations seeking new defenses against their political adversaries, but many of them found government becoming more and more obtrusive: there were more laws and governmental regulations.

Against this background, Congress inadvertently came to the rescue. Passage of the 1974 campaign reform law, as we have seen, led to the proliferation of hundreds of PACs. Traditional interests were quick to seize this opportunity to build linkages, through contributions, to key legislators. Today, many of the longer-established interest groups are the biggest contributors to members of Congress through PACs—the National Association of Realtors, the American Medical Association, the United Auto Workers of America, the National Association of Home Builders, and so on. But PAC formation represents just one response to the changed political environment. Increased lobbying, grass-roots pressure, information dissemination, and campaign contributions are components of today's political arsenal. Various trade, business, and labor organizations are demonstrating a good deal of adaptability in coping with Washington's changing political environment.

GROUP THEORY REVISITED:
A REAPPRAISAL

What about the future? Initially, it was James Madison who perceived numerous "factions" contending for political influence within the new nation. His response to this situation, woven into the fabric of the Constitution, was to establish an elaborate system of checks and balances, making it virtually impossible for any one set of interests to become dominant.

From Madison's time onward, these factions—later designated "interest" groups—came to be perceived essentially as materially oriented—business, labor, and agriculture. Recalling the position of twentieth-century writers such as Arthur Bentley, David Truman, and Earl Latham, these organizations were and are the "basic stuff" of politics. All politics revolve around the formation and activities of interest groups.

Ted Lowi, E. E. Schattschneider, and Mancur Olson, on the other hand, deplore the activities and perceived influence of organized interests. Their collective presence in our political system is disruptive and injurious to our democratic processes and institutions. Interest groups decentralize political power, thereby weakening the ability of the national government to address serious problems. The interest group system serves only the wealthy and large private corporations. Materially oriented groups have been the most successful in gaining benefits for themselves under the prevailing system.

While granting that a good deal of recent policy making—civil rights, consumerism, occupational safety—have been strongly influenced by economically oriented interest groups, Samuel Huntington[10] and William Lunch[11] theorize that ideology has also played a role apart from interests. Huntington, for example, argues that American politics undergoes periods of passion (or reform) that reflect our idealized social and political beliefs. He notes that the coming of age of public interest groups on both the political left and right is further proof of this heightening political ideology. The fact, too, that Washington is becoming a city of think tanks, public law firms and expert consultants points to the growing importance of ideas or causes.

Public interest groups, lest we forget, are interested in symbolic or intangible rewards—"clean government," "profile," a "nuclear freeze." Both Ralph Nader and Jerry Fallwell, in their own way, are seeking broad social changes in the directions sought by their established organizations. Neither the right nor left has a monopoly on political ideas or causes.

Certainly ideas or a cause can be compelling, as we noted in connection with the struggle over the Equal Rights Amendment. They are attractive and relatively neater and cleaner when compared with farm policies or policies on economic deregulation or monetary matters. Our rising educational levels are producing a growing number of political activists emotionally tied to certain causes. And, when employed by individuals who may lie at the political extremes, like the late Terry Dolan of the NCPAC or Jesse Helms or Jesse Jackson, the potential is great for periods of political divisiveness. Unfortunately, "true believers" usually shun the moderating devices of bargaining, compromise, and political pragmatism.

But even if Huntington and Lunch are right, and ideas or causes are advancing on interest-oriented politics, traditional group-based politics are far from dead. Washington's politics are still dominated by long-established interest groups, and the tactics and strategies of influence noted in earlier pages are still in vogue. And a great deal has been accomplished over the past quarter century as a result of interest group politics. Greater opportunities exist now for people to vote and participate in politics. The nation's environment is cleaner now, although much remains to be done. Also, despite the move toward deregulation, most Americans live fuller lives because of government's acceptance of greater social responsibilities. If we continue in the same direction nationally that we are now, policy making will still involve various combinations of groups— because as long as our constitutional guarantees continue, we as individuals will continue to establish organizations that give expression to our inevitably conflicting desires.

NOTES

[1]On the older legislative process, see Donald R. Matthews, *U.S. Senators and Their World* (Chapel Hill: University of North Carolina Press, 1960); and William S. White, *Citadel: The Story of the U.S. Senate* (New York: Harper, 1956).

[2]Samuel Eldersveld rejects arguments that political parties are "ineffectual" or "impotent." A few internal reforms would allow them to regain the stature they once had. See Eldersveld's *Political Parties in American Society* (New York: Basic Books, 1982).

[3]William M. Lunch, *The Nationalization of American Politics* (Berkeley: University of California Press, 1987), p. 257.

[4]For an excellent overview of deregulation, see Larry N. Gerston, Cynthia Fraleigh, and Robert Schwab, *The Deregulated Society* (Pacific Grove, Calif.: Brooks/Cole, 1988).

[5]Ibid., p. 88.

[6]Alfred E. Kahn, "Deregulation and Vested Interests: The Case of the Airlines," in R. G. Noll and B. M. Owen, eds. *The Political Economy of Deregulation: Interest Groups in the Regulatory Process* (Washington, D.C.: American Enterprise Institute, 1983), p. 132. Noll and Owen, incidentally, imply that deregulation is generating more democratic and open relationships between regulatory agencies and their clientele.

[7]Gerston, Fraleigh, and Schwab, *The Deregulated Society*, p. 106.

[8]See Ann Cooper, "Free-Wheeling Airline Competition is Apparently Here to Stay," *National Journal*, 16 (1984), 1085–89.

[9]Ann Cooper, "The CAB Is Shutting Down, but Will It Set an Example for Other Agencies?" *National Journal*, 16 (1984), 1822–23.

[10]Samuel Huntington, *American Politics: The Promise of Disharmony* (Cambridge, Mass.: Harvard University Press, 1981), especially Chapter 2.

[11]Lunch, *The Nationalization of Politics*, pp. 272–73.

BIBLIOGRAPHY

BOOKS

ADVISORY COMMISSION ON INTERGOVERNMENTAL RELATIONS, *The Transformation in American Politics.* Washington, D.C., 1986.

ALEXANDER, HERBERT E., *The Case for PACs.* Washington, D.C.: Public Affairs Council, 1983.

BAUM, LAWRENCE, *The Supreme Court* (4th ed.). Washington, D.C.: CQ Press, 1981.

BENNETT, JAMES T., and THOMAS J. DiLORENZO, *Destroying Democracy.* Washington, D.C.: CATO Institute, 1985.

BENTLEY, ARTHUR F., *The Process of Government.* Chicago: University of Chicago Press, 1908.

BERRY, JEFFERY M., *The Interest Group Society.* Boston: Little, Brown, 1984.

BLASI, VINCENT, ed., *The Burger Court: The Counter-Revolution That Wasn't.* New Haven: Yale University Press, 1983.

BOLES, JANET K., *The Politics of the Equal Rights Amendment.* New York: Longman, 1979.

BROWNE, WILLIAM P., *Private Interests, Public Policy, and American Agriculture.* Lawrence: University of Kansas Press, 1988.

CAMPBELL, ANGUS, PHILIP E. CONVERSE, WARREN E. MILLER, and DONALD STOKES, *The American Voter.* New York: John Wiley, 1960.

CHUBB, JOHN E., *Interest Groups and the Bureaucracy: The Politics of Energy.* Stanford, Calif.: Stanford University Press, 1983.

CIGLER, ALAN J., and BURDETT A. LOOMIS, eds., *Interest Group Politics.* Washington, D.C.: CQ Press, 1986.

CRAWFORD, ALAN, *Thunder on the Right.* New York: Pantheon, 1980.

CRONIN, THOMAS E., *The State of the Presidency.* Boston: Little, Brown, 1980.

DAHL, ROBERT, *Who Governs?* New Haven: Yale University Press, 1961.

DREW, ELIZABETH,   *Politics and Money: The New Road to Corruption.* New York: Macmillan, 1983.
ELDERSVELD, SAMUEL J.,   *Political Parties in American Society.* New York: Basic Books, 1982.
EPSTEIN, LEE,   *Conservatives in Court.* Knoxville: University of Tennessee Press, 1985.
FENNO, RICHARD F.,   *Congressmen in Committees.* Boston: Little, Brown, 1973.
GERSON, G. DAVID,   *Group Theories of Politics.* Beverly Hills, Calif.: Sage Publications, Inc., 1978.
GERSTON, LARRY N., CYNTHIA FRALEIGH, and ROBERT SCHWAB,   *The Deregulated Society.* Pacific Grove, Calif.: Brooks/Cole, 1988.
GITELSON, ALAN R., M. MARGARET CONWAY, and FRANK B. FEIGERT,   *American Political Parties: Stability and Change.* Boston: Houghton Mifflin, 1984.
GOULDEN, JOSEPH,   *The Superlawyers.* New York: Waybright & Tally, 1971.
GREEN, MARK,   *Who Runs Congress?* New York: Bantam, 1972.
GREENWALD, CAROLE S.,   *Group Power: Lobbying and Public Policy.* New York: Praeger, 1977.
HECLO, HUGH,   *A Government of Strangers.* Washington, D.C.: Brookings Institution, 1977.
HREBENAR, RONALD J., and RUTH SCOTT,   *Interest Group Politics in America* (2nd ed.). Englewood Cliffs, N.J.: Prentice-Hall, 1987.
IPPOLITO, DENNIS, and THOMAS WALKER,   *Political Parties, Interest Groups, and Public Policy: Group Influence in American Politics.* Englewood Cliffs, N.J.: Prentice-Hall, 1980.
JACOBSON, GARY,   *Money in Congressional Elections.* New Haven: Yale University Press, 1980.
KINGDON, JOHN W.,   *Congressmen's Voting Decisions* (2nd ed.). New York: Harper & Row, Pub., 1981.
KORNHAUSER, WILLIAM,   *The Politics of Mass Society.* Glencoe, Ill.: Fress Press, 1959.
LATHAM, EARL,   *The Group Basis of Politics: A Study in Basing Point Legislation.* Ithaca, N.Y.: Cornell University Press, 1952.
LOWI, THEODORE J.,   *The End of Liberalism,* New York: W. W. Norton & Co., Inc., 1979.
LUNCH, WILLIAM M.,   *The Nationalization of American Politics.* Berkeley: University of California Press, 1987.
MANN, THOMAS E., and NORMAN J. ORNSTEIN,   *The New Congress.* Washington, D.C.: American Enterprise Institute, 1981.
MATHEWS, DONALD R.,   *U.S. Senators and Their World.* Chapel Hill, N.C.: University Press, 1960.
McFARLAND, ANDREW S.,   *Common Cause: Lobbying in the Public Interest.* Chatham, N.J.: Chatham House, 1984.
MILLS, C. WRIGHT,   *The Power Elite.* London: Oxford University Press, 1956.
MOE, TERRY M.,   *The Organization of Interests.* Chicago: University of Chicago Press, 1980.
NADER, RALPH,   *Unsafe at Any Speed.* New York: Grossman, 1965.
NOLL, R.G., and B. M. OWEN,   *The Political Economy of Deregulation: Interest Groups in the Regulatory Process.* Washington, D.C.: American Enterprise Institute, 1983.
OLSEN, MANCUR,   *The Logic of Collective Action.* Cambridge, Mass.: Harvard University Press, 1965.
PERTSCHUK, MICHAEL,   *Revolt against Regulation: The Rise and Pause of the Consumer Movement.* Berkeley: University of California Press, 1982.

RANNEY, AUSTIN, *Curing the Mischiefs of Faction: Party Reform in America.* Berkeley: University of California Press, 1975.
ROURKE, FRANCIS, *Bureaucracy, Politics and Public Policy.* Boston: Little, Brown, 1976.
SABATO, LARRY, *PAC Power.* New York: W. W. Norton & Co., Inc., 1984.
SALISBURY, ROBERT H., ed., *Interest Group Politics in America.* New York: Harper & Row, Pub., 1970.
SCHATTSCHNEIDER, E. E., *The Semisovereign People.* New York: Holt, Rinehart and Winston, 1960.
SCHLOZMAN, KAY L., and JOHN T. TIERNEY, *Organized Interests and American Democracy.* New York: Harper & Row, Pub., 1986.
SMITH, HEDRICK, *The Power Game: How Washington Works.* New York: Random House, 1988.
SORAUF, FRANK J., *Money in American Elections,* Glenview, Ill.: Scott, Foresman, 1988.
STERN, PHILIP, *The Best Congress Money Can Buy.* New York: Pantheon, 1988.
TOCQUEVILLE, ALEXIS de, *Democracy in America.* New York: Colonial Press, 1899.
TRUMAN, DAVID, *The Governmental Process.* New York: Knopf, 1971.
WATTENBERG, MARTIN, *The Decline of American Political Parties 1952-1980.* Cambridge, Mass.: Harvard University Press, 1984.
WHITE, WILLIAM S., *Citadel: The Story of the U.S. Senate.* New York: Harper, 1956.
WILSON, JAMES Q., *Political Organizations.* New York: Basic Books, 1973.
ZEIGLER, HARMON L., and WAYNE PEAK, *Interest Groups in American Society.* Englewood Cliffs, N.J.: Prentice-Hall, 1972.

ARTICLES

BERRY, JEFFERY M., "Public Interest vs the Party System," *Society,* 17 (1980), 42–48.
CLARK, PETER B., and JAMES Q. WILSON, "Incentive Systems: A Theory of Organizations," *Administrative Science Quarterly,* 6 (1961), 129–66.
COOPER, ANN, "Lobbying in the '80's: High Tech Takes Hold," *National Journal,* September 14, 1985, 2030–32.
COSTAIN, DOUGLAS W., and ANNE N. COSTAIN, "Interest Groups as Policy Aggregators in the Legislative Process," *Polity,* 14 (1981), 249–72.
DENZAU, ARTHUR T., and MICHAEL C. MUNGER, "Legislators and Interest Groups: How Unorganized Interests Get Represented," *American Political Science Review,* 80 (1986), 89–106.
GLAZER, NATHAN, "Interests and Passions," *Public Interest,* Fall 1985, pp. 17–30.
GOPOIAN, J. DAVID, "What Makes PACs Tick: An Analysis of the Allocation Patterns of Economic Interest Groups," *American Journal of Political Science,* 28 (1984), 259–81.
GROSSMAN, JOEL, and STEPHEN WASBY, "The Senate and Supreme Court Nominations: Some Reflections," *Duke Law Journal,* (1972), 557–91.
HECLO, HUGH, "Issue Networks and the Executive Establishment," in *The New American Political System,* ed. Anthony King. Washington, D.C.: American Enterprise Institute, 1978, pp. 87–124.
KJELLBERG, FRANCESCO, "Do Policies (Really) Determine Politics? And Eventually How?" *Policy Studies Journal,* 5 (1977), 554–69.

LICHTER, ROBERT S., and STANLEY ROTHMAN,   "What Interests the Public and What Interests the Public Interests?" *Public Opinion,* April/May 1983, pp. 44-48.

MOE, TERRY M.,   "A Calculus of Group Membership," *American Journal of Political Science,* 24 (1980), 593-632.

O'CONNER, K., and LEE EPSTEIN,   "Amicus Curiae Participation in U.S. Supreme Court Litigation: An Appraisal of Hakman's Folklore," *Law & Society Review,* 16 (1981-82), 313-20.

ORREN, KAREN,   "Standing to Sue: Interest Group Conflict in the Federal Courts," *American Political Science Review,* 70 (1976), 723-41.

PFEFFER, LEO,   "Amici in Church-State Litigation," *Law and Contemporary Problems,* 44 (1981), 104-10.

ROBINSON, MICHAEL J.,   "Television and American Politics, 1956-1976," *Public Interest,* Summer 1977, pp. 2-40.

SABATIER, PAUL,   "Social Movements in Regulatory Agencies: Toward a More Adequate and Less Pessimistic Theory of 'Clientele Capture,'" *Policy Sciences,* 6 (1975), 301-42.

SALISBURY, ROBERT H., JOHN P. HEINZ, EDWARD O. LAUMANN, and ROBERT L. NELSON,   "Who Works for Whom? Interest Group Alliances and Opposition," *American Political Science Review,* 81 (1987), 1217-34.

SCHOLTZMAN, KAY L., and JOHN T. TIERNEY, "More of the Same: Washington Pressure Group Activity in a Decade of Change," *Journal of Politics,* 45 (1983), 351-77.

WALKER, JACK,   "The Origins and Maintenance of Interest Groups in America," *American Political Science Review,* 77 (1983), 390-406.

VOGEL, DAVID,   "The Power of Business in America: A Re-appraisal," *British Journal of Political Science,* 13 (1983), 19-43.

8895

INDEX